CATHOLICS IN ENGLAND

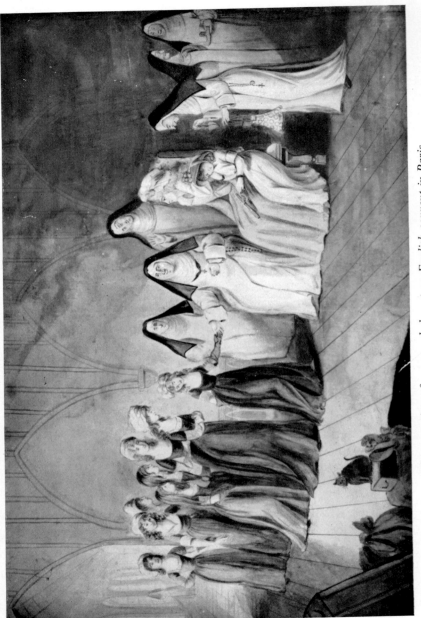

The reception of a new scholar at an English convent in Paris by Charlotte Jerningham, the scholar herself.

M. D. R. LEYS

Catholics in England
1559-1829
A SOCIAL HISTORY

LONGMANS

LONGMANS, GREEN AND CO LTD
48 GROSVENOR STREET, LONDON W1
RAILWAY CRESCENT, CROYDON, VICTORIA, AUSTRALIA
443 LOCKHART ROAD, HONG KONG
PRIVATE MAIL BAG 1036, IKEJA (LAGOS)
44 JALAN AMPANG, KUALA LUMPUR
ACCRA, AUCKLAND, IBADAN, KINGSTON (JAMAICA)
NAIROBI, SALISBURY (RHODESIA)
LONGMANS SOUTHERN AFRICA (PTY) LTD
THIBAULT HOUSE, THIBAULT SQUARE, CAPE TOWN
LONGMANS, GREEN AND CO INC
119 WEST 40TH STREET, NEW YORK 18
LONGMANS, GREEN AND CO
137 BOND STREET, TORONTO 2
ORIENT LONGMANS PRIVATE LTD
CALCUTTA, BOMBAY, MADRAS
DELHI, HYDERABAD, DACCA

PRINTED IN GREAT BRITAIN BY
THE CAMELOT PRESS LTD., LONDON AND SOUTHAMPTON

CONTENTS

The Frontispiece is reproduced by courtesy of The Essex Record Office

PREFACE

This book is not intended for specialists or for those interested in religious controversy; it is merely an attempt to examine the relations that existed between the Catholics in England and their neighbours during the years when the exercise of their faith was banned by the law. Much detailed research has yet to be done before a reasonable estimate can be made of their number at any given date, or a survey be completed of their circumstances in any particular area. This work is being undertaken on a considerable scale, by both professional and amateur historians; it is to be hoped that the inaccuracies and misunderstandings that are to be found in a large number of accepted authorities will be corrected as a result of their labours.

The sources I have consulted are too many to list; I have referred to some in footnotes. Volumes of the Catholic Record Society are quoted by the initials C.R.S. and the series number. Books quoted were published in London unless the place of issue is mentioned. Some of the archives I have used have not been calendared; part of those of the Midland District have been listed since I used them, and the Weld documents, now at Dorchester, are being sorted and calendared.

A Bibliography of Sources for Recusant History is being prepared; it will be of considerable size, for material is to be found in many books, in public records on the continent as well as in England, in parish registers, county court records etc. There are many collections of private papers in record offices and libraries, as well as others not yet available to scholars, like the Huddleston documents at Sawston Hall, and the Stonor collection. Much material used by earlier writers has been lost or destroyed; much has still to be found and preserved. It is to be hoped that those who have inherited letters and other documents of their Catholic ancestors will deposit them in a record office where they can be preserved and used. Much painstaking research also lies hidden in unpublished theses.

I have had the very great pleasure of receiving an astonishing amount of generous co-operation from people to whom I was a stranger. I have been allowed to use private archives; to see the unpublished material of many researchers; I have been given and lent rare books. I append lists of people to whom I am especially indebted, and apologize to anyone whose name I may have inadvertently omitted. To the Leverhulme Research Foundation I owe the financial help without which my work would have been impossible.

For permission to use private archives: The Abbot of Ampleforth; The Superior, the Bar Convent, York; John Arundell; and R. Bennison.

For permission to use unpublished research: Canon Foley; Rev. D. Holmes; Rev. Vincent Smith; R. O'Sullivan, Q.C.; C. Swan, D.Phil.; J. A. Williams.

For transcriptions of documents: Miss M. Akeroyd; Miss E. Halcrow; Miss M. Homes; Miss A. Sée; J. A. Williams.

For gifts and loans of books: W. C. Ainsley; Dom H. Aveling; M. Barrington; Miss Branney; The late Mrs Boyan; The Master of Campion Hall; M. Cleary; The Lord Clifford of Chudleigh; E. Esdaile; The Misses Guiney; Mrs Hopkirk; D. Jewsbury; F. B. Smith; Dom John Stéphan; Mrs Sutton; E. Thompson; M. Walker.

For information and suggestions: G. R. Batho; C. Burbridge; Mrs Cauley; Captain Charlwood; Rev. J. Crozier; Mrs Dodd; Mrs Stapleton O'Reilly; Rev. W. Pemberton; Miss P. Revill; F. Roberts; L. Ross; Canon Shanahan; Dom Aelred Watkin; Miss A. Whiteman.

Among many helpful archivists, I especially thank those of Beverley, Chelmsford, Dorchester and Exeter, and the City Librarian of York.

1

CHURCH AND PEOPLE IN SIXTEENTH-CENTURY ENGLAND

For 270 years, from 1559 to 1829, Catholics in England were deprived by law of their full rights as citizens. Although for part of this time their disabilities were shared by others who dissented from the national church, the Catholics were under the ban of specific laws and excluded from concessions. They formed a minority of a very unusual kind. A group within a nation which is distinct in fact, if not in law, from the bulk of the people is not uncommon; but generally such minorities are made up of men of a different race, or living in certain areas, or pursuing a particular aim, political or social. The English Catholics, however, came from every class and were scattered all over the country; only their religion divided them from their fellows. Peers of the realm, landowners, professional men, manufacturers, tradesmen, crafts-men, labourers, they held to a double allegiance—to their native land and to their traditional faith. When in 1559, after 20 years of uncertainty, the national church was established on the basis of a separation from Rome, they refused to conform. That they succeeded in remaining both English and Catholic was due to the character of the society in which they lived.

When Henry VIII died in January 1547, the country he had ruled was going through a period of rapid change, and there was no one with a personality and a status strong enough to control the forces which threatened peace. Henry had achieved much; he had continued the adaptation of old institutions to serve a power-ful monarchy; he had been one of the leading princes of Europe; he had broken with the pope and destroyed the monasteries without any violent departure from the dogmas and practices to which his people were accustomed. To maintain his system there was only a boy, not yet 10 years old, whose delicate health made it unlikely that he would live to manhood. In 1544 the king had been given the right to fix the order of succession to the throne; by his will in 1546 he laid down that Edward, if he died childless, should be followed by his half-sister Mary, with Elizabeth next in order.

BCE

That both princesses had been declared illegitimate counted for nothing. Sixteen men were to be his executors; quarrels between them were inevitable.

A pressing difficulty was that of finance. Henry could persuade his parliaments to expropriate the religious orders and break off relations with the pope, but he could not secure grants of taxes adequate to meet his expenditure. The profits from the sale of the great monastic estates were quickly exhausted, and he resorted to the disastrous expedient of creating money by minting coins of base metal. The old good silver pieces were hoarded, melted down or exported; the result was a rapid rise in prices and a dislocation of trade. His son's guardians continued this practice; the coins issued in 1551 were worth as silver only one-seventh of those current in 1526. It has been calculated that by 1558 the cost of living was four times as high as it had been in 1500.[1]

Traditional systems of trade and agriculture were already breaking down. The discoveries and exploitation of new lands by Portugal and Spain led to an expansion in overseas adventures and a dislocation of old markets. English landlords had for several years been breaking old customs and enclosing open fields to gain profit from sheep breeding. There was unemployment on a considerable scale, and much misery; to restore the rights of the peasants and stabilize agriculture was impossible, for no matter how many laws were passed, they could never be fully enforced.

Even the plans Henry had made for the church proved to be only temporary. The reformers felt that he had been half-hearted; they wanted a complete purification of dogma and practice on the principles laid down by the Protestant theologians of the continent. In choosing his executors Henry had tried to keep a balance between the more advanced and the more conservative of his councillors. Such a plan was bound to fail; in 1548 the Protestant party in the council forbade the use of Latin in the services and ordered the destruction of images in churches, and next year made the use of an English form of Common Prayer compulsory. Two years later the conservative bishops lost their sees, and in 1552 further changes were made by the publication of 42 Articles of Religion and a new Prayer Book.

The common people, already demanding redress of their economic grievances, in many places broke into open revolt. For instance, at Glapthorne, near Oundle in Northamptonshire, a merchant named John Johnson had secured a lease of the manor. He was a convinced Protestant, but, as is not uncommon among Christians of all denominations, his religion did not prevent him

[1] Clapham, J. E., *Concise Economic History of Britain* (1949), pp. 186–7.

from seeking wealth with the utmost vigour. In 1547 he had over 1,000 sheep pastured on the common land of the village, destroying the grazing rights of the cottagers. When to this invasion was added the abolition of the Mass, they rioted. Johnson's brother wrote to him regretting 'your neighbours' foolishness about the mass and the sacrament leading to a kind of seditious uproar'.[1] The government was appealed to and the ringleaders arrested; Johnson wisely secured their release after a few weeks, for he needed their labour.

There were many such small disturbances; far more serious were the Western Rising and Ket's rebellion in Norfolk, both in the summer of 1549. The men in the eastern counties were demanding economic redress; their leaders fully approved the new order in the church. The men of Cornwall and Devon rose in protest against the changes in religion. At Whitsuntide the Mayor of Bodmin, Humphrey Arundell of Yewtown, and a large number of the gentry and commoners of Cornwall and Devon marched on Exeter, demanding the restoration of the Mass. Their forces were undisciplined and armed only with pikes and bows and arrows. Professional foreign soldiers with guns were sent to deal with them; sympathetic risings in Wiltshire came to nothing; yet it took some months for the rebellion to be crushed. Fierce fighting near Honiton led to some fields being called Bloody Meadow for a long time; but the rebels were finally penned in the village of Clyst St. Mary, which was burned to the ground. Hundreds of men died, and the prisoners taken were massacred. In Exeter a priest was hanged, dressed in his vestments, from the tower of his church. Sporadic resistance continued in the high moorland country; Sir Anthony Kingston, sent down to deal with it, invited the Mayor of Bodmin to dinner and promptly hanged him. The bitter memories of the 12 weeks of struggle lasted long in the west.[2]

Edward's death in 1553 led to a reversal of policy. Attempts to prevent the accession of Mary failed; she was generally acknowledged as the true heir. The House of Commons begged her to marry an Englishman, for the idea of an unmarried woman as ruler was unfamiliar. She chose instead her kinsman, Philip, who next year became King of Spain and ruler of the Netherlands. Inevitably, England's foreign policy became subordinate to the interests of Spain, and a war with France led to the loss of the last cross-channel outpost, Calais.

Even among the common people, to whom the loss of Calais meant little, the Spanish marriage was unpopular. The Spaniards

[1] Winchester, B., *Tudor Family Portrait* (1953), pp. 190 ff.
[2] Rose-Troup, F., *The Western Rebellion of 1549* (1913).

provoked the strong resentment usually felt by people at the presence of foreigners whose manners are different and whose economic position is superior. Not many Englishmen would have agreed with Stephen Slater, who declared in 1585 that 'King Phillip was a father to Ingland and did better like an Inglyshe man than the Quenes Majestie did for that he wolde give them mete drynck and clothes'.[1]

Mary was an ardent Catholic, and her parliament in 1555 revoked the laws of Henry's reformation and submitted to the pope. The convinced Protestants fled, when they could, to the continent; those who remained were prosecuted as heretics.[2] Many of them were Anabaptists, belonging to a sect which flourished in Essex; Elizabeth also thought them dangerous, and five of them were burned as heretics during her reign. The Mass and the ancient rituals were restored, but if the acceptance of Catholicism was to be more than passive, an immense work of instruction was needed. For this the men were lacking; Mary, like Elizabeth, was seriously handicapped by the absence of adequately trained clergy.

Physically, too, the church had suffered. Much of its property had passed into lay hands; greedy men had stripped the lead from the roofs of parish churches, windows were broken, priests' houses pulled down. The visitations carried out by Archdeacon Harpsfield[3] in the diocese of Canterbury showed that in nearly every place structural repairs were needed, as well as the replacement of statues. Many of the parsons were reconciled to Rome, but there were also many vacant livings and no priests to fill them. Twelve men who had been bishops under Henry VIII retained or were restored to their sees; all were elderly, and most not distinguished for piety or efficiency. Seven of them died before 1559; so did eight of the 18 new bishops appointed by Mary, and four more died in 1559. Only four of them had gone abroad during Edward's reign, and thus had an opportunity of coming into contact with the ideas of the Counter-Reformation. The constructive work of Mary and the papal legate, Cardinal Pole, had barely begun when they died on the same day, 17 November 1558.

Mary had no child; the clearer legal title to the throne was held by Mary of Scotland, but she was abroad; her husband became King of France in July 1559. France was the traditional enemy of England, and in any case she was out of the way and had little chance to make a claim. Elizabeth was wholly English; her father had named her as next in succession; she was on the spot and

[1] Essex Assize Files, *Bulletin of Local Archivists*, No. 13, April 1954, p. 6.
[2] Hughes, P., *The Reformation in England*, Vol. III, pp. 254 ff. and 411.
[3] C.R.S., XLV and XLVI.

ready to act. There was no real doubt that she would be queen.

She had influential friends, and, as the many schemes for her marriage had come to nothing, she was not bound to any of the great rival families. An excellent education had developed her native ability, and the intrigues which had surrounded her had given her skill in evasion. She was only 25, so there were good hopes of an heir if she married. Under her Protestant brother and her Catholic sister she had outwardly conformed to the church established by law, but as the daughter of Ann Boleyn it was natural that her friends would be men who approved of Henry's breach with Rome. It was not expected that she would maintain Mary's counter-reformation, and the men who had fled abroad hastened back, full of zeal for the more radical doctrines of Zwingli and Calvin. Theologians from the various European centres of Protestantism bombarded her with long letters of congratulation and exhortation, but she was well aware that her father's, not her brother's, reformation would better meet the wishes of her people.

Her chief adviser, William Cecil, prepared the way for parliament to reverse Mary's ecclesiastical legislation. In the seventeenth century, John Strype the historian wrote that 'there was great opposition now made to the reformation of religion by many men at court. And had it not been for Cecil's wisdom, diligence, and interest in the queen, in all likelihood it had not proceeded with that roundness that it did'.[1] Opposition was expected from the bishops in the House of Lords, so four new peers were created to ensure a majority for the government.

When parliament met at the end of January 1559, it passed an Act of Supremacy, repealing all Mary's legislation and reviving a part of Edward VI's. All power and jurisdiction over the church were annexed to the crown, and all the clergy, judges, officials, university graduates—indeed, almost everyone in a position of authority—had to take an oath acknowledging the queen as Supreme Governor 'in all spiritual or ecclesiastical things as well as temporal.' Any person found guilty of defending the spiritual authority of any foreign prince or prelate was to forfeit all his property to the crown.

By an Act of Uniformity, the only legal forms of public worship were those of the book of Common Prayer of 1552, modified by the addition in the Communion service of words from the book of 1549, and by some alterations in the Litany. The rubric regarding Ornaments was also worded differently. The queen alone had power to change the rites and ceremonies. 'All and every person' in the land was ordered to attend church on Sundays or forfeit 12 pence—

[1] Strype, J., *Annals* (edn. 1823), Vol. I, p. 120.

then twice the daily wage of a labourer. Complete unity of church
and state was taken for granted in the sixteenth century; not only
in England had a change of religion followed on a change of ruler.
In Germany, after years of fighting, the peace made at Augsburg
in 1555 was based on the principle of *cujus regio, ejus religio*—
whoever ruled a state decided the religion of his people.

Those who had hated the innovations of Edward's reign, and
had been glad to hear Mass again under Mary, hoped that the new
queen would not enforce the law too rigidly. Elizabeth was reported to be no fanatic; she loved ceremony, and in spite of
ecclesiastical pressure insisted on vestments, ritual and music in
her own chapel. She did not hesitate to have Catholics in her
service; Ann Vavasour was her maid of honour, though she came
from a family known to be Papist; many of the gallants about her
succeeded in evading the obligation of attending service on
Sunday; William Byrd, a recusant, was responsible for the music
in her chapel. The Bishop of Norwich, John Parkhurst, was
distressed that she retained traces of popery; in 1563 he wrote,
'the cross, wax candles and candlesticks had been removed from
the queen's chapel; but they were shortly after brought back
again, to the great grief of the godly . . . The lukewarmness of
some persons very much retards the progress of the gospel.'[1]

So far as one can penetrate the mind of that enigmatic woman
Elizabeth, her religious position was that which Sir Robert
Naunton and other commentators defined by the odd phrase
'Church Papist'. This designation was applied to those to whom
the church meant the church in England, with English clergy,
free from interference by Spaniards, Italians, Scotsmen or any
other foreigners. They tolerated the services which some continental reformers called 'an unhappy compound of Popery and
the Gospel', but they preferred the Mass and all that went with it,
especially prayers for the dead and the invocation of familiar
saints. The compromise implied by this name seems to have suited
a large number—perhaps the majority—of Englishmen in the early
years of Elizabeth's reign. As late as 1567 many vicars in Yorkshire were reported as saying 'the communion for the dead' and
keeping crucifixes, holy water stoups and so on in their churches.[2]
In the same year Archbishop Parker declared that in the diocese
of Chichester 'in many places they keep their chalices, looking for
to have Mass again'; in 1571 John Northbrook spoke of the many,

[1] Caraman, P., *The Other Face* (1960), p. 48.

[2] Dickens, A. G., article in *Yorkshire Archaeological Journal*, Pt. 138, 1941,
pp. 157 ff.

especially of the clergy, who 'have Gospel talk but yet a Romish faith'.[1]

Such an attitude was not surprising. The pageantry of the great festivals of the Christian year, with their colourful vestments and processions, and all the merry-making that accompanied them, were part of the traditional life of the country, for which no substitute had been provided; their reappearance would be welcome to townsman and villager alike. To them, 'papacy' did not imply an active appreciation of the importance of the pope; most of them were willing to take the oath which denied his jurisdiction over England. They probably wanted to retain Henry's reformation of 1540, when transubstantiation, prayers for the dead and auricular confession were approved by act of parliament. If they were ordered to attend service at the parish church, they would, by occasional and outward conformity, avoid the penalties laid down by law; they did not feel that an immediate choice had to be made between the laws of England and those of Rome, especially after the frequent alterations of recent years.

Mary had been forced to recognize that a restoration of their lands to the religious orders was impossible, so the many families who now owned them felt themselves secure. Some had qualms; the Petres in Essex obtained a letter from the pope confirming their rights of ownership of monastic estates. In religion this family, like many others, pursued an erratic course; sometimes the head of the house would conform while his wife and children secretly attended Mass. There was a general feeling that the church settlement of 1559 might not endure—a view which was shared by several of the trained theologians in the universities. Cambridge had housed many of the reformers, yet even there several fellows of the colleges clung to the old ways. Philip Baker had been elected Provost of King's College in 1559; in 1565 he was accused of hoarding 'Popish stuff', missals, pyxes, vestments and so on. When he was ordered to destroy them, he refused, saying 'That which hath bin may be again.' John Caius, another Cambridge man, had refounded the old Gonville Hall and given his college the name of Gonville and Caius. He was a man of wealth, who had studied at Padua and won fame as a physician. He also was reported in 1565 for 'keeping within his College copes vestments albes . . . all kind of mass bookes . . . with all massinge abominations and calleth them the colledge treasure.'[2] Both these men were fully competent to judge of the theological issues

[1] Caraman, P., op. cit., pp. 32 and 34.
[2] Swan, C. M., unpublished thesis, Cambridge: *The Catholic Reaction in the Universities of Oxford and Cambridge during the Reign of Queen Elizabeth.*

involved in the acceptance of the Elizabethan settlement, yet did not feel it their duty to resign their positions.

Ordinary laymen generally took the oath of supremacy when requested. William Lord Vaux of Harrowden was in 1559 a wealthy and gay young man. He held office as justice of the peace in 1578 and 1579, and performed other functions under the government. Yet he showed small respect for the official religion, and claimed, when cited in 1581 for failure to attend church services, that his own estate was a separate parish. He was a keen sportsman, and in the same year sent his bear on tour in the country round about. A bear-baiting was arranged at Chesterton, close to Cambridge, on a Sunday at sermon time, and naturally the undergraduates flocked out to see the dogs attack the bear. The proctor sent his beadles out to stop the show. The local constables should have helped the university officials, but when the bearward refused to go away they instead 'violently shoved and thrust the beadle upon the bear'.[1]

Already Vaux was recognized as a Catholic at heart; in 1571 he had by a deed given one Douglas, a priest, a regular payment of £10 a year. When the oath was proffered to him in 1581 he would not take it; from being a 'Church Papist' he had become a 'recusant', a declared rejector of his legal obligation.

John, Baron Stourton of Stourton, in Dorset, was not so honest a man. He conformed to the law, and was sufficiently trusted to be appointed one of the commissioners for the trial of Mary, Queen of Scots, in 1586; yet he retained two priests in his house, planning that when he was at the point of death he would be reconciled to the religion in which he really believed. As it happened, he died very suddenly in 1588, when both priests chanced to be away, and the story ran that his penitent ghost appeared to a priest saying Mass. His son Edward was brought up a Catholic, but he too conformed after being imprisoned in the Tower of London. Later on, however, the Stourton family were so stoutly recusant that, by 1704, they were seriously impoverished.[2]

The country gentlemen who took the same line as the great nobles were very numerous. John Bold, for instance, was Sheriff of Lancashire in 1576 and, as a follower of the Earl of Leicester, joined the Protestant Association in 1581. Yet the very next year he was reported to have a priest in his house and to have Mass said there for the local Catholics. When Weston, a Jesuit, knew him, he had retired from public life.[3]

[1] Anstruther, G., *Vaux of Harrowden* (Newport, 1953), p. 98.
[2] Oliver, G., *Collections* (1857), pp. 95, 97.
[3] Weston, W., *Autobiography*, trans. Caraman, P. (1955), p. 55.

Even the retainers of some of the recusant families were, as the priests called them, 'schismatics'. William Suffield, a Norfolk man and a weaver by trade, was attached to the Wiseman family, which was strongly Catholic: they not only maintained priests in their houses, but many of them went abroad to train for the priesthood. Suffield, although a 'Church Papist', was, so to speak, lent by them to a Jesuit, John Gerard,[1] and was arrested in a house belonging to this priest. Yet he resisted all attempts to make him tell the secrets he knew, or in any way betray his master.

Such men, in all walks of life, were very common in the sixteenth and seventeenth centuries. The Benedictine monk, Augustine Baker, was a shrewd observer; he wrote that 'the greatest part of those who in their judgements and affections had before bin Catholickes, did not well discern any great fault, novelty or difference from the former religion, that was Catholick, in this new sett up by Queen Elizabeth, save only the change of language'. They 'as it were unawares to themselves, became neutrals in religion'.[2]

This 'neutrality' of so many of the gentry may explain the ease with which successive sovereigns had secured changes in the national religion, and also the remarkable contrast between the severity of the laws passed against Catholics and the laxity in their enforcement. The gentlemen of the shires and the merchants of the towns were growing in wealth and taking an increasing share in the government. They sat in the House of Commons; though the representation of the shires was fixed by custom, the monarch could at will give boroughs the right to send members. In the reign of Henry VII there were 296 M.P.s. Henry VIII increased them by 31 for Wales and 14 more for English boroughs; under Edward VI 34 more were added, under Mary 25, under Elizabeth 62; so by 1603 they numbered 462. The places they represented were often villages; it was the ambitious men who wanted to play a part in national affairs who secured their charters.[3] Some of the 'faithful Commons' were genuinely interested in politics; others merely wished for increased importance at home and a chance of making friends at court. The cost in time and money was not great; during the whole 45 years of Elizabeth's reign the Commons sat for only 33 months. During this time much legislation of importance was dealt with, and something like a party emerged, constantly urging more drastic changes in the church. Elizabeth several times rebuked the Commons for their boldness; she abruptly dismissed or prorogued parliaments,

[1] Gerard, J., *Autobiography*, trans. Caraman, P. (1951), p. 55.
[2] C.R.S., XXXIII, 16.
[3] Neale, J. E., *The Elizabethan House of Commons* (1949), p. 147.

even though this meant the loss of money grants she badly needed, and she frequently vetoed bills passed against her wishes.

Care was taken to ensure that some members would speak for the government; they were usually Privy Councillors. Part of the duty of William Cecil, whom Elizabeth appointed secretary to her council, was to try to secure the passage of government bills. The principal secretary was an important man, for the chief organ of the Tudor government was the council. Its members were chosen by the monarch, and they exercised the prerogative rights of the crown, which included the promulgation of proclamations, sometimes of so wide a scope as to be practically laws; the exercise of undefined judicial power; the appointment of officials, paid and unpaid; the granting of licences and privileges. The secretaries had a growing number of officials to assist them, but under Elizabeth none of them was ever free to make policy or to ensure that it would be carried out. All political decisions of importance had to be acceptable to the queen, a woman of strong will and varying moods. The day to day administration—the collection of taxes, the arrest and detention of criminals, the trial of minor offenders—lay in the hands of the local gentry appointed as justices of the peace. They were practically unpaid; their honourable status provided adequate compensation. It was very rare for a man to refuse or to resign a commission as justice.

Amateurs however are seldom completely efficient and reliable, and how strictly these gentlemen enforced the laws and regulations depended on local conditions. There were many possibilities of delay or negligence when to carry out the government's orders would be disadvantageous to their kinsmen and friends; men like Shakespeare's Shallow and Slender, in *Henry IV, Pt. II*, were to be found in every county. Warrants issued by a justice were valid only in his own district; there was no regular police force, only untrained and incompetent village constables. Active lawbreakers could avoid arrest by moving from one place to another; to deal with them, 'pursuivants' were sent by the government with warrants valid for the whole country. Their captives could be taken to London or kept in some local jail, along with the men arrested by the justices, for trial by the judges of assize on their next circuit.

Prisons were regarded as temporary lodgings where accused persons were kept until they were tried; only slowly did it become customary to sentence convicted persons to definite periods of detention. Most jails were run by private enterprise; their inhabitants had to pay for food and lodging, and it was only when their money and that of their friends was exhausted that the government reluctantly paid a pittance to the jailers. Men accused of grave offences were questioned before their trial, in the hope of securing confessions or information; torture might be employed to break down obstinate resistance. As a rule, punishment of people found guilty of offences was corporal—execution, branding, flogging, the pillory—or financial, fines or confiscation of property.

One of the astonishing things about the Tudors is that they maintained a powerful government with such inadequate means of compulsion. There were very few regular soldiers; the navy was very small—in 1575 it contained only 24 vessels of all types. In time of war, untrained men were called up, and merchant ships hastily armed. Elizabeth had to take constant heed of the opinions of the wealthy landowners and merchants, who could if they chose raise men and ships, who sat in the Commons and ran the administration of the shires. Prompt and decisive action was taken if necessary, but usually the queen and her council moved with the utmost caution.

Scotland, across a border difficult to defend, and Ireland, separated only by a narrow sea, were both possible sources of danger. Mary Stewart, whose claim to the throne of England was a strong one, returned from France to Scotland when her husband died in 1561. Fortunately for Elizabeth, her rival had to deal with factious nobles and a strong Protestant opposition led by John Knox. Elizabeth did not at all approve of the fiery reformer who had published *The First Blast of the Trumpet against the Monstrous Regiment of Women*, but his enmity towards Mary was most convenient. English agents kept in close touch with the opponents of the Queen of Scots, and considerable sums of money were found for their assistance.

Ireland presented a more complicated problem; it was a foreign country which had been partially conquered but never subdued. If it were abandoned, England's enemies could use it as a base for invasion. Yet it was most difficult to quell; and the introduction of the Prayer Book helped not at all, for it alienated the people. All through her reign Elizabeth had to meet the cost of expeditions to put down rebellions, using men and money that she could ill spare. It was not only in the nineteenth century that Ireland was 'the grave of reputations'; a Venetian ambassador called it 'the Englishman's grave'.[1]

The powers most likely to attack Elizabeth, whether via Ireland, via Scotland, or directly, were France and Spain. Luckily they were bitter rivals and unlikely to combine. In France civil

[1] Quoted by Neale, J. E., *Queen Elizabeth* (1934), p. 352.

wars began in 1562 and went on spasmodically until 1589; a genuine desire on the part of some reformers to make France Protestant was used as a cloak for baronial attacks on the crown. Henry of Navarre became a Catholic in 1593 to secure his throne, but as he had led the Protestant party he retained their support.

Philip II of Spain was the monarch most immediately interested in English affairs. His empire was vast; he ruled over Spain and the Netherlands—the modern Holland and Belgium; he inherited the immense areas of Central and South America which had been discovered in the wonderful age of exploration and conquest. From their mines came gold and silver, from their coasts pearls, from their forests timber and countless other goods. In 1580 to these possessions, which kept Spanish ships crossing and recrossing the Atlantic, were added the colonies and trading stations of Portugal in Brazil, Africa and the Indian Ocean. The marketing of an immense variety of commodities was carried on to a large extent in the busy cities of the Netherlands, whence goods flowed into Europe up the great highway of the Rhine. The English Channel was therefore of supreme importance to Spain; the great merchant ships were always liable to attack by pirates. Philip's marriage to Mary had secured an alliance with England; to retain it, he offered his hand to Elizabeth, but was refused. Open enmity would imperil Spanish communications, so his aim was to secure English neutrality. He was an ardent supporter of the Counter-Reformation, but he was also a ruler with countless and pressing problems.

To be on good terms with Spain was highly advantageous to Elizabeth in the early years of her reign. Later on, as England clearly took her stand on the Protestant side in Europe, neutrality became harder to maintain. In 1568 Philip had to deal with revolts in Spain and above all in the Netherlands, where religion combined with personal grievances to inspire a resistance which in 1609 led to the independence of the northern part of the Low Countries. Here, as in Scotland, the Queen of England could give semi-secret support to the rebels of her potential enemy.

The third great European power, the Holy Roman Empire, was also faced by internal strife arising from the Reformation, and in addition was menaced by invasion from the Moslem Turks. Attempts made by the pope to get united action for the defence of Christendom proved vain. The popes were themselves territorial princes, but their concern with England was based on their spiritual power. It so happened that during Elizabeth's reign there were no fewer than ten popes, some of them ruling for very brief periods. Since 1545 a great council, known generally as the Council of Trent, had been discussing and re-stating doctrines challenged by Luther, Zwingli, Calvin and other reformers. It drew up regulations for the elimination of abuses and the discipline of the clergy. The Catholic Church was prepared to enter the theological battle-field, but for political action it had to depend on the princes of Europe. Their adhesion must be secured.

Papal agents therefore approached Elizabeth; no matter what shadow lay over her birth, she was the actual ruler of England. Polite messages were delivered to her in May 1560, and it was suggested that a nuncio, an official representative of the pope, should call on her. Philip of Spain was alarmed at this proposal; he knew England far better than did the officials of the Vatican, and realized that even if she wished to Elizabeth could hardly revert to Mary Tudor's policy. He did not want to be asked to intervene by force if she rejected proposals from Rome, so he exerted diplomatic pressure to delay the embassy. This suited Elizabeth well; it was not until May 1561 that her council formally refused to grant a passport to a papal nuncio.

The customary means of dealing with recalcitrant heretics, even great princes, was solemn excommunication. It is just possible that, had Pius IV excommunicated Elizabeth in 1560, some of the many waverers in England might have been affected. When in 1570 Pius V issued the bull of excommunication, *Regnans in Excelsis*, it was far too late; the only effect of his formal release of the people from their allegiance to their queen was to create immense difficulties for loyal Catholics. Yet it took a long time for the Vatican officials to realize that in the political field these solemn condemnations had little effect. In 1596 some of the cardinals were wondering whether a threat of excommunication would ensure that James VI of Scotland would conform to Rome in return for papal approval of his claim to the throne of England.[1] James had indeed been carrying on negotiations with the papacy, but the idea was quite absurd. Even more fanciful were other schemes mooted in Rome during the last years of Elizabeth's life—that France and Spain should jointly choose a king of England and place him on the throne by force of arms when the queen died, or, failing this, should apportion the British Isles between themselves.[2]

Indeed, since the middle of the sixteenth century no pope had had any effective way of enforcing his wishes by arms or even by diplomacy; but the spiritual prestige of the papacy had been

---

[1] D'Ossat, Cardinal, *Lettres*, . . . *au Roy Henri le Grand . . . 1594–1604*, February 1596 (Paris 1627).

[2] Op. cit., February 1597, p. 375.

enormously enhanced by the Council of Trent. Uncertainties had been removed, abuses acknowledged, and means for reform made more effective. The new organization of the Society of Jesus, established in 1540, placed directly under the pope's orders a rapidly growing body of priests of all nations, ardent and willing to carry the faith to the heathen in far distant lands or to undertake the delicate tasks of reconciling lapsed Catholics and converting heretics. Victory for the Church must now be won by personal and individual effort, by priests, secular or belonging to the orders, who were fired with an apostolic zeal and trained in controversy to meet rational arguments. That a great historic and international organization took time to realize this, and that the character and problems of its English adherents were for so long not fully understood, added enormously to the difficulties of the English Papist recusants.

The story of these English Catholics can be understood only when it is realized that it had for background a complicated pattern of political intrigue and genuine religious zeal; of selfless idealism and selfish opportunism, heroic courage, cruelty, enthusiasm, apathy and reckless folly. The curious variations and apparent contradictions in the history of the recusants and of their opponents can be followed only if it is recognized that many influences wholly distinct from religious faith played a part in moulding their lives.

2

THE QUEEN AND THE PAPISTS

Elizabeth was determined to establish her popularity so firmly
that no enemy, foreign or domestic, would secure substantial
support. In this she succeeded so well that the myth she created
became generally accepted. She was Gloriana, the Virgin Queen,
the embodiment of the aspirations of the poets and adventurers
who thronged her court. Like Napoleon Bonaparte, she became a
legend in her lifetime as well as for posterity.

As a moral basis for her sovereignty she had to establish a church
acceptable to the people she ruled. She could not adopt either of
the two religious systems which had a logical basis; Calvinism had
been shown in Scotland to be fundamentally anti-monarchic; to
submit to Rome would be to undo the settlement on which her
own claim to rule was founded. Both creeds held the rights of
sovereigns to be limited, the one appealing to the scriptures, the
other to traditional belief. Of the two, the extreme Protestants
seemed the more dangerous to her; she had observed their un-
popularity when Edward was king. Unlike the convinced Catholics,
they had no scruples in obeying the law, taking the oath and
attending church services, so they were able to sit in parliament
and express their convictions. They claimed that as parliament
had legalized the breach with Rome and the subsequent changes,
it could eliminate the abuses they saw in the church organization
of 1559. Both at court and in the council they had powerful
friends, in particular William Cecil.

Elizabeth's leniency to the Papists alarmed her secretary,
whose Protestantism was sincere in spite of his having served
Mary Tudor. It was chiefly his doing that in 1561 passports were
refused to the papal nuncio; he adopted a plan which he used
frequently later on, the 'discovery' of a popish plot. In April
1561 a priest was captured as he was leaving England; several
people were arrested for attending Mass; the nephew of Cardinal
Pole was sent to the Tower. Cecil explained his actions in a letter
of 8 May to Sir Nicholas Throckmorton, the English ambassador
in Paris. 'When I saw the Romish influence toward, about a month

past, I thought it necessary to dull the Papists' expectations by discovering of certain Mass-mongers and punishing them.' He went on 'I meant no evil to any of them, but only for the rebating of the Papists' humours which, by the Queen's Majesty's leniency, grow too rank.'[1] Some of the captives who could pay heavy fines were released after a few months, but others remained long in jail.

In spite of this, a few Catholics were elected to the parliament of 1563, but they were outbalanced in numbers and influence by the extreme reformers. The customary sermon at the opening of parliament was preached by the Dean of St. Paul's, who stressed the need for strong measures against the Papists. Sir Nicholas Bacon, the Lord Keeper, in his opening speech lamented that the 'common people in the country universally come so seldom to Common Prayer',[2] and asked the queen and her bishops to take disciplinary action.

There was no difficulty in getting legislation passed, but the Commons showed their independence by amendments which completely altered the government's draft measure, making it 'most penal, sharp and terrible'.[3] The oath of supremacy[4] was to be administered to practically every man in any position of importance—lawyers, minor officials, private schoolmasters and many others; only peers of the realm were exempt. Anyone who refused to take it was subject to the penalties imposed by the statutes of *Praemunire*, which had been passed in 1353 and 1393 to prevent appeals to the papal courts from judgements made in English civil courts; they would be deprived of their lands and goods. If the oath were tendered a second time, to refuse was high treason, punishable by death.

Penal action, however severe, was merely negative; the church itself must be made acceptable. In 1562 and 1563 the convocation of the clergy discussed and approved Thirty-nine Articles of Religion, based on Cranmer's Articles of 1553. Most were carefully worded to permit a wide variance in interpretation but three explicitly denied the theology of Rome.[5] When parliament

---

[1] Read, Conyers, *Mr. Secretary Cecil and Queen Elizabeth* (1955), p. 211.

[2] Neale, J. E., *Elizabeth I and her Parliaments 1559–1581* (1953), p. 96.

[3] Neale, op. cit., p. 117.

[4] A man had to swear 'that no foreign prince, person, prelate, state or potentate, hath or ought to have any jurisdiction, power, superiority, pre-eminence or authority, ecclesiastical or spiritual within this realm.' Full text in Prothero, G. W., *Statutes* etc. (3rd ed.), p. 7.

[5] In Article XXII: 'The Romish doctrine concerning Purgatory, Pardons, Worshipping and Adoration, as well of Images as of Reliques, and also invocation of Saints, is a fond thing vainly invented, repugnant to the Word of God.'

Article XXV: 'There are two Sacraments . . . Baptism and the Supper of

met again in 1566 the Articles were given legal sanction, though the Protestants in the Commons took the opportunity to demand alterations in the forms of service. Controversy over these, and over ritual, such as the use of the sign of the cross in baptism, and the wearing of vestments, continued throughout Elizabeth's reign. Sermons and tracts gave much trouble to the queen and her bishops, and in successive parliaments bills and petitions were introduced in spite of prohibitions.

It was easier to define dogma than to supply men of good character and intellectual conviction to fill the vacant livings and replace the 'massing priests' of Mary Tudor. The bishops' powers over the appointment of clergy were limited, for many laymen had rights over their parish churches. The most important was that of advowson, by which a candidate could be nominated for a vacant benefice; the number of advowsons in lay hands had been greatly increased when the monastic lands became private property. Catholic landowners lost this right when James I transferred it to the universities, but in many cases they, like their conforming neighbours, had some control over the churches on their lands.[1] Graduates of the universities were alone eligible for ordination, so a reform of the teaching given them was urgently required.

The oath of supremacy had been tendered to all senior authorities in 1559. When the commissioners arrived in Cambridge, they found that the Vice-Chancellor and two other heads of colleges had already left; they dismissed four more and another one resigned. Yet in King's College, a notorious papist, Philip Baker, was elected Provost. Horne, the Bishop of Winchester, was an ardent reformer, but he warned Cecil that if all recalcitrant fellows were dismissed from their posts few teachers would be left. In Oxford, nine heads of colleges were dismissed or forced to resign. Hart Hall, later Hertford College, had no chapel, and became a refuge for Catholic students. The colleges were intended as inexpensive residences for poor scholars, so for years Catholic parents went on sending their boys to the universities, to live in lodgings and work with the fellows who were still openly Papist. As yet, the oath had to be taken only when a man received his degree, and even then the proctors were often negligent in demanding it.

the Lord.' The others are 'not to be counted for Sacraments of the Gospel'.

Article XXVIII: 'Transubstantiation (or the change of the substance of Bread and Wine) in the supper of the Lord . . . is repugnant to the plain words of Scripture . . . The Sacrament . . . was not by Christ's ordinance reserved, carried about, lifted up, or worshipped.'

[1] See Chapter 14, p. 202.

Cce

The conservatism of the universities was demonstrated when the purification of the college chapels was undertaken. The removal of crucifixes, statues and pictures led to open resistance. In 1561 six Oxford undergraduates were sent to the Tower for trying to prevent the removal of the crucifix from their chapel. Four years later the commissioners paid another visit and ignoring protests had the windows with 'Imyges', or with inscriptions asking for prayers for deceased donors, smashed, and publicly burned the vestments and missals. The altar plate that had not been hidden was removed, sold, or melted down.[1] An attempt to win over the traditionalists by the authorization of a Latin translation of the Prayer Book for use in college chapels had little effect.[2] In 1568 Bishop Horne had to remove the senior fellows of Corpus Christi college by force; they obstinately refused to elect his nominee as their President, and chose instead a man who had been ejected as a Papist. More and more of the fellows were dismissed or left; at one time only three of the Cambridge colleges had heads. Undergraduates also went away; many of them went to the Inns of Court to continue their education. The College of Physicians also attracted students; all through the penal times Papists were engaged in the medical profession.

Elizabeth tried to win the universities by her personal influence. In 1564 she visited Cambridge; the customary orations and festivities were followed by a less happy incident. When she left for Hinchingbrooke, undergraduates followed her and performed a play for her amusement. In their Protestant zeal they went too far; they caricatured Queen Mary's bishops, and one lad dressed up as a dog ran about with a sacramental Host in his mouth. The queen was extremely angry. Her visit to Oxford two years later was wholly successful. Two men in particular pleased her by the skill of their Latin orations. One was Edmund Campion, who died at Tyburn as a Jesuit; the other Tobie Matthew, who became Archbishop of York.

The differing fates of these two men symbolized the results of the reform of the universities. Those who accepted the Elizabethan settlement had a splendid career open to them if they were ordained; those who rejected it had to leave England and seek their training for the priesthood on the continent. The way for them was prepared by William Allen, a Lancashire man, a notable scholar who in 1556 had become Principal of St. Mary's Hall,

---

[1] See Oman, C., *English Church Plate* (1957).

[2] Swan, C. M., unpublished D.Phil. thesis, Cambridge, on the *Catholic Reaction in the Universities . . . during the Reign of Elizabeth* contains valuable information on this subject.

later absorbed by his own college, Oriel. In 1561 he refused to take the oath and went to the university of Louvain, in the Netherlands. Next year he went home to Lancashire, for, like other Englishmen, he found the climate of the Low Countries unhealthy. It is surprising how often during the sixteenth and seventeenth centuries Catholics left the safety of their refuges on the continent to go back, for their health's sake, to their native land, though death was the penalty for their return.

Three years later he went to Mechlin (Malines) and, after he had been ordained, lectured there on theology. Latin was a living language among educated men; a Master of any university could teach in any other. In 1567 he went on a pilgrimage to Rome; a meeting with a professor from Philip of Spain's new university at Douai made him decide to go there. He found at Douai (spelt by Englishmen Douay or even Doway, which was how they pronounced it) another Oxford man, Richard Smith, a scholar of international repute. Allen, like Smith, was made a professor, as were Thomas Stapleton and Owen Lewis (or Lewis Owen), and students leaving Oxford followed their former tutors to this new foundation.

Allen determined to found a special college for Englishmen who aspired to the priesthood. Many had already gone to various centres in Europe, but a purely English institution would attract still more. There they could be trained to write the English books which were urgently needed to answer the arguments of the Protestants and stimulate the faith of people tempted to conform. A new Oxford, on Flemish soil, was his desire. He found generous co-operation; the university gave its approval, its members gave money and goods, as did three Benedictine abbots and other local patrons. By Michaelmas 1568 Allen was able to open his college in two large houses in Douai. He began with four students, but the number grew rapidly. The training was rigorous and the standards high, yet in 10 years' time 77 Englishmen had qualified for ordination. *Hence 'Allen Hall' at Ware*

An English translation of the Bible was begun; versions existed that preceded Wycliffe's,[1] but they were rare and out of date. Large portions of Scripture were familiar to Catholics, but theologians held that so much of the sacred text was obscure that explanation was necessary for the ordinary man. Now that the Bible was the sole authority recognized by the Church of England,[2] it was important that an accurate translation should be available.

[1] Kenyon, F. G., *Our Bible and the Ancient Manuscripts* (1896).

[2] Article VI: 'Holy Scripture containeth all things necessary for salvation'.

By 1582 the New Testament was printed at Rheims,[1] where Allen's college obtained a temporary home when war made Douai unsafe. While in some cases a rather pedantic desire for accuracy led to the use of such words as 'concorporate', 'celestials, terrestrials and infernals', much of the translation was in vigorous contemporary English, and was freely used by the scholars who produced in England the Authorized Version of 1611. The Douay Old Testament was published in two volumes in 1609 and 1610. Besides this great work, a Catechism and a number of other books, controversial and devotional, were written and smuggled into England.

Meanwhile, the situation had worsened for the Catholics at home. Elizabeth had encouraged the enemies of her heir, Mary of Scotland, and they had succeeded in defeating her. In 1567 she was forced to abdicate, and her baby son was crowned king; she herself was accused of complicity in the murder of his father, Darnley, and imprisoned. Next year she made a dramatic escape and fled to England, to the great embarrassment of her sister queen. Though Elizabeth had strong views on the rights of monarchs, she had no wish to help Mary regain her throne. The accusations of the Scots gave her a good excuse for keeping the royal refugee under guard in Bolton Castle, while a commission of inquiry investigated the charges.

The tribunal met at York; it was headed by the Duke of Norfolk. He was a widower, and his friends suggested that he should marry Mary. When Elizabeth heard that this was being discussed, she closed the sittings at York, added more commissioners to continue the inquiry in London, brought Mary further south and in the autumn of 1569 sent Norfolk to the Tower. This was a blow for the nobles of the northern shires. They had cherished hopes of placing Mary on the throne of England and themselves regaining the power they had lost when in 1537 Henry VIII established his Council of the North. When Elizabeth summoned the Earls of Northumberland and Westmorland to court they decided to resist, though they knew their chances of a successful rebellion were poor.

The rising of November 1569 was the last of the many revolts of great barons against the crown; though some of the leaders were Catholics, the restoration of the papacy was not their main aim. It was an ignominious failure; no support came from other regions, and within two months the Earl of Westmorland had escaped to the continent. Northumberland fled to Scotland, was imprisoned,

[1] Carleton, J. G., *The Part of Rheims in the Making of the English Bible* (1902).

and in 1572 sent to England for execution. Six hundred of the villagers who had been enrolled were hanged; it was not only they who suffered from the reckless folly of their lords. Substance had been given to the charge that Mary Stewart and her co-religionists were a threat to the peace of England.

News of the rising did not reach Rome till February 1570, and in a distorted form. The holy friar who was Pope Pius V was led to believe that the Catholics of England were in arms for their faith, and he felt it his duty to justify them by declaring that Elizabeth had no right to her throne. A papal court pronounced her a heretic, and the pope issued a bull declaring her deposed. The people of England were released from their allegiance and forbidden to obey her laws.

The whole procedure with regard to the bull *Regnans in Excelsis* was peculiar.[1] It was declared valid even in places where it had not been promulgated, yet it was not sent to any of the Catholic princes. This gave them, and also some hesitant Catholics in England, an excuse for holding that it was not binding on them. Copies were smuggled into England; John Felton secured one and fixed it on the door of the Bishop of London. He was arrested and executed for a rash act which was patently illegal. The Spanish ambassador also managed to obtain a copy of the bull and sent it to his king. Philip knew the harm that Pius had done to the Catholics in England; he tried to counteract it by writing to Elizabeth saying that he disapproved of the pope's action. If Pius V had simply declared Elizabeth and her church heretical, it might have affected the considerable number of Catholics who had felt that outward conformation was no great sin. To forbid them to obey all the laws of their country, and to declare their queen deposed, was to play straight into the hands of their enemies who now had an excuse for branding all Papists as traitors.

When a new parliament assembled in April 1571 Cecil was not in the House of Commons; Elizabeth had made him Lord Burghley. The preacher stressed the need for unity in religion; 'this liberty that men may openly profess diversity of religion, must needs be dangerous to the Commonwealth . . . One God, one king, one faith, one profession, is fit for one Monarchy and Commonwealth.'[2] To carry this principle into effect, government speakers introduced bills to increase the penalties for non-conformity and add the reception of the Sacrament at least once a year to the obligation of attending service on Sundays. All beneficed clergy were to accept the Articles of Religion and declare them valid. The

[1] Hughes, P., *The Reformation in England*, Vol. III (1954), pp. 272 ff.
[2] Neale, J. E., *Elizabeth and her Parliaments 1559–1581* (1953), p. 185.

Protestants in the Commons demanded changes in the Articles and in the services; they passed amendments to the bills which led the queen to veto them.

Legislation against Catholics presented no difficulty. An act made it treason to call the queen a heretic; even to discuss the question of the succession to the throne would now involve the penalties of *praemunire*. Another act referred directly to the bull of 1570, which it declared had been procured by 'divers seditious and very evil-disposed people' to assist them in reconciling 'weak, simple and ignorant people' to Rome. The introduction of any bull would henceforth be high treason, and anyone who consented to be absolved from his oath of allegiance to the queen was to be reckoned a traitor unless he publicly confessed his errors and declared that he wished to be re-admitted to the Church of England. The importation of 'crosses, pictures, beads or such-like vain and superstitious things' might lead to the forfeiture of land and goods for those who received them as well as those who brought them in. The same penalty applied to everyone who left the country without leave.

The bull and its consequences formed a turning-point in the lives of the Catholics of England. The suggestion that they had 'procured' the bull was contrary to the truth; the pope's action was for them a most unwelcome shock. They deeply resented the implication that it was their duty to overthrow the queen, heretic though she was, but they had to recognize that compromise in religion was no longer possible. What Sir Simonds D'Ewes later called their 'wilful obstinate separation' from the national church was inevitable. Many of the Church Papists gave up the struggle and conformed, at any rate outwardly : the convinced Catholics decided to face the consequences of their fidelity to their faith.

Elizabeth knew perfectly well that the majority of her Catholic subjects were loyal; her hope was that as new generations grew up more and more would conform. But there was no doubt that as long as Mary Stewart was in England she would be a centre of disaffection; there was a serious risk of a change in the policy of Spain, and Elizabeth was not prepared for open war, though she was very willing that private enterprise by English sailors should interfere with Spanish trade. One of these adventures gave an opportunity of learning something of Philip's plans. John Hawkins had been attacked in 1567 at San Juan d'Ulloa, and several of his men had been captured by the Spaniards. He sent an agent to Spain to negotiate for their release, and this opened the way for a double intrigue. Philip hoped to get into touch with an Englishman of good standing and persuade him to act as his agent with

Mary; Elizabeth could trust Hawkins to keep her informed of anything he could learn about Spanish plans.

Philip fell into the trap. Hawkins let it be understood that he was disaffected, so a free pardon for his raids on Spanish ships and ports was given to 'Achines de Plimua' (the nearest a Spaniard could get to Hawkins of Plymouth). Some of his sailors were released and returned home, and he was sent a gift of a costly ring along with another ring and a letter to be given to Mary. Before he delivered the letter Hawkins copied it, and the royal prisoner's reply was also studied by English officials.[1]

Watch was always kept on the Spanish ambassador, and this led to the discovery of a plot which like most of the schemes hatched by Mary's friends was quite impracticable. The ambassador and an Italian banker called Ridolfi revived the idea of marrying Mary to the Duke of Norfolk, who had been released from the Tower in 1570. Spanish troops from the Netherlands were to invade England; but their commander held that action must first be taken in England. Ridolfi's correspondence was seized; the duke was arrested, tried for treason, and finally executed. Elizabeth had an affection for him and his family; she delayed four months before she signed his death warrant, and allowed his eldest son Philip to keep the title of Earl of Arundel he inherited from his mother, and a portion of the family estates.

The Spanish ambassador was ordered to leave England. Hawkins accompanied him to his ship and arranged a cipher for future correspondence. Mary and her friends went on writing letters, nearly all of which were read by English officials, although the revolt in the Netherlands in 1572 made it very improbable that any help would reach her from Spain.

The Ridolfi plot was valuable propaganda for use against the Papists, yet the laws which could have made the exercise of their religion almost impossible were not strictly enforced. Not only would it have been difficult to carry out the law all over the country, it might well be dangerous to antagonize them and their friends. Priests were sought for, but lay people were to a great extent left alone; the queen herself continued to ignore the recusancy of men whom she liked or respected. As late as 1580 she considered making Edmund Plowden Lord Chancellor; he was the most distinguished lawyer of his day but was notoriously Catholic. His refusal of the honour was boldly worded: 'I find no reason to swerve from the Catholic faith in which you and I were brought up. . . . I should incur your displeasure, if it be your Majesty's

[1] Tenison, E. M., *Elizabethan England*, Vol. II, pp. 194 ff. (1933). Privately printed, and based largely on European sources.

royal intent to continue the system of persecuting the retainers of the Catholic faith.'[1] Yet when he was accused of hearing Mass, he was allowed—which was most unusual—to cross-examine the witnesses. He asked the man reputed to be the priest if he would swear that he was ordained. When he refused, 'then the case is altered; no priest, no Mass,' said Plowden. This phrase, 'The case is altered, quoth Plowden' passed into common use among the lawyers, who continued for many years to use his writings on English law as standard authorities. In Plowden, who died in 1585, lived on the tradition of Sir Thomas More, and the queen was far too shrewd to evoke the memory of that most popular of Chancellors by making a martyr of another honoured lawyer.

When laymen were accused of recusancy, the charge was generally brought by a personal enemy. In Cornwall, Sir Richard Grenville was sheriff in 1576; he and his friend Sir George Carey were on bad terms with two very wealthy Catholic families, the Tregians of Golden Manor and the Arundells of Lanherne. Francis Tregian had been at court, but had incurred the queen's displeasure, so Carey knew it was safe to attack him. He induced Grenville to take a strong force to Golden Manor on pretence of seeking an escaped criminal; when he searched the house a priest was discovered. Cuthbert Mayne was an Oxford man who had gone to Douay; among his papers was a copy of the fatal bull. He and Tregian were arrested; Tregian was told that if he would conform the priest's life would be spared. He refused, as he knew Mayne would have wished, and the priest was executed as a traitor at Launceston in 1577. Tregian was kept in and out of prison until in 1601 he was released, in spite of protests from Sir George Carey who had taken possession of his estates. In 1603 Carey died; Tregian went abroad, and on his death in 1608 his son bought back the property.[2]

Sometimes the feud was within a family. Henry Norwich, of Northamptonshire, was a keen Protestant; his nephews, Simon and Edward Norwich, were Catholics. At Kettering market, in April 1566, they quarrelled; Edward said that 'having a little staff in his hand, he did with the same give a little blow': his uncle said that the blows were 'vehement and mighty'. The young man was charged at the quarter sessions with assault; Henry was not satisfied with the result, and in 1578 asked the court of Star Chamber to hear his complaint; the delay, he said, was due to his having been falsely accused of thefts from the church at Brampton. In Henry's petition, Edward's 'little blow' had become a full

[1] Caraman, P., *The Other Face* (1960), pp. 200 and 92.
[2] Boyan, P. A., and Lamb, G. R., *Francis Tregian* (1954).

scale attack by several Papists with all sorts of weapons. Nephew Simon was charged along with his brother; he was accused of harbouring priests and—an important point for his uncle—hearing Mass at the 'armitage' in the woods near his house. Henry himself wanted to get hold of this ancient hermitage, which had been a place of pilgrimage. When the last hermit left, Simon had annexed it and given shelter there to a Catholic family which had been in trouble in Kent. Though his nephew was sent to prison, Henry failed to get the hermitage; Simon was released in 1583, bought the property, and went on harbouring priests. Six years later, he was again arrested, and remained in prison, except for a brief release to allow him to settle his affairs, until his death in 1593.[1]

In most areas, the laws against Catholics were very slackly enforced. For many years it had been difficult to carry out the religious policy of the government in Essex. In 1550 the reformers had found it 'troubled with the frenzy of the Anabaptists',[2] several of whom were burnt to death for heresy in the reign of Edward VI. Nearly a fifth of the heretics burnt under Mary came from Essex; even under Elizabeth five Anabaptists met a similar fate, and many parsons lost their livings for being ultra-Protestant. Papistry was also strong in this county; in 1577 it was reported that 'There be divers bold disorders and riotous assemblies of divers Papists at Colchester . . . They maintaine lakyn' (devotion to our Lady) 'in great boldness . . . They have got into their felowshippe a Justice of the Peace' who 'shadoweth them'.[3]

Two brothers, George and William Binkes, tailors of Finching-field, were charged on 25 September 1577. William was reported to have said, 'What manner of religion we have here in England I knowe not, for ye preachers now do preach their own inventions.' George, said a witness, had proclaimed, 'The Masse is good', that 'Images are good and ought to stand in the church to put men in remembrance that such saints there were, and that the crosses in the highways ought to stand to put men in remembrance that Christ died upon the cross.' Neighbours had quarrelled with the Binkes for saying these things, but the brothers were merely bound over to keep the peace.[4]

The Essex court records again and again show lists of Papists who ought to be presented, and against many of the names is written 'not to be found'. On one list the under-sheriff noted

[1] Anstruther, G., *Vaux of Harrowden* (Newport), 1953), pp. 57 ff.
[2] Hooper to Bullinger, June 1550. See Hughes, P., *The Reformation in England*, Vol. II (1953), p. 141. For the executions, see ibid, p. 261.
[3] P.R.O., S.P. 12, 120, No. 6. Transcribed by Canon Foley, Harlow.
[4] Essex Calendar of Records, Vol. III.

that Edmond Danyell and others had been committed to William Golding for safe keeping, but he had allowed them to cross into Suffolk and so escape arrest. When Golding was arrested, the bailiff was assaulted, and he escaped.[1] During all the time of persecution only one Catholic, John Payne, a priest from Douay, was executed in Essex, at Chelmsford in 1581.

Perhaps the friendship shown by Elizabeth to the Petre family had something to do with the inadequate enforcement of the law in their neighbourhood. Sir William Petre conformed, and the queen visited him at his grand new home, Ingatestone Hall, in 1561. He married a notorious Papist, but in 1582 Elizabeth forbade local officials to take any action against her. Her son, Sir John Petre, was like his father a Church Papist; though his wife had twice been presented as a recusant, he was in 1591 appointed a commissioner for enforcing the laws against priests. A similar case occurred in Surrey where Sir Nicholas Saunder,[2] who had a Papist wife, was a member of the commission; his family was on friendly terms with William Cecil, Lord Burghley. To have good friends at court was usually a guarantee of safety for a Catholic.

[1] Essex Calendar of Records, Vol. III.
[2] Walker, M. L., *The Manor of Batailles*, Surrey Arch. Soc. X. (1956).

3

THE SECRET INVASION

During the 1570s, those Englishmen and women who were determined to adhere to the Catholic faith were forced to recognize that a national reconciliation with Rome, if it were to come about, would certainly be postponed for many years. They were glad to get the books smuggled in from Douay, but they needed priests; for many of the old, or 'Marian', clergy had died or had conformed, and without Mass and the Sacraments Catholicism could not survive. They had sent their sons abroad to be ordained, and the young men begged to be allowed to return. Allen's men were restive, and in 1574 three of his priests, Lewis Barlow, Martin Nelson and Henry Shaw, adventured across the Channel.

They were the first of a continued stream of 'seminary priests': six years later 100, and by 1603 about 450, Douay men had slipped back secretly to their native land. They were young, well trained in theology, full of ardour; to assist the faithful and reconcile the lapsed they were willing to face imprisonment, torture, and martyrdom in a peculiarly horrible form. By the law of England they were traitors, and, perhaps to terrify like-minded men into submission, the execution of a traitor was barbarous in the extreme. The condemned man was drawn through the streets on a hurdle to a gallows erected in some open space where a crowd could watch his agony. He was hanged by the neck, but before he could die he was cut down, half-strangled. Then he was laid on the ground and his living body slashed open and the vital organs dragged out. The corpse was beheaded and cut into four pieces which were displayed on gateways or walls for public execration. In rare cases, by the direction of a merciful official, or being himself moved with pity, the executioner would jerk the rope so that the victim died before the disembowelling.

Up to the last moment it was possible for the Catholic to save himself. As he stood with the rope round his neck he was given a chance to declare his submission to the Church of England; most of the priests took this opportunity to address the people, justifying their faith and declaring their loyalty to their queen.

Sometimes they were stopped by their executioners or shouted down by the crowd; sometimes they were heard with real sympathy.[1] In later years their last words were printed, as were those of high-waymen and other criminals, and sold as broadside pamphlets. Many Catholics went to these spectacles, to witness a death more agonizing than that of burning at the stake, and to pray for the sufferer. They remembered his dying words, they collected when they could fragments of his body or clothing or the straw on which his blood was spattered, and treasured them as relics. Songs, ballads and tales were written and passed from hand to hand, and stimulated reverence for the martyrs among the lay folk and emulation among their fellow priests.

Far from drying up, the stream of young men who left home to study for the priesthood grew greater. Some joined one of the religious orders, and in later years a number of them, chiefly Benedictines and Franciscans, were allowed to serve on the English mission. More were attracted to the new and exciting Society of Jesus, especially after 1573, when a Portuguese Jesuit named Alvarez, who was on his way to the West Indies, was forced to land at Southampton. He found refuge among the Catholics of Hampshire and Sussex, who were protected by Henry Wriothesley, the second Earl of Southampton. Although he had been involved in the Northern Rising and sent to the Tower, the Earl's powerful friends had secured his release in 1573.

The Earl's cousin, Thomas Pound (or Pounde), was one of those who listened open-eared to the Jesuit's description of his Society. He tried to organize a party of his friends to go with him to join it, but only one of them, his page-boy Thomas Stephens, managed to escape abroad. Eventually he became a famous missionary. Pound himself was arrested in 1575: the Earl of Southampton secured his release but in 1580 he was again arrested and taken to the Marshalsea prison. As time went on, more and more young men became Jesuits. William Allen did nothing to dissuade them: he was on very friendly terms with the Society, which he greatly admired.

Pound and others like him were busy helping the priests as best they could. Sometimes the missioners arrived disguised as sailors, soldiers, or merchants in one of the ordinary ships plying across the Channel. They called themselves by false names, to protect their kinsfolk, for there were many English government agents in the ports of the Netherlands and France to watch their movements. Sometimes they could get passage on a fishing-boat

[1] After 1592 priests were for a time prohibited from addressing the crowd (C.R.S., LII, 47).

which would drop them on a lonely stretch of coast: the creeks of the Essex shore of the Thames estuary were convenient. Those from the north of England often tried to land on the coasts nearer to their homes; the Lancashire bays and estuaries, the Furness peninsula, the Humber estuary and the little ports further north were often visited by boats which landed a priest or two and hastened away. Whenever feasible friends at home were warned to expect them, but often this was impossible, and like escaping prisoners they hid by day and walked by night until they reached a safe refuge.

London was the goal of many of the priests, for there, in the very heart of England, they found both the best field for their work and the best concealment. Strangers, conspicuous in the countryside, were unnoticed in the busy streets of London. In a report on conditions in England, written probably by William Allen in 1575–6, he spoke of the Inns of Court as a centre for Catholics, 'frequented by all the gentry of almost the whole nation.' Here, he said, 'Ours have in recent years made wonderful headway, both by personal intercourse—for nowhere do men lie hid more safely than in London—and especially by books in the vulgar tongue'.[1] Lodgings were available in Gray's Inn and Chancery Lane; many of the Catholic nobles had town houses, and the large households of other rich men often contained Papists, who concealed priests without the knowledge of the master of the establishment. Indeed at one time a priest was in rooms owned by the chief of the pursuivants employed to track down the missioners. In the suburbs, it was often possible to rent a house for a short period and then to move to another before the coming and going of Catholics seeking their pastor became too noticeable.

When in 1580, in answer to the pleas of Allen and of their own English members, the Jesuits agreed to allow some of their priests to work in England, it was to London that they went. The first to arrive was Robert Persons (or Parsons); he managed to land at Dover, disguised as a soldier, and slipped up to London at night in a tilt-boat in which the Queen's musicians, who had been performing in Kent, were returning home.

> Persons arriving on foot with no horse could get no lodging, and was forced with great danger of being discovered to go up & down half a day from place to place, to wit from ye break of day until noone, at what time he resolved to adventure into ye prison of ye Marshalsea & to ask for a gentleman prisoner there named Mr. Thomas Pound, in whose chamber he dined.[2]

[1] C.R.S., IX, 65.   [2] C.R.S., II, 200.

Persons' account shows that the men across the Channel had been informed of Pound's imprisonment; it also illustrates one of the peculiar features of the Elizabethan penal system. Discipline in the jails varied immensely, but in many of them, and especially in the Marshalsea at that time, there was open traffic with the outside world. Indeed, at one time London Catholics used to come constantly to the priests imprisoned there, to hear Mass, to go to confession, even to get married.

The Jesuit went on:

> And here now after dinner came unto him the good angel which God his eternal providence had appointed should be ye chief temporal means of assisting ye first mission of ye Society in England. I mean Mr. George Gilbert who was a young gentleman born to good lands in Suffolk and some other countries.

Persons already knew Gilbert; the young man had been a Puritan, but while travelling on the continent he had met an English Jesuit in Paris whose arguments changed his views. In Rome Persons had acted as his godfather when he received the sacrament of confirmation. Now he set to work to form an association among his friends to keep up a correspondence with the continent and to meet and conceal priests on their arrival. Between them they built up a regular 'underground movement', in which young men passed the priests from one place to another. Gilbert himself in 1583 drew up instructions for the guidance of Jesuits and other missionaries: as soon as one lands 'he should seek out some gentleman to be his companion'. The advantage of procuring a map of the area in which the priest planned to work was pointed out: to ask for directions might be to arouse suspicion. All the advice given was practical, and included sensible hints on how to deal with the heretic friends of their guides and hosts.[1]

Shortly after Persons landed he was joined by a colleague who was perhaps the most remarkable of all the men who died a traitor's death at Tyburn. Edmund Campion had left Oxford for Douay in 1572: when Cecil heard of his flight he said, 'It is a great pity to see so notable a man leave his country, for indeed he was one of the diamonds of England.'[2] As a scholar, an orator and a poet, he held a high position among the many able men and distinguished

---

[1] Portions of Gilbert's Memorandum have been printed in Caraman, P., *The Other Face* (1960), pp. 119 ff. and 125 ff. Gilbert himself was so closely pursued that he had to leave England in 1581; he joined the Jesuits, and died in 1583.

[2] Quoted by Waugh, E., *Edmund Campion* (1935), p. 61.

writers of his day. His pupils at Oxford had loved him, and his wit was combined with a personal charm and genuine charity that made him almost irresistible.

Persons and Campion got into touch with priests and laymen, among them Thomas Pound, who suggested that it would be a good plan for the Jesuits to make it clear that their work was religious, not political: Campion at once set to work and produced his famous 'Brag'. It was addressed to the Privy Council; in it he spoke of Elizabeth as 'My Sovereign Ladye'. He stated that his aim was to prove the truth of the Catholic faith and win England back to its observance; he had been strictly forbidden to 'deal in any respect with matters of State or Policy of this realm.' He and his fellow Jesuits would 'never despair of your recovery, while we have a man left to enjoy your Tyburn, or be racked with your torments, or consumed with your prisons'.

Copies of the 'Brag' were widely distributed; prisoners in the Marshalsea and other jails, priests already at work, laymen who had been almost in despair, were heartened and encouraged. Cecil and his associates were extremely angry; they feared Campion as an individual, for many of the council had heard of his brilliant career at Oxford, and they believed that the Jesuits were dangerous and unscrupulous. Campion moved about the country, visiting various houses, preaching and exhorting: again and again he eluded capture in spite of the efforts made by government agents. Persons stayed mostly in London, where he printed pamphlets in reply to attacks made on the 'Brag'.

Every effort was made to discover and capture the Jesuits and their helpers. Nicholas Roscarrock, a young Cornishman and a member of the Inner Temple, belonged to Gilbert's association for helping priests.[1] One of these priests, who had been a friend of his when he was at Oxford, was discovered hiding in Roscarrock's London house, so the young lawyer was arrested and on 5 December 1580 taken to the Tower. Every effort was made to induce him to betray his friends; the priest was tortured and then laid on the snow under the window of Roscarrock's room so that he might see what suffering would await him too if he did not give way. He still held out, in spite of being himself racked soon afterwards; his name (as Rose Caricke) appears with that of Thomas Pound in the list of prisoners in the Tower in March 1583 'for matters of religion' who are to 'paye their owne dyet &c.' They were still there two years later, 'for religion only committed & for intelligence with Jesuites & priests, two dangerous men and

[1] For a brief biography of Roscarrock and a specimen of his verse, see Guiney, L.I., *Recusant Poets* (1938), pp. 199 ff.

apt for anie practise: fitt they should be banished.'[1] Roscarrock
was released in 1586, as were many of the others, for room was
needed for new prisoners, but by the end of 1595 was back in the
Fleet. However, he had powerful friends and was eventually
released: he died peacefully, a very old man, at Naworth Castle
in Cumberland, where Lord William Howard had given him a
home, whence he corresponded with his antiquarian friends. He
was one of the lucky ones; not many of his fellow prisoners
escaped so easily.

Although many people were arrested, Elizabeth and her advisers
were well aware of the extent of the influence exerted by the
writing and preaching of the Jesuits and those whom they stirred
up to activity. Parliament had not met for five years; it had been
prorogued again and again to avoid any comment or interference
by the Commons while the queen was engaged in complicated
negotiations about a possible marriage. Money was very badly
needed for the costs of her diplomacy as well as the normal
expenditure, and the chances of getting an adequate grant would
be greatly improved if the patriotic Protestantism of the members
was aroused.

There was no general election; the parliament of 1572 was recalled in January 1581. After a brief brush with the Puritans, the
main business was introduced in an extremely able speech by
Sir Walter Mildmay.[2] He spoke of the dangers that surrounded
the queen, and in particular of 'a sort of hypocrites, naming
themselves Jesuits' whose aim was 'to stir sedition', and who were
influencing people who had conformed to return to recusancy.
The Commons at once set to work to draft bills for granting taxes
and for dealing drastically with the Papists. Elizabeth herself
was probably responsible for a modification of the original measures,
but even in their final form they were sufficiently stringent.[3]
It was declared treason to 'withdraw any of the Queen's Majesty's
subjects' from their obedience to her or 'to withdraw them for
that intent from the religion now by her Highness' authority
established.' The wording should have been a safeguard for a man
like Campion, who expressly denied any wish to 'withdraw people
from their natural obedience', but 'intent' is difficult to prove,
and the law courts took it for granted that every priest who
'reconciled' a man who had conformed was *ipso facto* a traitor.
'Aiders or maintainers' of proselytizers were also to be accounted

[1] C.R.S., II, 229, 238.
[2] For this speech see Neale, J. E. *Elizabeth and her Parliaments 1559–1581*
(1953), pp. 382 ff.
[3] Texts in Prothero, *Statutes*, etc. (3rd edn., 1906), pp. 74 ff.

traitors. The penalties for saying or hearing Mass were increased, and the fine for failure to attend church services was raised to £20 a month—a sum that would, if it had in fact been levied on all recusants, have reduced them to beggary. Another act, against seditious words and rumours, was not so harsh, for many of the friends of the Puritans in Parliament might be charged with criticism of the government, but it was sufficiently severe: a man convicted might have both his ears cut off in public, unless he preferred to pay 200 marks (about £130) and be imprisoned for three months. By this time definite terms of imprisonment were being used as a punishment. A censorship of the press had already been imposed by a Star Chamber ordinance of 1566; in 1586 a further ordinance prohibited all printing, except by persons having a government licence, and appointed censors to examine all new books.

In spite of these laws Campion and many other priests continued a successful campaign. Small hand presses could be quickly erected and dismantled, and on these the Jesuits produced effective propaganda. In 1581 a pamphlet printed at Stonor, deep in the woods near Henley, caused a great sensation. It was in Latin and gave ten reasons for rejecting Protestant teaching; it was aimed at the clergy, and copies were distributed in Oxford, some being placed in the University Church of St. Mary. The Bishop of London was ordered to produce counter-arguments, and refutations of Campion's points were hastily written by professors and theologians. Persons too was busy in and around London, often in imminent danger of capture. Campion paid brief visits to Yorkshire and Lancashire; his popularity was so great that his presence in any area soon became known, in spite of all precautions. In July 1581 he was discovered, with three Douay priests, at Lyford Grange near Faringdon in Berkshire. He was taken to the Tower; the queen herself questioned him, and he was offered a splendid career if he would conform. Rumours were spread that he had yielded: after being tortured, he was forced to carry on a theological controversy, and was constantly questioned in an attempt to break his spirit. If he could be persuaded to conform, it would discredit his church; if he could be made to confess to a political aim, the government would be justified in attacking the Papists; failing both these, he might be made to give information about the people he had visited and the priests he knew. The months he spent in the Tower were a period of agony, mental and physical, ending on 1 December at Tyburn. Two other priests suffered with him; Campion's last words were a prayer for 'Elizabeth, your Queen and my Queen, unto whom I wish a long quiet reign with all prosperity'.

Dce

One of the spectators, Henry Walpole, was so moved that he went back to his chambers in Gray's Inn and wrote a long poem in praise of Campion;[1] it was printed, and though the printer was discovered and lost his ears, he did not reveal the author. A year later Walpole went abroad, and eventually became a Jesuit. He was one of many young men inspired by Campion to follow his example. Robert Persons returned to the continent, where he continued to work, organizing the training of missionaries, raising funds from Philip of Spain and others, setting up new seminaries, writing books, and keeping in touch with the Jesuits who went to England and with the friends of Mary of Scotland.

The activities of some of the ardent Catholics, however, did much to contradict the very point which Campion had stressed, that a man could be both a loyal Catholic and a loyal subject of the queen. To them, the only hope of a tolerable life seemed to lie in replacing Elizabeth by Mary; and as parliament was demanding the death of the Queen of Scots, immediate action seemed necessary. Foreign aid, which in any case would have been unacceptable to many English Papists, could not be secured. Mary's own son, James, a boy of 16, was so deeply embroiled with his rebellious subjects that in 1583 he actually asked Pope Gregory XIII for aid.[2] A French army was attacking the Spaniards in the Netherlands. Yet this was the time when Francis Throckmorton (or Throgmorton) decided to attempt to release Mary from her captivity and proclaim her Queen of England. The pope, still very badly informed about England, had been listening sympathetically to the schemes of the refugees in Rome, and Mary was writing letters to everyone whom she thought likely to assist her. Francis Throckmorton was attached to her household; his uncle, who had conformed, had been Elizabeth's ambassador in Paris, where he had been friendly with the girl who was then expected to be the future Queen of France. Francis acted as go-between for Mary and the French diplomats; a spy of the English government who worked in the house of the ambassador reported his visits, and in November 1583 he was suddenly arrested. As a conspirator, he had been extremely inefficient; in his house were found several incriminating documents, including a list of Catholics whom he hoped to use in a plot for Mary's release. The Duke of Guise was to invade Sussex, and the Catholics were to be bidden to raise forces to co-operate with him. After he had been racked three times, Francis told all

---

[1] A contemporary copy is in the Bodleian Library. The verses are printed in full in Jessopp, A., *One Generation of a Norfolk House* (1879), p. 106, and in part in Guiney, L.I., *Recusant Poets*, p. 178.

[2] Tenison, E. M., *Elizabethan England* (1933), Vol. IV, p. 40.

he knew. This did not save him: he was executed in May 1584.

The Spanish ambassador had also been in touch with Throckmorton; he replied to the protests of the English government with rather vague denials, and recounted Spain's own grievances—the raids made by Englishmen on Spanish shipping, the aid given to rebels in the Netherlands. He was ordered to leave the country; his royal master was extremely annoyed by the revelation of these constant intrigues. Philip wrote to his agent at the Vatican to point out how dangerous were such plots, known to so many people. He was not prepared to go to war with England, and he could well guess what harm such irresponsible people were doing to the Catholics in England and to Mary herself.

Burghley and Walsingham published accounts of Throckmorton's plot, emphasizing Elizabeth's danger; the assassination of William the Silent, the leader of the rebels in the Netherlands, served to remind people of the perils run by princes. A Scots Jesuit was captured, who told of earlier schemes for freeing Mary; it appeared that there was a wide and complex net of conspiracy. During October and November 1584, while elections were being held for a new parliament, the council appealed to all Englishmen to join a new association for the protection of the queen. Its members swore to 'pursue to utter extermination all that shall attempt or give consent to anything that shall tend to the harm of Her Majesty's person'. Moreover, they vowed to prosecute to the death any 'pretended successor by whom or for whom'[1] any attempt should be made against the queen.

It was now accepted that any Catholic, however loyal he might be to Elizabeth, might be taken to be 'aiding' conspirators if he were aware that someone was corresponding with the imprisoned queen. Priests, in particular, were placed in a most difficult position. If a penitent confessed that he had been involved in a plot, he could be forbidden to continue in it, but the knowledge which he must not reveal was a serious danger to the confessor. Many priests did suffer torture and death as a result of their loyalty to the seal of the confessional. The thousands of people who took the oath of the association were all given licence to kill, without being answerable to the courts, anyone suspected of plotting, even Mary herself. Such a breach of the common law of England was unique.

When parliament set to work in 1585, the association was made legal, but Mary of Scots was to some extent protected; if a rising took place, a commission was to inquire into the matter before she could be declared incapable of succession to the crown. Once

[1] See Neale, J. E., *Elizabeth and her Parliaments 1584–1601* (1957), p. 17.

her complicity had been established, it was the duty of 'all her Highness' subjects' to pursue her to the death. Mary was not mentioned by name; the act referred to 'any person that may pretend title' to the throne. It was clear that parliament wanted her death, but that the queen had serious scruples. Another act was 'Against Jesuits and Seminary Priests': foreign priests were not included, for, as was said in the debate, it was 'our home Jesuits who did all the hurt amongst us', since 'Englishmen would not be led with strange priests.'[1] It declared that the aim of these native priests was to stir up rebellion; they were to leave England within 40 days or be adjudged guilty of treason. Anyone who had been educated in a seminary, even if he had not been ordained, was included, and heavy penalties were imposed on all those who sent children abroad.

The Catholics bitterly resented the declaration that their priests were traitors and themselves disloyal. Some of them, including Lord Vaux, Sir John Arundell and Sir Thomas Tresham, drew up a petition to Elizabeth protesting that the 'priests pray every day for your Majesty'. Catholics were being forced to choose between being nominal traitors to their queen or actually betraying their God: 'let not us your Catholic native English and obedient subjects stand in worse peril . . . than the Catholic subjects of the Turk.'[2] Richard Shelley managed to present this petition to Elizabeth as she was walking in Greenwich Park. He was promptly arrested and sent to the Marshalsea prison, where he died—'which was the sum of the answer'.

The fears of Lord Vaux and his friends were fully justified. Henry, his eldest son, had taken the place of Gilbert as the leading spirit among the young men who supported and cared for the missionaries. The new law made the peril to the priests acute, and yet their continued presence was essential to the survival of Catholicism. Precautions were taken against the spies known to be employed by Burghley and Walsingham, but it was impossible to guard against those who, through hope of reward or through fear, remained apparently Catholic but were in touch with the English government.

In 1584 a captured priest gave the government a good deal of information about Vaux and his activities: they were told that Henry Vaux 'keepeth in the manner of a serving-man one Bridge, alias Gratley, a seminary priest'. This man turned informer, and entered the service of Philip Howard, Earl of Arundel. The Earl had become a Catholic in 1584; his position at court embarrassed

[1] Neale, J. E., *Elizabeth and her Parliaments 1584–1601* (1957), p. 38.
[2] Anstruther, G., *Vaux of Harrowden*, p. 155.

him, and Grateley persuaded him that he ought to leave the country.[1] He was caught in the act and charged with treason; the evidence that he had 'maintained' seminary priests was clear. He was not executed, for this might have antagonized his fellow peers, but was kept in the Tower until his death in 1595.

The strange story of Anthony Tyrell, another Vaux protégé, shows the psychological strain under which many priests suffered. Among his acquaintance was Anthony Babington, a young man of 25, who had been one of Mary Stewart's pages, and was a friend of the Vaux family. An optimistic and ill-balanced man named Ballard, who had once been a priest but had ceased to act as such, persuaded Babington that to assassinate Elizabeth would be a meritorious act, since only by her death could Mary be brought to the throne. Such an idea was not uncommon in the sixteenth century; many European observers fully expected Elizabeth to arrange for Mary to be killed privately, preferably by poison, and there is good evidence that the queen would not have been displeased had such an act been undertaken.[2] But Ballard was closely watched by an agent of Walsingham whose reports, signed "A.B.', gave full details about Babington and the other young men involved. Tyrell was arrested in August 1586 and Babington soon after. After torture, Tyrell promised to conform, and Mr. Justice Young ordered him to remain in prison and keep in close touch with the other Catholic prisoners, especially the priests, who were crowded in as arrest followed arrest. He was to continue to say Mass and hear confessions. But he could not keep up the deception, and the men who shared his cell discovered, although they had been torn into small pieces and carefully hidden, letters written by Lord Burghley and copies of Tyrell's replies. The priests in the prison summoned Tyrell and confronted him with this evidence; he confessed his treachery and promised to repair as far as he could the harm he had done.

It was soon realized that he was no longer useful to the government while he was in prison, so he was released and sent to Norfolk as a spy. Again he repented and wrote an account of his temptation and his fall.[3] Men were sent to arrest him, but the local Catholics helped him to escape abroad, where he wrote his autobiography for Father Persons, the Jesuit. But he could not settle down; he returned to England and gave himself up. He was ordered to make

---

[1] The documents in Arundel's case are printed in C.R.S., XXI. See also Weston, *Autobiography*, ed. Caraman (1955), p. 238.

[2] Neale, J. E., *Elizabeth and her Parliaments 1584–1601* (1957), pp. 139–41.

[3] This was sent to Verstegen in Antwerp in April 1593. C.R.S., LII, 134.

a public denial of the Roman faith at St. Paul's Cross, and a great show was prepared. One of the finest of the Elizabethan orators, John Reynolds, preached an introductory sermon. Tyrell followed him to the pulpit, but his first sentence showed that he had changed his mind about his recantation, and was planning to confess his treachery and his faith in Catholicism. He was dragged from the pulpit and taken back to prison, scattering as he went leaflets among the crowd; one was secured by a Papist and used later on in propaganda.

Again he was tortured, and again he submitted and was set free. In 1588 he obeyed orders and made his public recantation at Paul's Cross; he was rewarded by two small livings in Essex. His conscience still troubled him; he married, yet felt that he was still a priest and bound by his vow of chastity. In 1601 he had to give evidence against the Jesuit William Weston; this so troubled him that he tried in the following year to escape abroad. He was again sent to prison and again released, but finally he managed to get across the Channel. He died reconciled to his church.

When Tyrell was first arrested in August 1586 he had plenty of companions in misery, for the opportunity was taken of seizing any prominent Catholics who could be suspected of collusion, or at least sympathy, with Babington. Many prisoners had been released to make room in the jails for them, for the government had known of the conspiracy and had laid its plans well before the plot was officially discovered. Babington and Ballard were executed as traitors, and with them several other young men who had probably known nothing more than that there was a plan to liberate Mary Stewart. Babington himself stated, 'Before I met this Ballard I never meant nor intended to kill the Queen':[1] and he probably spoke the truth. Before he died he incriminated many of his friends, and even Mary herself. As had happened before and was to happen again, when romantic and ardent young men conspired without adequate knowledge or foresight, the plot was disastrous to the cause they had at heart, and very useful to those whom they detested. Burghley had long wanted an opportunity to move directly against Mary, and the act of 1585 had provided the machinery for dealing with her. Elizabeth's scruples had made it essential that there should be evidence of her implication in something other than a simple escape from custody; Babington's plot was just what was wanted. A special commission was sent to Fotheringay to try the Queen of Scotland.

Parliament had been prorogued and was not due to meet again

[1] Quoted by Caraman, P., in *William Weston* (1955), p. 106. In Weston's *Autobiography* and the editor's notes there is interesting material on Babington.

until November; so it was dissolved and a new one elected to meet in October 1586. Elizabeth herself did not attend the opening; she withdrew to Richmond, for she was unwilling to take an active part in what everyone knew to be inevitable, the condemnation of a queen. On 12 November she told a deputation from both Houses that in the act of 1585 'You have laid a hard hand upon me—that I must give direction for her death, which cannot be but most grievous, and an irksome burden to me.'[1] Though Mary was found guilty in November, the queen did not sign the warrant for her execution until February 1587; even then, so she said later, she did not expect it to be put into force until she gave the word. But Burghley and Walsingham took no chances; the warrant was sent off, and on 8 February Mary, still denying that she had known of the plan to assassinate Elizabeth, was beheaded at Fotheringay.

When the news reached London, bells were rung and bonfires lit, but Elizabeth felt the shock acutely. So did all the courts of Europe; the actual execution of one reigning princess by the order of another seemed outrageous in an age when sovereignty was venerated. The Pope, Sixtus V, had held a high opinion of Elizabeth: 'she is certainly a great queen and were she only a Catholic she would be our dearly beloved.'[2] Now he felt it his duty to issue a bull condemning her and proclaiming a crusade against her.

To the English Catholics, it seemed that all hope of freedom had ended. Even those who had had no share in plans for overthrowing Elizabeth had hoped that she would die unwed, and that Mary would be her heir. Babington's criminal folly had laid them open to the charge which they and their priests had tried so hard to prove false, that to be a Catholic in England involved disloyalty to the queen. There seemed to be no need for parliament to pass any further acts against Papists, but in 1587 another statute not only ordered a stricter enforcement of the existing laws but introduced a method of conviction of recusants new to English law. A suspected Papist who was summoned to attend at the assizes, and did not put in an appearance, could be 'proclaimed' by the clerk of the court to attend the next assize; if he did not then surrender himself for trial he was declared a recusant convict, although no evidence had been called and no official investigation made. A man could henceforth be declared guilty of an offence involving severe penalties without undergoing any trial at all. This arbitrary procedure was doubtless aimed at the recusants who had managed to escape arrest by moving from place to place. To be a recusant convict involved—in theory, if not always in practice—

[1] Neale, J. E., *Elizabeth and her Parliaments, 1584–1601* (1957), p. 119.
[2] Neale, J. E., *Queen Elizabeth* (1934), p. 284.

a deprivation of all civil rights; for instance, a debtor, sued for payment by a recusant, could plead that his creditor was a convicted Papist and therefore unable to bring an action in the courts. In 1592 another procedure, based on the normal law, was evolved to deal with the men who, though they themselves had conformed, had Catholic wives. As married women had no control over their property, they could claim to be unable to pay the £20 a month fine, even if they had been convicted. Now the government began to sue the husbands for the debts arising from their wives' unpaid fines. Henceforward no Catholic could feel any security, and according to the law the practice of their religion was almost impossible. Many did indeed suffer in body or in their property, though the very severity of the law led to sympathy from local officials and a corresponding failure to carry out their duty.

The success of Elizabeth's government in dealing with the Catholics did not however lead to peace and harmony in church and state. The Calvinists held that, now that the evils of Papistry were clearly revealed, all traces of Rome must be removed from the Church. The episcopal system was attacked in a series of tracts; the Puritans in the Commons were constant in their demands for change. Already in 1585 Elizabeth had upbraided those who were 'overbold with God Almighty' and declared them 'dangerous to a kingly rule'—a view that was shared by Mary's son James in Scotland. Yet for the rest of her reign, and under her successors, the Presbyterians and Independents remained in active opposition to the church established by law. As they had no conscientious objection to the oath prescribed by the Act of Supremacy, and were for the most part willing to attend and even to conduct services in the churches, they were not liable to prosecution by lay courts except for unlicensed printing of propaganda. Though their public 'exercises' had been prohibited, and their preachers might fall under the ban of the ecclesiastical court of High Commission, they were well organized and had many sympathizers, even among the queen's own councillors and courtiers. It is not surprising that many continental observers, in view of this double opposition to the religious policy of the queen, believed that Elizabeth could not count on the loyalty of her subjects.

Even before Mary's execution, England's relations with Spain had been subject to increasing strain. Raids on Spanish shipping carried out by Englishmen were regarded as purely private enterprises even though a share of the booty might go to the queen. Aid to the men fighting Philip's government in the Netherlands took a more obvious form when in the autumn of

1585 Elizabeth's favourite, the Earl of Leicester, took an English force into the Low Countries and accepted an official position at the head of the Dutch rebels. This could hardly be ignored, and Philip prepared for war. Neither side was ready for immediate action; England in particular was ill-prepared. The death of Mary of Scotland perhaps strengthened Philip's determination to deal with a country which was so persistently a nuisance to him; that the might of Spain would triumph seemed certain. A great fleet collected in Cadiz harbour; in April 1587 Drake, in a brilliantly executed raid, destroyed it. The invasion had to be postponed.

Preparations in England began with the preventive detention of many leading Catholics; they were ordered to live in the houses of bishops and other supporters of the government. This plan of using bishops as unofficial jailers was often followed; sometimes the idea seems to have been that they might succeed in persuading their guests of the errors of Roman theology. These precautions were probably unnecessary, for Mary's death had altered the situation profoundly. As long as she lived, most Catholics had anticipated that she would succeed Elizabeth, even if they were unwilling to take violent steps to hasten the event. Had Philip appeared earlier as her rescuer, they might have felt bound to support him; but now his victory would involve either submission to Spain or the accession of James of Scotland. Although some Papists shared the hope of the politicians in Rome that James might be induced to accept his mother's faith, many despised him for so calmly acquiescing in the very lame excuses Elizabeth had given for the execution of a queen. To secure their religious freedom as a result of a national defeat in war was not at all what the majority of Catholics wanted. Instead, many of their leaders begged to be allowed to join in the fight against the invaders from Spain. Sir Thomas Tresham had had much of his land confiscated, had paid heavy fines, and had been sent to prison: he refused to admit that Elizabeth was head of the church, but offered to swear to defend 'her royal person from violence' and 'this realm from invasion against all persons without exception, be it Prince, Pope, or potentate'.[1] Sir Thomas Arundell had been allowed to go abroad to fight under the Emperor Rudolph, Philip's kinsman, against the Turks; he had won renown and great rewards, out of which he sent £100 to England to help Elizabeth to buy arms. They were typical of many: but their protestations of loyalty were not believed, or at any rate not heeded.

The defeat of the Great Armada relieved the queen's government

[1] Anstruther, G., *Vaux of Harrowden*, p. 176.

of an immediate danger, though the possibility of further attempts in England and Ireland could not be ignored. The total extinction of Papistry now seemed a less impossible task, and Burghley set about it with vigour, tempered with caution lest the friends of Catholics should be antagonized. In the act of 1581 rewards had been made available for anyone who obtained the conviction of a Papist: the money paid by the offender was to be divided into three: one third for the queen; one to 'such person as shall sue for the same'—that is, the informer; one for the 'relief of the poor in the parish where the offence' was committed. This last was in practice made available for local expenses or additional rewards; Dr. Jessopp wrote in the mid-nineteenth century, 'I have never met with the faintest trace of evidence that the poor of the parish in any one case benefited.'[1]

To secure the arrest of a well-to-do Catholic was thus quite profitable, but it was still generally necessary to send pursuivants to carry out the actual seizure of the accused. In some areas new justices were appointed in the hope that they might prove more active in the enforcement of the law than those too closely bound to their Papist neighbours by ties of friendship or even of blood. To ensure convictions a device known to the Catholics as the Bloody Question was used: would they defend England against the pope himself if he invaded the country? This question offended the accepted principles of the common law in two ways—the accused was required to answer, not on a matter of fact, but on an improbable possibility: and if he replied No, he condemned himself.

There are very many examples of the use to which the Bloody Question could be put: it was dreaded by all who fell into the hands of the law. Robert Bickerdick had twice been found not guilty by a jury at quarter sessions of aiding a priest; he was taken away from the normal courts to York Castle for trial as a traitor. He was asked, 'If the Pope should invade the realm, what part he would take. He answered he could not tell at present what he would do in time to come, more than God should put into his mind. The judge said that he blew treason out of his mouth', and he was condemned and executed for high treason. When some of the local gentry questioned whether Bickerdick's words were 'treason by any statute or law' the judge was angry, and said that his duty was merely to give judgement.[2] Such an attitude was not uncommon; the evidence given in very many cases would never have been admitted in ordinary trials, and even where a

---

[1] Jessopp, A., *One Generation of a Norfolk House* (1879), p. 216.
[2] Grene, *Collections*. Quoted by Caraman, P., *The Other Face*, p. 231.

jury was used they would have been brave men indeed to acquit a prisoner accused of treachery.

A new word was coined by the wits at Elizabeth's court to signify the hunting down and torture of Papists—'*topcliffizare*'. Richard Topcliffe became a sort of symbol of brutality, unscrupulousness and greed, yet he played a prominent part in the suppression of Papists from 1584. He appears frequently in the prison lists as being responsible for the committal of captives, examining suspects, or having prisoners delivered to him personally. He was a man of good family and education; he sat as a member in the parliaments of 1572 and 1584, and frequented the court. Elizabeth was friendly to him, but gave him no official position save the vague one of 'the Queen's servant'. He must have had some charm or ability, for in spite of notorious scandals he remained in favour. He once boasted to a priest named Portmort, whom he was questioning, about his relations with the queen, suggesting a familiarity that was certainly untrue; the prisoner managed to write down his words and smuggle them out of the jail, but it was Portmort, not Topcliffe, who suffered.[1] In 1592 he had the Jesuit poet Robert Southwell in his power; he wrote to Elizabeth that the prisoner should be made 'to stand against the wall, his feet standing upon the ground and his hands stuck as high as he can reach' to enforce him to speak. This was an ingenious form of torture which replaced that of the rack; men who had had their limbs practically dislocated showed the effects plainly when they were brought to trial. 'The wall', which meant hanging by the hands with the feet barely touching the ground, left little outward mark save for the swollen and crippled wrists, though it caused a displacement of the organs of the body which was agonisingly painful. Southwell endured his sufferings without speaking, so, it was reported, 'The Queen called Topcliffe a fool'. She sent other people to help to break down the Jesuit's resistance, but they too failed.

The inquisitor was himself arrested in 1592, but was soon released and made one of the commissioners for the discovery of Jesuits and seminary priests. Even his seduction of a woman prisoner led only to a brief incarceration in 1594, and in 1595 he was able to harry Southwell in public at his trial in such a way as to scandalize even those who were accustomed to such mockeries of justice. For a while he was out of favour at court, but when he died in 1604 he was in possession of large estates secured in a variety of unsavoury ways.

[1] Devlin, C., *Robert Southwell* (1956), p. 274: a brief account of Topcliffe and his methods is given in this book. Portmort's notes are printed in C.R.S., LII, 97.

Topcliffe was outstanding, but there were many others who enjoyed both witnessing sufferings and building up fortunes from rewards or bribes. The danger of capture, and the certainty of torture unless they betrayed their associates, might well have been expected to hinder priests from coming to England, and laymen from welcoming them or allowing their sons to join their ranks. Instead, it seems to have stimulated the desire of young Englishmen to play a part in what they saw as a glorious adventure. In 1590 a large coloured map of Lancashire was made for the use of the Privy Council, to whom the Bishop of Chester had reported that 'The Papists every where are growen so confident, that they contempne Magistrats and their authorytie.'[1] It showed an extraordinary number of Papist estates with their owners' names, some of which Burghley marked as particularly important.

In England, and all over the continent, where many spies watched the English Papists, immense efforts were made to safeguard the priests. In the later sixteenth century new houses were being built and older ones enlarged and made comfortable in the latest style with great windows and chimneys. Elaborate hiding-places were constructed in a great many mansions—in chimney-breasts, under the roofs, beneath staircases, in the thickness of the walls, between floors, even in disused sewers—whence arose legends of underground passages. Granville Squiers published in 1934 a book on *Secret Hiding Places*. In it he described 112 'priest holes' in Catholic houses which he himself examined; 93 others almost certainly existed, but the houses have been altered, damaged or destroyed; and there must have been more of which no trace or record remains. These refuges are fascinating examples of the ingenuity of their constructors and the endurance of those who used them.

Nicholas Owen, a Jesuit lay brother nicknamed 'Little John', was exceedingly clever at devising and constructing these 'hides'. He made them wherever he went, even in houses which the Jesuit priests he accompanied had merely rented for a short time. Many a priest, Jesuit or secular, escaped arrest as a result of his work; but the refuges were usually too small for any one to live long in them, and a persistent search, sometimes lasting for days, generally led to the discovery or the surrender of their occupants. Father John Gerard, S.J., escaped by hiding in the Wisemans' house, 'Braddocks', in Essex; he had been betrayed by John Frank, a member of the household. Shortly afterwards, on 23 April 1594, he and 'Little John' were both caught in London. Gerard was sent to the Tower, from which he made a dramatic escape three

[1] C.R.S., IV, 162. The map is reproduced in this volume.

years later; Nicholas Owen was tortured but gave away no secrets, and his release was obtained by some Catholic gentlemen who needed his help badly enough to pay good money for his freedom.[1]

Most of the priests who were taken had been betrayed, either by men like John Frank, who were employed by the government, or by weaker brethren who, like Anthony Babington, were induced by torture to tell all they knew. That they were not all caught was due to the obstinacy and ingenuity of the lay folk they served, and the blind eyes turned on them by many local officials. Sometimes this acquiescence in law-breaking was secured by bribery; the government was not a generous paymaster, and it seemed well worth while to many Catholics to pay this sort of blackmail. More often, however, the reason was the reluctance of the neighbours of a Catholic family to get them into trouble, especially as a number of the conforming gentry owed their membership of the established church to convenience rather than to conviction. In some cases they tried hard to persuade friends or kinsmen to conform; a very old and ill man, Nicholas Gerard of Bryn in Lancashire, was carried to church by his brother's orders, but the obstinate old man started singing the psalms in Latin in so resonant a voice that he had to be removed with haste.[2]

Even though they might themselves feel fairly secure, the future of their children was a constant source of anxiety to the Papists. One of Burghley's 'by-ways' for eliminating Catholicism was to take children away from their parents 'under cover of education'.[3] A woman whose husband was in prison or in exile often tried to conceal the birth of a child for fear that it should be taken from her. In one instance a husband, Henry Hubert (or Hubbard), had gone abroad; he returned secretly with the Jesuit Father Weston in 1584. He knew that his wife was expecting a child, and that she had hidden in the house of a friend, but he dared not go himself to visit her. The priest called at the house, but had great difficulty in getting into contact with her, and had to produce a jewel belonging to her husband to prove that he was a true messenger and not a spy.[4] Such precautions were not unnecessary; when Thomas Haughton, one of a prominent Catholic Lancashire family, died in 1589, his young heir, Richard, was

[1] See Caraman, P. (trans.), *John Gerard* (1951), for the full story of these adventures. Owen died in 1610 after being tortured in the Tower.

[2] Myerscough, J. A., *A Procession of Lancashire Martyrs* (1958), p. 84.

[3] His *Memorial* of 1584 in the Petyt MSS. is quoted and discussed in Devlin, C., *Robert Southwell*, p. 330.

[4] Caraman, P. (trans.), *William Weston*, pp. 4–5.

taken from his mother and made the ward of Sir Gilbert Gerrard, the Master of the Rolls. Sir Gilbert brought the boy up to be a Protestant, and before he came of age married him to his daughter.[1] Some mothers, like Lady Vaux, succeeded in buying back the wardship of their sons.[2]

Even when both parents were living, their children were not safe. Two of the sons of Sir Henry Jerningham, of Costessey in Norfolk, were sent to school in London by government order. In 1593 the plague was raging in the city, and Sir Henry got leave to bring his sons home; but he was told 'Wee doe look that in the mean time your Children bee brought up and instructed bye a School-master known to be well affected to Religion'. The Jerninghams remained staunchly Catholic, so the plan failed.[3]

Once four boys of one family were all arrested—Thomas, Robert, Richard and John Worthington—when they were staying at Sankey Hall near Warrington. Their father was a recusant and their uncle a well-known Jesuit, so in February 1584 Sankey Hall was raided and the boys taken off for questioning. At first only the two elder ones were sent to prison in Preston; they refused to give information or to promise to attend the parish church, so the other two were brought in. The youngest, John, was kept without food and then given wine to make him talkative when he was brought before the court. He, too, was obstinate, and when closely questioned became so violently sick that he had to be taken out of court. The Bishop of Chester took the child, who was only 12 years old, into his own house, but John would answer back and argue when attempts were made to convert him. The bishop ordered the two elder boys to be flogged, but in vain; so Thomas, who was 16, and Robert were put in heavy irons. When it was decided to send them to school for instruction their keeper had to carry the irons under his cloak. The two boys started arguing with the schoolmaster, doubtless to the delight of the other pupils, so this plan had to be abandoned; they and their youngest brother John were sent to prison in Manchester. Richard was lucky; he was put in charge of a Dutch Protestant who treated him kindly. Thomas and John managed to escape from their prison, and Robert was rescued by friends as he was being removed to Chester.[4] The three boys safely reached their Jesuit uncle, who decided to take them to Douay. They joined a party of travellers, but were betrayed, and the dreaded Topcliffe himself claimed their

---

[1] C.R.S., XV, 155.
[2] Anstruther, G., *Vaux of Harrowden*, p. 231.
[3] Jessopp, op. cit., p. 216.
[4] Myerscough, J. A., op. cit., pp. 53 ff.

horses as his perquisite. Robert and John managed to escape; Father Worthington was sent to the Tower and later banished; and Thomas went to the Gatehouse prison. Mrs. Worthington succeeded in freeing Richard from his Dutch guardian by promising to pay for his board and lodging as if he were still in custody, and he, with his brothers Robert and John, got across the Channel to Rheims. Robert died soon afterwards as a result of all he had suffered, and Richard survived him by only four years. Thomas eventually escaped and settled in Louvain; John became a Jesuit priest.

To question children when houses were being searched for priests was often profitable to the officials: not many were as obstinate as the Worthington boys or as quick-witted as Frances Burroughs. This girl had been adopted by a widow, Eleanor Brookesby, whose house at Great Ashby (or Ashby Magna) in Leicestershire was a convenient refuge for priests as it was near the border of Warwickshire. As the lady was a Vaux, she was highly suspect, and searches of her house were frequent. When pursuivants came, Frances was usually sent to open the door; although she was only 11, she was very clever at handling them. One day the dreaded knock came while Mass was actually being said: Frances ran down with a lady, and found to her dismay that the men had already been admitted and stood with their drawn swords in the hall. She cried out to them, 'Oh, put up your swords or else my mother will die for she cannot endure to see a naked sword.' Rushing to get wine for her so-called mother, the girl made such a commotion that the priest was got safely into hiding and the chapel dismantled before the pursuivants got upstairs. Eventually Frances became a nun, and told the story to her fellow nuns who recorded it in the Chronicle of St. Monica's, Louvain.[1]

In one well-known case it was a child who betrayed the woman who had given him a home. Margaret Clitherow was the wife of a butcher in York: she had become a Catholic and was known to harbour priests; but she was so beloved for her charity that it was hard to get evidence against her. The little boy who was questioned did not in the least realize what was involved, and gave enough information to secure her arrest in 1586. When she was brought to court, she took a most unusual step—she refused to plead, for by English law a person who refused to answer to a charge could not be found guilty and thus no property could be confiscated. She saved her children's inheritance, but at the price of an appalling death by the 'peine forte et dure'. What precisely this meant is recorded in the sentence passed

[1] Quoted by Anstruther, G., *Vaux of Harrowden*, p. 181.

on another brave woman, Jane Wiseman, who followed Margaret Clitherow's example in 1598. When she refused to be tried by a jury, the sentence was 'that the said Jane Wiseman' should 'naked, except for a linen cloth about the lower part of her body' be laid on the ground on her back, 'and upon her body in every part let there be placed as much of stones and iron as she can bear and more; and as long as she shall live, that she have of the worst bread and water'; 'on the day she eats she shall not drink, and on the day she drinks she shall not eat, so living till she die.'[1] In Jane's case this sentence was not carried out, for Elizabeth 'rebuked the Justices of cruelty and said she should not die',[2] so she remained in prison until 1603 when, with other captives, she was released on the accession of James I.

There are countless stories, available in many books, of the escapes, tortures and deaths of men and women who made a point of the fact that they were suffering for their religion, as a formal conversion would have saved them. Naturally, the majority of those executed were priests, and most of them died in or near London.[3] Of the 56 laymen and three women, 37 suffered death in the provinces; probably far more died in prison, but it is not easy to get precise information. There was often sympathy for the victims; after the execution of two laymen in 1583 the Hampshire justices reported that many 'poor husbandmen and Artificers' had suddenly refused to go to church, saying that they wanted the Mass.[4] In Yorkshire the number of those who failed to attend service on Sunday grew, instead of diminishing. In 1578 the archbishop's visitation inquiries showed only 21 named offenders; in 1582 there were 329, in 1584, 417, in 1590, 587. It has been suggested that by 1603 there may have been 3,000 Papists in Yorkshire, when allowance has been made for the custom of naming only the head of a household, and for the deliberate omission of names.[5]

It seems certain that many people who had seen no harm in

---

[1] C.R.S., V, 367.   [2] Gerard, John, *Autobiography*, p. 228.

[3] A summary of numbers can be found in Hughes, P., *History of the Reformation in England*, Vol. III (1954), pp. 338 ff. In a pamphlet issued in 1960 by the Catholic Truth Society, Caraman and Walsh give a chronological list based on the latest available information of *Martyrs of England and Wales, 1535–1680*.

[4] Cotton MSS., Titus B III, fol. 81. Quoted by Dr. Swan in thesis cited in Chapter 2.

[5] Dickens, A. G., articles on Romanist Recusancy in Yorkshire, *Yorkshire Archaeological Journal*, Pt. 138 (1941), and Pt. 145 (1948). See also Aveling, H., *Post-Reformation Catholicism in East Yorkshire*, E. Yorks Local Hist. Soc., 1960.

occasional attendance at their parish church were induced to absent themselves by the arguments of the priests from overseas. Some of the seminarists were employed near their own homes, and they far outstripped the incumbents of the parishes in their zeal and in their influence. The Archbishop of York could do little to hinder their efforts; though the Council of the North, centred on York, was generally co-operative, he lacked support in the rural districts. There was much pluralism and apathy among the local parsons, and often the justices were protectors rather than prosecutors of their Papist neighbours. Not merely in the north, but all over England, only when a parson was infuriated by the open disregard of his parishioners, or when a quarrel arose over property, was the normal Englishman inclined to act as informer.

Even in the central courts in London some judges were disinclined to enforce the law. Recorder Fleetwood lost his post for his slackness in proceeding against Catholics. An example of his leniency was given in a report sent to Antwerp from England in 1592; he warned a lady that Justice Young planned to search her aunt's house for the priest who lived there.[1] Probably he, like other English lawyers, disliked the reputation that the English courts were establishing for tyrannical procedure. When at The Hague in 1593 an emissary of the Earl of Essex charged Peter Philips, the musician, with planning the assassination of Elizabeth, he was infuriated at the demand made by the judges for precise proof; it was reported that he exclaimed, 'O Papist Papyist yf I had the in England I would make short woorck of the.' This ill-judged remark was translated for the benefit of the court, and the president said 'that he knew well enough what the justice of England was but it should not be so here'.[2]

[1] C.R.S., LII, 40.   [2] *Recusant History*, IV, No. 2 (1957), p. 52.

4

PLOTS AND COUNTER-PLOTS

'We had a late Quene and she was a blodye Quene.'[1] Katherine
Gawen, gentlewoman and Papist, was indicted in 1603 for saying
these words. Not many people felt as strongly as she did, but
criticism of Elizabeth was growing during the last few years of
her reign. It was a time of tension; Archbishop Whitgift was
dealing severely with the Protestant opposition; widespread
poverty had led to the passing of a series of acts designed to
relieve the poor and assist the economy of the villages. War with
Spain continued; raids on the fleets and ports of both old and new
Spain met with varying success. Sometimes the organizers of
these expeditions made great profits, and sent handsome gifts to
the queen.

Yet Elizabeth remained very short of money. She had replaced
the bad English currency by new coins, but prices were rising all
over Europe. Taxes granted by parliament were inadequate for
her needs, even if they had been properly collected; she got more
and more into debt, in spite of selling land. Her two ablest councillors
died, Walsingham in 1590 and Burghley in 1598, and though
after a good deal of intrigue Robert Cecil became secretary, he
had not the same influence as his father. Elizabeth was more
amenable as she grew older; she rewarded her favourites with
patents giving them a monopoly in dealing with some commodity
and so provoked angry complaints in parliament. She went
further with her chief courtier, the Earl of Essex; though he had
shown himself domineering and incompetent, she sent him in
1599, with a considerable army, to put down rebellion in Ireland.
He not only failed to obey orders; he returned to England having
offered peace terms to the Irish which amounted to a surrender.
Elizabeth had to dismiss him from his offices, but retained her
personal affection; he repaid her by plotting a rising in London and
in the end she was forced to order his trial and execution.[2]

[1] Hist. MSS. Commission, Various I (1901), p. 73.
[2] Elizabeth's anguish was recorded by Marc Gheeraerts in a remarkable
portrait; it was lent in 1937 by Lord Methuen to an exhibition at Bristol of
Art Treasures of the West Country.

In such circumstances it was not easy to placate parliament. A simple means was to add to the laws against the Catholics; in 1593 all convicted recusants were forbidden to travel more than five miles from their homes. Such a restriction, if properly enforced, would not only have prevented laymen from evading arrest by moving from one house to another, it would also have limited the activity of their chaplains. Yet the number and the success of the priests continued.

William Allen was made a cardinal in 1587, as a tribute to his general supervision of the English candidates for ordination. He and Robert Persons the Jesuit worked closely together, trying to ensure that there were adequate colleges for the instruction of the seminarists, sufficient funds for their support, and care taken over their admission lest spies should creep in among them. From 1568 Allen and Persons had been concerned over the English hospice in Rome. This was an ancient hostel for pilgrims; many young Englishmen had gone there to the embarrassment of the elderly priests in charge, who were not at all suited to manage a seminary. In 1578 the authorities in Rome agreed that the buildings and the revenue should be used for training priests. The first Rector appointed was an elderly Welshman, who naturally favoured men who could speak Welsh; if Catholicism was to survive in Wales they were badly needed. Unhappily, the English students resented this, and in 1579 many of them left the college and went round Rome begging for money to pay for their journey home. Allen persuaded the Roman authorities to put the college into the Jesuits' hands; the Society was not anxious to take over another seminary but agreed, and from 1586 an English Jesuit managed the English College in Rome.

In 1594 Cardinal Allen died, and there was no one of similar vision and ability to succeed him. His foundation at Douay continued with varying fortunes, surviving personal disputes, shortage of money, and the dangers of the wars so frequent in the Low Countries. The secular priests sent to England from Douay and Rome had to face other and more subtle dangers than torture and death. It was hard for them to maintain their own high standards; some lived isolated lives, others were forced into unwelcome companionship. In 1580 a special prison for priests had been established in a semi-ruined castle at Wisbech in the Isle of Ely; here they were herded together, with very slight opportunity for contact with the world outside. The government had found that priests in the ordinary jails exercised considerable influence over their fellow prisoners, as well as over the Catholics who brought them food and clothing.

It was in Wisbech in 1584 that the last of the Catholic bishops
in England died; the only other survivor died in Rome the next
year. The secular priests had now no one at all to advise and
control them, save a Cardinal Protector in Rome. Yet it seemed
impractical to choose another bishop, with no cathedral, no chapter,
and to whose nomination the government would certainly not
assent. An Archpriest was appointed, with authority over the
Catholic clergy of England and Scotland—a fantastic task for
any man, even though he was empowered to commission 12
assistants. The man chosen, George Blackwell, was directed to
seek the advice of the superior of the Jesuits in England. This
greatly annoyed the secular clergy, and widened a breach, already
apparent, between them and the Jesuits; this antagonism had
lasting repercussions on English Catholic life.

The sons of Ignatius were a disciplined force, bound by regulations to which they managed to adhere to a surprising degree.
One of their number was Provincial, in command of all the rest,
sending them where they were needed and controlling their
activities. As each provincial in turn was executed, imprisoned, or
broke down in health, another was appointed. Every year all the
Jesuits who could possibly manage it met together, to renew
their vows and inspire and comfort each other. Full reports of
their work were sent to the General in Rome, smuggled overseas
or written when they were out of the country. Thus much more is
known about the Jesuits than about the secular clergy in England
who far outnumbered them but who had no obligation to make
records which might, if discovered, mean death for their patrons
and themselves.

Some of the most powerful Catholic families, like that of Vaux,
chose Jesuits as their chaplains, and the comparative safety they
could give their priests not unnaturally led to some jealousy.
When they found their Archpriest was in close contact with the
Society, many of the secular priests protested. They sent two
envoys to Rome in 1598 with a list of their grievances against
the Jesuits; in particular, their propaganda against the English
government was thought to exacerbate a situation already sufi-
ciently unpleasant. The keen desire of the 'Appellants', as they
were nicknamed after making a second appeal to Rome in 1600,
was to invent an oath of loyalty so phrased as to make it clear
that Catholics accepted the pope as a spiritual, not a political,
authority. That the English government at this juncture would
have accepted such an oath, and ceased to insist on conformity
to the national church, is so highly improbable that it reveals
how desperately the English priests longed to be rid of the stigma

of disloyalty. Indeed, Elizabeth's government was only too glad to fan the flames of discord between regulars and seculars.

In 1588 William Weston, S.J., was removed from prison in London to Wisbech. He found the priests confined there were not, as had originally been planned, in solitary confinement. Their friends had given them necessary furniture and had smuggled in the equipment for saying Mass; they were allowed to employ local boys as their servants. Two boys had been so impressed by their masters that they stopped attending the parish church. Although they were put in the stocks, they remained obstinate; one of them got away and eventually succeeded in reaching Douay and being ordained. The other was sent to a special prison for boys at Ely, and complaints were made to the council that the prison at Wisbech was 'as dangerous as a seminary'. Yet Weston found that many of the prisoners were not maintaining high spiritual standards, and suggested that their life should be organized in a regular routine. Some of the seculars approved the Jesuit's plans, others strongly objected, and 'stirs' and quarrels added to the disharmony between the Jesuits and the other priests.[1]

To the laity it mattered little whether the priests who heard their confessions and whose Masses they attended were seculars or Jesuits; it was not until later that they became involved in the unhappy controversy. The great majority stayed at home, evading the law as best they could, but fear of arrest, or sentence of banishment, drove many laymen overseas. Some went to Rome, some to Paris, but the greater number was to be found in the Netherlands. The King of Spain granted them sinecure offices or small pensions, but as time went on and their numbers grew, his payments became more and more erratic. Men, once well-to-do and now too old to work, were forced to beg for bread; some actually died of starvation. Their misfortunes were used as propaganda by the English government; in 1595 a pamphlet was published in London on the 'Usage of the English fugitives by the Spaniard'. Verstegen, the chief agent of the Catholics in Antwerp, had to admit that 'our miseries are such in truthe as that our Catholique friends in England may thereat be much agreaved.' It was 15 months, he wrote, since any money had come from Spain, in spite of 'lies and deluding promises . . . God comfort us and send us meanes to live withoute depending upon any forraine friends'.[2]

[1] Caraman, P., *William Weston*, pp. 139 ff, and C.R.S., LI, *The Wisbech Stirs.*

[2] C.R.S., LII, 96, 214, 219.

The exiles could only hope that, when Elizabeth died, her heir would allow them to return to their native land. Father Persons in Rome, Henry IV in France, and Philip III who succeeded to the Spanish throne in 1598, were all busy making plans, but none of them could be sure what policy James of Scotland would follow. Father Persons wrote a book on the legal title to the throne of England; the pope considered influencing James by a threat of excommunication. James himself had no doubts; he was already in touch with Sir Robert Cecil and ready to move as soon as he got news of the death of Elizabeth.

When her end came, in March 1603, many of the English Catholics shared the view of Katherine Gawen, who, after her rude remarks about Elizabeth, went on to say, 'Nowe we have a Kinge whoe is of our religion and will restore to us our rights.'[1] They trusted that James, the son of Mary Stewart, when he was free of the tiresome Scots Protestants, would be generous to her co-religionists even if he did not actually join her church. Clement VIII carried on a friendly correspondence with the new king through the English ambassador in Paris, and the leaders of the lay Catholics welcomed him with enthusiasm. Sir Thomas Tresham in Northamptonshire, and Sir Benjamin Tichborne in Winchester, took it on themselves publicly to proclaim his accession.

James reached London in May; he was aware of the danger of antagonizing the Papists, and not sure how strong they were. Catholics and their friends were invited to court and were included among those to whom knighthoods and other honours were distributed. More important, a very large number of those in prison for their religion were released, priests as well as laymen. The new king was convinced that the state of war with Spain must be ended on reasonable terms; more than immediate policy was concerned, for he believed that the preservation of peace in Europe would be greatly to the advantage of his kingdom. The relief to Catholics was one move in his diplomatic game.

Another opportunity of placating the Spaniards was given by some extremely futile plotting directed against James. An ex-priest, Watson, and a number of malcontents both Catholic and Puritan, schemed to get rid of him and place his cousin Arabella Stewart on the throne. Their aims seem to have been personal rather than national or religious. Father Garnet, the Provincial of the English Jesuits, learnt of the plot and wisely informed the council; James was so grateful that he promised to remit the fines on recusants. Sir Walter Raleigh was implicated by the statement of the men who were arrested; that he was seriously involved is

[1] Hist. MSS. Commission, Various I (1901), p. 73.

unlikely, but he was certainly discontented, for James had removed him from his post as Captain of the Guard. He was sent to the Tower, which delighted his enemies in Spain. As he had always been strongly anti-Catholic, his disgrace gave further encouragement to the recusants.

The Puritans also hoped that the Scots' king would adopt their policy for the church, but when they met him in conference in 1604 James made it perfectly clear that he disliked Calvinism and upheld the Elizabethan system which harmonized with his view of the divine rights of a monarch. The reformers were disappointed but not silenced, for they could state their case in public when James summoned his first parliament in 1604.

The drain of expenditure on the war with Spain ended when peace was made, but the king's needs were even greater than those of the late queen. He had debts of his own, as well as those he inherited; he had a family to maintain in royal state, courtiers to reward, and Scotland to administer. There was no division between the monarch's personal revenue and the national finances, so every jewel bought by the king reduced the sums available for government spending. Only parliament could give him aid, and James worsened his relations with the Commons by making Robert Cecil, whom he kept on as secretary, a peer. Trouble began immediately, for though the king in his opening speech denounced the pope, he went on to attack 'puritans and Novelists', who were he declared, 'a sect unable to be suffered'. The Commons retorted by drawing up an apology; it was not formally presented to James but he knew its terms. It contained not only demands for church reform, but expressed a view of the constitution radically different from that of the king.

The first shots had been fired in the long-drawn struggle that ended in the execution of James's son. Only on one matter was there agreement. The Catholics had been emboldened by James's friendly attitude; priests began to arrive almost openly, and now that peace had been signed Spain no longer need be placated. So the parliament was allowed to re-enact all the Elizabethan penal laws affecting Catholics. This was an unexpected blow for them; the laymen had anticipated continued relief, and the priests had rejoiced in the number of conversions and reconciliations. Katherine Gawen again spoke out. She was charged in 1605 with declaring that at James's accession she had spent much money on 'bonfires and otherwise to show joy at his coming, but it is indeed a King as good as no King'.

The Papists did not think that James himself was really unfriendly; many of them thought that he had been forced to give way before pressure in parliament. Once again a group of hot-heads, ignoring the realities of the situation and the advice of priests and wiser men, engaged in conspiracy, this time against the House of Commons. The three leaders were all about thirty years old, and had already played some part in politics. Robert Catesby was heir to considerable estates, and related to many of the leading Catholic families. He had been involved in the plot of 1601 which led to the execution of the Earl of Essex and to heavy fines and imprisonment for Catesby. In 1602 he and Lord Mont-eagle had sent Thomas Winter to Spain to ask for intervention when Elizabeth died, but so weak a deputation had carried little weight. When James succeeded peacefully and came to terms with Spain, Monteagle gave up hope and conformed to the established church.

Catesby's plan was to destroy the House of Commons by an explosion. He enlisted Winter's aid; Winter in turn brought in Guy Fawkes, whose name was to become a byword. They rented a house next to the hall where the Commons sat, acquired a quantity of gunpowder, hid it under firewood in the cellar, and put Fawkes in charge. James had prorogued parliament, and Catesby found the expense of maintaining the house more than his funds would bear. When he heard it was to meet again in November 1605, he approached his cousin Francis Tresham, confiding his plans and asking for money.

Tresham had been involved in the Spanish plan of 1602 and was a man of wealth. He strongly disapproved of Catesby's scheme, and asked whether any priest had been consulted about its morality. When Catesby said No, he declared that he held it damnable, and 'that thereby the Catholics wilbe utterly undone whether it be affected or noe, ffor if it be effected, what can the Catholics doo, what strengthe are they of, as of themselves, having no forrayne power to backe them?'[1] Tresham could not persuade his cousin to give up the plan, but urged him to delay until parliament had taken yet more steps against the Catholics. He also warned Catesby that the government probably knew all about the plot, but he promised him £100, and more in the future, and urged him to consult a priest. This Catesby did, but to no avail, as he would not listen to advice from anyone: in spite of dissuasion, he went on with his crazy scheme.

Tresham was right; the Earl of Salisbury was well aware of what was going on. This was shown by the clearing of prisons to make way for new inmates, as had been done before the official discovery

[1] Wake, J., 'The Death of Francis Tresham'. In *Northamptonshire Past and Present*, Vol. II, No. 1 (1954), pp. 36 ff.

of Babington's plot in 1586. It did not need the letter of warning which Tresham sent to Lord Monteagle for the discovery to be made, though this served well as the official reason. There is a copy of this letter in a contemporary hand in the archives of the Darrells of Calehill in Kent, now in the Record Office at Maidstone,[1] which suggests that it was circulated to other people before or immediately after the seizure of Guy Fawkes on the night of the 4/5 November 1605.

Fawkes was no hero; under torture he told all that he knew, and was then executed. Catesby was more fortunate; he was killed in resisting arrest. Thomas Winter and his brother Robert who had joined him both confessed fully before their death.

The plot suited Salisbury so well that later on he was suspected of inventing or initiating it. There is no doubt, however, that there was a genuine conspiracy; what the government did was to publicize it to horrify the country, and to accuse of complicity Catholics who had never heard of it, and would certainly have condemned it. Widespread arrests were made though Robert Cecil knew perfectly well how few were actually involved; he had been alarmed by James's attitude to the Catholics, and the plot was a perfect excuse for increased rigour against them. Parliament appointed a special commission to consider the punishment of the traitors; but several people were executed, some without a proper trial, before it had met.

A number of prominent Catholics were sent to the Tower. Henry Huddleston, with two priests and four of his servants, were taken, but 'whatever torture they be put to'[2] they swore that they knew nothing of any plot. Sir Everard Digby's house was ransacked by the High Sheriff of Buckinghamshire when he was taken to the Tower, and his wife wrote to Salisbury[3] protesting. 'He hath not left the worth of one penny . . . not so much as great tables and standing chests, that could not be removed without sawing and cutting a-pieces.' Even her own as well as her husband's clothes had been taken, and the parlour floor removed. Orders were given for the loot to be returned, but were hard to enforce. Sir Arthur Throckmorton seized Francis Tresham's personal property including a thirteenth-century manuscript which he presented to Magdalen College, Oxford. Tresham was already a sick man: he died in the Tower in 1606.

The Tower was the only prison in which torture could safely be used, for in all others people came and went with some freedom.

[1] Darrell MSS., Z 8/3.
[2] Anstruther, G., *Vaux of Harrowden*, p. 307.
[3] Ibid., p. 325.

In February 1606 leave was given to torture inferior prisoners, 'but if they put them to the manacles then cause them to be kept still in the Tower.'[1] What was wanted from these prisoners was proof that priests had approved of the conspiracy. That some did know of it is certain; but under the seal of the confessional.

The Jesuit Father Garnet was the man most closely in touch with Catesby and his friends. It was suspected that he was in Worcestershire in Hindlip Castle, and a very thorough search was made. After three days 'Little John' (Nicholas Owen, the maker of hiding places) and another Jesuit lay brother came out; they had had nothing but one apple between them to eat. Perhaps they hoped that their surrender might end the occupation of the house, but it did not, and on the eighth day Father Garnet and Father Oldcorne came out of the hole in a chimney-breast where they had been unable to stand upright, and with no means of sanitation. They were taken to London; after being tortured five times, Oldcorne was sent to Worcester and hanged, drawn and quartered. Garnet was at first well treated in the Tower; he was a man of good birth and very high reputation. There was no evidence that he had countenanced the plot; in fact he had written to Rome asking for a formal condemnation of all such schemes. He was allowed to communicate with Anne Vaux and other friends; like many other Catholics he used orange juice as invisible ink. These letters were read and copied by the authorities, and are extant; they could not be used against Garnet, for they would have been evidence in his favour.

Salisbury tried to spread it abroad that Garnet had admitted his complicity. Yet in a letter to the Earl of Mar he wrote that although 'Walley' (a code name for the Jesuit) had sworn that he had tried to dissuade the plotters, he would be executed as a traitor, for 'it is expedient to make it manifest to the world how far those men's doctrinal practice reacheth into the bowels of treason, and so for ever stop the mouths of their calumniation that preach and print our laws to be executed for difference in point of conscience.'[2]

Garnet was tortured only once, and after trial was executed on 3 May 1606. James gave orders that he should be allowed to hang until he died, and the dismemberment of his body caused pain only to those who looked on at the loathsome proceeding. The secretary to the Spanish ambassador reported that 'when the executioner showed his head and bade "God Save the King", there was not one would bestow an "Amen", but instead thereof fell

[1] B.M. Add. MSS. 11402. Quoted Anstruther, op. cit., p. 341.
[2] S.P. 14/19, No. 27. Quoted Anstruther, op. cit., p. 352.

upon the hangman.'[1] One Catholic spectator secured a straw from the basket into which the head was thrown. It was believed that the priest's likeness appeared on the bloodstained straw, which was treasured as a relic; and the story of the martyr was added to the legends repeated by recusants throughout the years to come.

Many of the Catholics who could manage to do so fled to the continent; one priest, Father Tesimond, knocked out his captor and hid in a boat carrying a cargo of dead pigs. Unmarried women and widows often joined convents already established; some of them founded new congregations of English nuns. Many of the men joined the Spanish forces, for the idea of national armies did not then exist in Europe: soldiering was a career, or a way for young men to prove their valour. Private persons formed their own troops or regiments: there might even be a private army, like that of Wallenstein in Central Europe during the Thirty Years War, which made him practically an independent power, able to bargain with both sides. Other refugees practised a profession; Peter Philips, John Bull and other musicians were employed by grandees or as church organists and music teachers.[2] Those untrained to a craft lived on what money could be smuggled to them from England, or on scanty and uncertain doles from the King of Spain and other sympathizers.

The great mass of English Papists remained at home, and with them parliament proceeded to deal, passing in 1606 still more laws against them. The 'Church Papists' were hit, for a new law made it impossible for them to escape by an occasional attendance at service; they now had to receive the sacrament at least once a year or be fined on an ascending scale. Churchwardens were ordered to report the names of those absent from church, including their wives, children and servants, every year to the quarter sessions. Householders were responsible for the attendance at church of all their dependents.

Many Catholics, including some priests, had found it possible to take the oath of loyalty to James. Now a new form was drawn up, which stated that those who took it considered 'damnable' the pope's claim to excommunicate or depose a prince, and pledged themselves to report any 'traitorous conspiracies'. Rome was asked whether Catholics could take this oath: as might have been expected, a bull of 1606 prohibited it. Every person indicted for recusancy was to be asked to take this oath or incur the penalty of *praemunire*—loss of property. If a person went abroad without

[1] Gerard, John, *Autobiography*, trans. Caraman (1951), p. 201, footnote.
[2] See Petti, A. G., 'Peter Phillips', *Recusant History*, Vol. 4, No. 2 (1957).

having sworn, he 'shall be a felon'. To reconcile to the See of Rome, or willingly to be reconciled, was declared traitorous.[1]

Another act prohibited recusants from coming near the court without a specific summons. They were also forbidden to have a house in London, as many of them in fact did, unless they worked there at a trade and had no other abode. The detection of Catholics was encouraged by rewards of up to £50, from forfeitures imposed, to be given to those whose information led to the conviction of anyone who said Mass or was present at Mass. The professions were closed to all convicted recusants: they could not practise officially as doctors or lawyers or be employed in the state's service in any way. Licences of exemption heretofore had been given by two justices of the peace; now four were needed, or the Privy Council itself. Convicted women lost all their rights to act as executors or guardians and to inherit their husbands' chattels, and were deprived of two-thirds of their inheritance or jointure.

All 'recusants convict' were declared excommunicate, which debarred them from going to law except in cases involving landed property. No Catholic could be the executor of a will or guardian of a child. No marriage was valid unless solemnized in the national church, the parties to an illegal marriage performed by a priest had no claim on each other's property, and their children would, in theory, be illegitimate. If a child were not baptized in church a fine of £100 was due, and for a clandestine burial a fine of £20. Yet Catholics continued to be baptized, married and buried by their own priests; only rarely did Protestant kinsmen take advantage of the laws and claim their lands.

To send children overseas was prohibited, unless they were apprentices or servants of merchants, or enrolled as soldiers or seamen, or their parents had procured a special licence for their journey. Boys already overseas were ordered to return within six months, and any child who had been out of the country had to take the oath of allegiance when he was 18, or lose his property, which meantime would be administered by the nearest Protestant kinsman. No Papist could have any weapons save those which the justices agreed were necessary for his defence: any other arms could be seized if four justices issued a warrant. The magistrates could also search suspect houses for imported books and destroy any they found; rosaries, crucifixes and such things were to be destroyed, although a 'crucifix or other relic of price' might be returned to its owner after the image on the cross had been defaced.

The extreme severity of these laws could still be avoided in

[1] The text of the act is in Prothero, G. W., *Select Statutes*, etc. (1906) pp. 256 ff.

districts where neighbours were friendly. Sometimes the seizure of a recusant's land in lieu of annual fines could be a great advantage to him. Some of the leases preserved in the archives of the Chichesters of Arlington indicate how the law affected that family.[1] Amyas Chichester and Mary Chichester, widow, were punished for their recusancy in 1606 by the seizure of their chattels and two-thirds of their lands. Their personal property and a 41 years' lease of the land were given to William Anes. In 1608 Anes was granting leases to W. Moore and J. Poyntz, and these two men, with Anes and Amyas Chichester, were in that year leasing out farms. The strong inference is that the three gentlemen were friends of the family, and the Chichesters' loss more nominal than real. Amyas was able in 1609 to sell standing timber to a carpenter of Tiverton for the large sum of £216, which shows his control of valuable woodland.

The family was an obstinate one, and in 1628 John Chichester had two-thirds of his land taken and leased to Lewis Incledon for £3 6s. 8d. a year. Incledon then assigned the lease back to John; so it appears as if this fortunate recusant was in fact paying only £3 6s. 8d. instead of the £240 which would have been his annual fine for non-attendance at church. This is a very unusual case, where the preservation of deeds seems to demonstrate what could happen when circumstances—distance from London, strong friendship of neighbours—were favourable. In other places, where full advantage was taken of the confiscations, well-to-do families were often reduced to poverty.

The reporting of recusants to quarter sessions could also be very imperfectly done. Sir John Yorke of Nidderdale in Yorkshire did not belong to one of the old-established families; he obtained the Nidderdale estate by marrying a Catholic heiress. Although he decided to 'goe to the Churche for the saving of his goods'[2] his brothers as well as his wife were recusants, and he was closely linked with Catholic families in the district. He had some connection with Robert Winter, yet he was not even questioned after the Gunpowder Plot. The local parson was so much under his influence that in 1606 he took his list of recusants to Sir John before he sent it in; as, although there were four or five hundred people in the parish, he stated that only two or three attended service, and sometimes none at all, his list must have been a formidable document. Sir John scratched out the names of his friends and

---

[1] Chichester MSS., Nos. 50/11/4, 15 and 16; 50/11/23; 50/11/4, 18 and 19; 50/11/17, 3 in Exeter City Library. In other cases speculators got the leases and the family was ruined. See *Recusant History*, Vol. IV, No. 5., p. 189.

[2] Howard, C., *Sir John Yorke of Nidderdale* (1939), pp. 11 ff.

servants, 'and then gave him the bill again and thanked him.'

At York Assizes in 1609 the law was actually invoked against men who had attacked recusants.[1] Thomas Marr and Richard Braithwaite were accused of ill-treating Dorothy Scroope, 'she being aged about 60 years and very sickly'. They had broken into her house and arrested her as a recusant, and 'put her on a barrow and took her to Thirsk, a mile and a half from her house.' After getting 45s. from her, they released her; but she complained of the bruising she had suffered from being bumped about in a wheel-barrow, and her friends said they feared she would die. The men were also accused of robbing other recusants. Their arrest was ordered, and four local gentlemen commissioned to inquire into the charges of 'oppressions and extortions &c.' against recusants and others.

Even when Papists were properly indicted at quarter sessions they might escape. Sir Thomas Posthumus Hoby, a strong enemy of Rome, reported that some of the justices in the East Riding of Yorkshire, 'fearing that divers of their friends, tenants &c. should be indicted and thereby discovered to be recusants', arranged that at the January quarter sessions of 1615 the unusual number of 21 magistrates should attend, 'thus obtaining a good majority'. Then, 'by putting idle things to voyces the [to vote] moving needless questions, adjourning for dinner unnecessarily', they so delayed proceedings that the lists were not dealt with at all.[2]

In Devonshire, Richard Reynell, who lived near Crediton, was indignant with the failure of the Exeter justices to deal with recusants. He had sent men to arrest priests, 'but they had notice of all your proceedings. . . . And old Baggot was seen ryding to and from ye Popish Houses. But I have sent for old Baggot. I marvel how they should so speedily have notice of your doings and letters.'[3] Reynell had some justification for his resentment at the non-enforcement of the law: a Devonshire man, a Jesuit, who was arrested in Exeter in 1621, not only had a chalice and paten and other necessities for the saying of Mass, but a number of devotional and controversial books. Pursuivants from London were sent for, and he was taken to the capital, but merely imprisoned and released in 1625.[4]

In 1605 the Bishop of Hereford reported his difficulties in dealing

---

[1] Meynell MSS. at Ampleforth Abbey. Vol. I.

[2] Legard, Sir J. D., *The Legards of Anlaby and Ganton* (London, 1926), p. 33.

[3] Quoted by Oliver, G., *Collections* (London, 1857), p. 8. He ascribed the letter to the year 1621.

[4] Oliver, op. cit., p. 6.

with the Catholics on the borders of Wales. If he sent a few men to arrest priests and recusants, they were driven off; a large force could not be concealed, and the suspects fled in time to the forests and hills. On Corpus Christi day the sheriff had attempted to arrest 30 or more men who had assembled; they were armed and put up so stout a resistance that only five were captured.[1] All along the Welsh border there was great toleration for the Catholics; Abergavenny was a strong centre for them.

It was not only in these remote areas, but even in counties like Oxfordshire and Berkshire, that Papistry was able to flourish; parish churches in many places still have tombs and grave slabs with inscriptions that show the faith of the recusants there laid to rest. Parsons were put in a difficult position when local squires refused to conform. Should the deaths and births in their families be entered in the parish register? Occasionally children were entered as 'base born', for their parents had not been married in the church; more often they were recorded normally, especially when, though a priest had baptized the baby, the appropriate fee had been paid to the incumbent. At Twyford, in Hampshire, deaths among the Wells family were entered in the register,[2] though sometimes the burial was described as 'clandestine' or 'private', and once with a note, 'No bell or fees'. At Sefton in Lancashire interment of Catholics in the parish church was prohibited, and William Blundell of Crosby made a private graveyard for them, after melancholy difficulties had been found in the decent disposal of the bodies.[3] Generally, however, it seems to have been possible for the coffin to be taken to the churchyard after the Catholic rites had been performed by a priest, and the actual burial was carried out by the incumbent.

Sometimes a Catholic family had legal rights which must have embarrassed the authorities. The Eystons of East Hendred in Berkshire owned an aisle of the parish church; they also had an ancient chapel where their priest said Mass.[4] In Lancashire the Westbys had a private chapel in the church at Kirkham, and in 1618 an ancient chantry chapel at Great Singleton was sold to the local Papists and used for Mass.[5] Yet in spite of the very large number of examples that can be found of Catholics who escaped the penalties imposed by the law, they were continually aware of their insecurity. Their safeguard lay with the uncertain favour of the monarch; parliament was inimical, but it met rarely and had

[1] C.R.S., II, 289 ff.   [2] C.R.S., XXVII, 47 ff.
[3] Blundell, M., *Cavalier* (1933), p. 244.
[4] Humphreys, A. L., *East Hendred* (1923), p. 287.
[5] C.R.S., XV, p. 562.

no administrative power. James could not repeal the laws, but if he chose he could by his open disfavour reduce the number of prosecutions, and he could always exercise his royal prerogative of pardon. It was to him that the priests and their flocks looked with hope ever renewed in spite of disappointments; though his shifts of policy affected many sections of English society, for the Catholics they might mean life or death.

5

POLITICS AND PAPISTS 1612–28

The death of Robert Cecil, Earl of Salisbury, in 1612 ended a period in the story of the Catholics. He had maintained the Elizabethan principles and methods of dealing with them; severity or lenience depended mainly on the situation in England. When he was gone, there was no obvious person to follow him as the king's chief adviser; the popular Henry, Prince of Wales, died that same year, and his brother Charles was only 12. James's aims were clear—he wanted a strong government depending on himself, and peaceful relations with his brother sovereigns. He was humane, and disliked barbarous executions; the religion of Rome fitted his theory of monarchy better than did Calvinism. Yet the fines paid by some recusants, and the sale of exemptions and licenses to others, brought in money he badly needed. He was a poor judge of men, and his strong personal affections induced him to accept the ideas of the favourites he cherished, so he never pursued a clear line of policy.

He found the existence of the Papists useful in his foreign policy. He could offer benefits to them as a consideration in his bargaining with Spain, with whom he was anxious to maintain peace. Europe was in a state of flux; Henry of Navarre had died in 1610, the Emperor was still struggling to maintain his own authority and the Catholic faith against the ambitious princes of Germany. James envisaged himself as able by skilful diplomacy to act as a balancing force. In 1613 he chose Frederick, Elector Palatine of the Rhineland, as the husband of his daughter Elizabeth; lest this should indicate that he was allied to the Protestant party in Europe, he revived the idea, first considered in 1604, of a Spanish bride for his heir. This would not be popular, but the handsome dowry of an Infanta would be a compensation. Negotiations were begun, and in 1613 Diego Sarmiento, later Count Gondomar, came as ambassador from Spain. He soon established a considerable influence over James, to the annoyance of the reigning favourite, George Villiers, and of the strongly Protestant Archbishop of Canterbury, George Abbot.

FCE

These two persuaded the king to release Raleigh from the Tower and fit out an expedition to annex a gold mine in Guiana. Raleigh promised to respect Spanish sovereignty in the area, and Gondomar was promised that, if he came to blows with Spaniards, Sir Walter would be hanged. The ill-found venture was a disastrous failure; Raleigh's own son was killed when attempting to seize a Spanish settlement, and no gold was found. Sir Walter returned in 1618 and was beheaded under the sentence passed on him in 1603 for his share in Watson's conspiracy. The death of an Elizabethan hero added to the indignation felt over the plan of a marriage alliance with Spain.

Next year, a barrier to James's schemes was raised by his daughter Elizabeth. She was an ambitious woman; when the nobles of Bohemia who had revolted against the Emperor invited her husband to be their king, she urged him to accept. The forces Frederick could muster were quite inadequate to withstand the armies of the Empire; he was driven out of his own territory as well as out of Bohemia. Though James had not been consulted he wanted to restore the Palatinate to his son-in-law. If Spain were friendly, this might be done.

The king had failed to grasp two important points; the defeat of Frederick had made an English alliance unnecessary for Philip of Spain, and had roused English feeling to a high pitch. A popular song, which like other political effusions survived to become an unintelligible nursery rhyme, expressed public opinion.

> I had a little nut tree, and nothing would it bear
> But a silver nutmeg and a golden pear.
> The king of Spain's daughter came to visit me,
> And all for the sake of my little nut tree.

That the nutmeg, symbol of the spice trade, would be lost to England by a Spanish alliance was firmly believed; the idea that Spain was the barrier to the expansion of trade, not only in the Americas, but also in the Indies, died very hard. When a clash came at Amboyna in the Spice Islands in 1623, it was the Dutch who tortured and killed English merchants who attempted to break into their trading area, but there was nothing like the outcry that would have resounded had Spaniards been responsible. There were complaints, and demands for compensation, but the Dutch were good Protestants.

Catholicism and Spain were inseparably united in the minds of the men who sat in the Commons when James reluctantly called a parliament to vote him some money. Every priest, especially all Jesuits, became for them a secret agent for Spain.

There were many other causes for opposition; the king had been raising money in ways considered unconstitutional and spending it freely; they detested his favourite Villiers, made Duke of Buckingham in 1623, who had now adopted a pro-Spanish policy. The only point on which the king yielded to their demands was that he promised to enforce the laws against recusants. Each session ended with a prorogation or dissolution before any adequate taxes had been voted.

James did not wish the penal laws repealed, for they could be used to placate Gondomar by the release or pardon of priests. He often intervened on behalf of recusants for humanitarian reasons as well, as he did in 1612. In that year occurred the last burning alive of heretics in England; one was an Arian, who denied the divinity of Christ, the other an Anabaptist. That the bishops who were responsible for the fate of these two men would tolerate Papists was improbable, and George Abbot, Archbishop of Canterbury, showed he had something of the brutal humour of what may be called the Topcliffe era.

There were several priests in the Gatehouse prison, and order had been given that they should be kept in solitary confinement. When they asked for a relaxation of the rule, Abbot directed that they should be 'dumped together in a worse place'. A number of them were put in a room so small that they could not lie down; in answer to protests, the Archbishop replied, 'they should lie one upon the other, and he that was undermost, when he was weary, might lie at the top.'[1] Two of the many priests captured were executed. One of them complained that he had been kept lying in a damp dungeon, loaded with chains; this was reported to the king, who was very angry, and for three years he would allow no further executions. This was the longest break in the death roll of priests since 1577.

In 1616 James did not exert his privilege of mercy; four priests, all Douay men, were executed. The story of one of them, John Maxfield, was unusual; directly after his death an account of his life and death was written in Latin and widely read, for a second edition was printed. An English translation was made by the musician John Bolt, who had taken refuge in the Netherlands.[2]

Maxfield had been born in prison, where both his parents were confined. In 1603 he was sent to Douay; though his training was interrupted by bad health, he finished his studies, was ordained, and in 1615 arrived in London. Three months later he was arrested

[1] Westminster Cathedral Archives, XI, No. 44. Quoted by Anstruther *Vaux of Harrowden*, p. 417.
[2] Printed in C.R.S., III, 30 ff.

just as he had finished saying Mass: he did not deny that he was
a priest. He was sent to the Gatehouse prison, and after some time
made an attempt to escape by letting himself down from a window,
but as he reached the ground a man saw him and seized him. His
jailers were very angry and loaded him with irons; he was then
placed, bent double, in a dungeon where the 'wormes & creeping
beastes which that filthie place engendred' tormented him. When,
after 70 hours, he was taken out, he was in such a state of naked-
ness and dirt that the man who caught him in his attempted
escape gave him his cloak, so that 'he might more decently go
through the streets' to Newgate. After his trial and condemnation
many people visited him, and so much sympathy was aroused
that the authorities tried to prevent demonstrations at his execution by providing an alternative spectacle, 'a woman who had
killed her husband, to be burned at Smithfilde'; but in spite of
this counter-attraction, when the journey to Tyburn began at
5 a.m. a large number of his friends and admirers were ready to
accompany him. English Catholics, foreigners from the embassies,
and above all 'Spaniards mounted upon goodly horses, rode two
by two in a long trayne both before & on each side' of the hurdle,
defying the attempts of the guard to beat them off. At Tyburn the
gallows had been decorated with summer flowers, and the executioner was persuaded to let Maxfield hang until he was dead.

This demonstration by the Spaniards and the Catholics in
London did not lead to any corresponding anti-Catholic movement
among the people: indeed in the seventeenth century such executions more often led to expressions of horror and sympathy than
to satisfaction among the spectators. In the north of England,
Bishop James of Durham had reported in 1615 that there was 'a
flocking of priests together' in Newcastle, 'wherein there was,
within these few years, not one recusant.' One of these priests
was William Southerne,[1] whose family lived in the neighbourhood;
in 1605 he had returned to work there after studying in Poland
and other countries. Bishop James employed a man known as
Christopher Newkirk to find out and report on priests; he was
said to be a Pole by origin, and a surgeon, and may have been the
'Pollonyan fisission' who in 1593 was rewarded by the authorities
in Newcastle.

By pretending to be a Catholic, Newkirk succeeded in persuading a man, who acted as a liaison officer between the priests
and the people, to take him to see Southerne. The priest lived in
humble quarters, 'where a woman dwelleth . . . selling some small
commodities in her shop, as Ropes, Red herrings and some salt

[1] Forster, A. M. C., article in *Recusant History*, IV, No. 5 (1958), pp. 199 ff.

fishes, and many small trifles.' Newkirk disarmed suspicion by talking about Poland; then, by going to confession and attending Mass, he won the priest's complete confidence. After a few days Southerne visited him: 'I entertained him friendly with wine, pears, walnuts and east country gingerbread.' They talked about other priests in the district, but for some reason the Bishop of Durham did not attempt to arrest any of them.

Three years later a priest, who had abandoned his faith, denounced Southerne and secured his arrest. The President of the Council of the North arranged an immediate trial, and he was found guilty of treachery because he refused to take the oath of allegiance or to admit that he was a priest. There was a delay of six days while the authorities searched for a man who would be willing to carry out the horrible rites of the execution, but eventually one was found, and on 30 April 1618, Southerne underwent his fate, with a smile on his face when he died. When the Spanish ambassador heard the story, he was so indignant that he threatened to break off negotiations; to pacify him, James promised to dismiss Lord Sheffield, the President who was responsible for the execution, and also ordered the immediate release of all the priests who were in prison. There were a great many of them; the names of over 70 are known. They were commanded to leave the country, and when Gondomar went back to consult with his king he took with him about 100 English priests, so contemporaries said. Not many of them remained abroad; they came back and resumed their work.

'The interposing of foreign princes and their agents' on behalf of English Papists was resented by the parliament of 1621; but it could influence the king only by refusing grants. Catholics who were arrested knew that they had a fair chance of escape; when in 1622, to hurry on his Spanish plan by showing his clemency, James again ordered the release of those in prison, it was said that there were 400 priests and 4,000 laymen affected by the order.[1] These figures may be exaggerated, but there is no doubt that there was a very large number of Catholics in the country and that they were amply provided with priests. Besides the Jesuits, members of the older orders were working in England; the Benedictines had refounded their English congregation, and from 1618 there was a Franciscan national province, but the missionaries remained predominantly secular priests, and their organization was far from satisfactory. It was difficult for the Archpriest to exercise any real authority, and the danger from unworthy priests, or even unwise ones, was still very real. In 1618 the Archpriest was troubled

[1] Davis, G., *The Early Stuarts* (Oxford, 1952), p. 206.

about the scandal caused by priests going to the theatre in London; the playhouses were, not without justification, looked on as meeting-places for disorderly people of all ranks. Many of the priests in the ordinary jails had considerable freedom, provided they were present at night, and during the day some of them went to the theatres. As they had to live on the alms of the lay Catholics, who might well be shocked to see them spending money on such amusements, there was every ground for Archpriest Harrison to prohibit attendance at public theatres, though he allowed priests to go to private performances. An outcry, led by an elderly priest of good character, greeted this decision, and the ban had to be withdrawn.[1]

Petitions to Rome for the appointment of a bishop were renewed, and in 1622 a commission of cardinals investigated the situation. King James was approached: he was told that only one bishop would be appointed and that he would not be given a title derived from an English see. Under these conditions, the king could see no harm in agreeing, and in 1623 the selection was made. It seems extraordinary that a man of 70 should have been nominated for so difficult a duty, but to find a priest known in Rome and respected in England was not easy. William Bishop had been one of the envoys sent to Rome by the English priests in 1603; he was created Bishop of Chalcedon, an ancient see in Asia Minor, and given authority over the whole of England, Wales and Scotland. When on 31 July 1623 the bishop landed secretly at Dover, he had to walk for over 12 miles before he found a safe refuge. He showed amazing energy for a man of his years; at Cowdray in Sussex he administered the sacrament of confirmation to 400 people. His wide knowledge of the English clergy was a great help to him; he chose 20 archdeacons and put them in charge of districts, and set up a chapter of canons to advise him and help in administration. But his very energy shortened his career; his strength failed and he died early in 1624.

Richard Smith was chosen to succeed him; William Bishop had appointed him a canon, although he was then living in Paris. Smith was 58, a Lincolnshire man who had studied in Oxford and Rome. From 1602 to 1609 he had been chaplain to Viscountess Montague at Battle Abbey in Sussex, but had left to go to Paris where a small college had been founded in which priests continued their studies and wrote books of theology and scholarly propaganda. The new bishop knew Richelieu well, he had been the Cardinal's tutor in theology, and the French ambassador in

[1] Semper, I. J., article on 'Jacobean Playhouses and Catholic Clerics', *The Month*, July, 1952, p. 28.

London was told to help him as much as he could. He reached London at the end of April 1625.

He boldly travelled over the rough English roads in a coach drawn by four horses; for this he was criticized, rather unfairly, for his only alternative was to ride as his medieval predecessors had done—the riding apron and gaiters survive as an episcopal uniform. By April 1627 he could report that he had visited every part of the country, administering the sacrament of confirmation and meeting his clergy. His difficulties were great: there were many priests, but the secular colleges found it hard to know precisely what their men were doing when they were in England. The Jesuits and Benedictines were under the orders of their immediate superiors, and challenged Smith's claim that their 'faculties' to hear confessions and administer the sacraments must be granted by him. Often he had no means of telling whether a man was in fact a priest.

This obscurity was shown in the case of Tobie Matthew, the eldest son of the man who had, with Campion, delighted Elizabeth at Oxford[1] and later became Archbishop of York. Like his father, the younger Tobie was clever and witty; he distinguished himself at Oxford and became an intimate friend of Francis Bacon. He was a member of the last parliament of Elizabeth and of the first of James. In 1604 he planned a tour in Europe; his father, who knew that he numbered Catholics among his friends, made him promise not to visit Italy or Spain. Tobie broke his word and went to Italy; there he fell in with some English Catholics and was received into their church.[2]

When he came home, he concealed his change of religion from most of his acquaintances except the Archbishop of Canterbury. When he was asked to take the oath of allegiance, Matthew refused; he was sent to the Fleet prison, where various divines tried to convince him of his errors. When a severe epidemic of the plague attacked London, he was released, and in April 1608 obtained leave to go abroad. James refused to allow him to return, so he went to Rome and studied at the English College; he was ordained in 1614. He then went travelling, and when in France made friends with George Villiers. In 1617 Villiers got permission for Tobie to return to England. Hardly anyone knew that he was actually a priest; he lived like a normal man of his class, save that he refused to take the oath. Although this caused another banishment, his influential acquaintance at court again procured his return. He knew Gondomar well, and through him

[1] Supra, p. 18.
[2] Mathew, A. H., Ed., *The Conversion of Sir Tobie Matthew* (1904).

and Villiers was on good terms with the king, who used him in negotiations with Rome about the proposed Spanish match.

Prince Charles and George Villiers, Duke of Buckingham, grew impatient at the slow progress of the plans for the marriage, and in 1623 tried to force the pace by journeying to Madrid. The notion that the King of Spain would yield to the persuasions of a romantic lover was quite absurd, and Charles, who was disappointed in the Infanta, found himself involved in a course of hard bargaining in which Philip, who had been made even less willing for the match by Villiers' conduct, had all the advantage. James sent Tobie Matthew to advise and help his son; when in the end the Prince returned, angry and disappointed, Tobie was knighted.

That a known Catholic, even if his priesthood was concealed, should play such a part at court was of course very encouraging to his co-religionists. How great their numbers were in London was publicly demonstrated by an incident in 1623. At Hunsdon House, in Blackfriars, a very large congregation had gathered to hear a sermon from a well-known Jesuit. The floor of the room collapsed under the weight; many people were injured, and it was said that nearly 100 were killed. As the story was reported in a letter to Rome, the dead included '10 persons of worth, one Minister, a Protestant'.[1] It is highly probable that a 'minister' was present, for theological arguments between Papists and members of the established church were being carried on freely; Tobie Matthew held such 'disputations' before James himself. Augustine Baker, a Benedictine monk, argued and corresponded with John Selden, the jurist, and there were many similar personal friendships.

In spite of Tobie's intervention in Spain, James had to drop the plan for a Spanish match which he had pursued for years, to find some other means of assisting Frederick, and to seek another wife for his son. Alliance with France was the obvious course, and a suitable princess was available in the youngest daughter of Henry IV, born shortly before her father's assassination in 1610. In 1624 an embassy in Paris began negotiations for the hand of Henrietta Maria; at the same time in England a parliament was summoned, for the king's financial position was desperate, and the breach with Spain might make the Commons more amenable.

To a certain extent, this hope was realized. Funds were voted for war in Germany on behalf of the Elector, but the Commons demanded in return that all the laws should be duly executed against priests and 'generally against all Popish recusants'; that

[1] Transcriptions of the letters of Mary Ward, in the Bar Convent, York.

all priests should be forced to leave the country by a fixed date
and not allowed to return; and that 'upon no occasion of marriage
or treaty or other request in that behalf from any foreign prince
or state whatsoever, you will take away or slacken the execution
of your laws against Jesuits, priests and popish recusants'. This
the king promised to the Commons, and the Prince of Wales
followed him by swearing in the House of Lords that Catholics
should not benefit from his marriage.

They soon broke their word, for Cardinal Richelieu insisted on a
secret clause in the marriage treaty that the penal laws against
Catholics should be abolished; both James and Charles signed
this pledge. Promises were made that Henrietta Maria should
have her own chapel, and chaplains and waiting ladies of her
choice. James ordered the release of all persons imprisoned for
their religion, but the pope was well aware that the promise in
the treaty would not be kept.[1] Before the marriage took place,
James died, in March 1625.

The accession of Charles I did not seem to affect the position
of his Papist subjects in any marked way. Though he did not share
his father's interest in theology, the new king was devoutly
attached to the church of which he was the head, and believed
that he was divinely appointed to rule a united nation; all his
subjects should be loyally submissive to the established constitution of church and state. His immediate inheritance was an
acute financial crisis, and his chief friend and adviser was the
Duke of Buckingham. It was to him, and to the French girl who
was to wed the king, that the Catholics must look for help. Unfortunately for them, Buckingham was both unreliable and
unpopular.

In June 1625 the first parliament of the new reign assembled.
The policy of aid to Frederick, which the Commons had demanded,
was proving extremely expensive, but as usual the members
would not vote large sums to be expended at the king's pleasure.
They made a small grant, accompanied by a demand for the
strict enforcement of the laws against recusants. This was promised;
but the Commons went on to demand church reform and to
criticize Buckingham. Charles dissolved the parliament in August,
hoping that by raids on Spanish ports he might get both booty
and a popular victory. The expedition sent in October met with
disaster. Buckingham himself was not in command of the fleet,
but it was on his shoulders that people laid the blame.

Plague was rampant in London in the summer of 1625, and
this prevented people from enjoying the pageantry that should

[1] Oman, C., *Henrietta Maria* (1936), p. 24.

have accompanied the marriage and coronation of the king. The new queen had reached Dover in June, after being married to Charles by proxy in Paris in May. With her came 15 priests and a bishop, a number of French ladies and courtiers, and a group of English people, including Sir Tobie Matthew, who had crossed to Boulogne to accompany her. At Canterbury a second marriage took place. When her husband was crowned in February 1626 Henrietta Maria was absent, as she refused to take part in a Protestant ceremony. Already quarrels had broken out between the newly wedded pair, exacerbated by Buckingham on the one hand and the French courtiers on the other. The young queen had just grounds for complaint. Little had been done to make ready for her coming; in 1623 Inigo Jones had been commissioned to prepare Catholic chapels in the royal palaces for the Infanta, but they had not been completed for the substitute bride. A makeshift chapel was arranged in her apartments at Whitehall; when the first Mass was celebrated there, 'the King took order that no Englishman or woman should come near the place.'[1] In the summer of 1626, despite all his vows and Henrietta Maria's tears, Charles sent her French priests and courtiers back to their own country.

It was the French ambassador, rather than the queen, who was able to give some practical help to the English Catholics. Nineteen priests were released from prison at his request, and his chapel was open for the use of the London Papists. In 1626 this led to a sensational fracas outside Durham House, a great mansion by the Thames which was the London residence of the Bishop of Durham. Thirty of the rooms had been taken over for the French embassy, the bishop 'crouding up himselfe and his whole ffamily (being great) into the worst and basest Roomes of ye House'.[2] It was reported on 22 February that there was 'daily Resort of Multitudes of Englishe Subjects of more than a hundred at once to Masse' there, '& that in this time of the Parliamt sitting'. Warrants were issued for the arrest of these people 'when they are thence departed, either by water or by land', for the embassy was French territory, and could not be entered by London constables.

On Sunday, 26 February, a body of pursuivants and constables waited outside the great gate of Durham House, whence a short passage led to the street. When Mass was over, the 'ffollowers of the ffrench Ambassador tooke upon them with their swords in their hands to carry the English Papists by strong hand through

---

[1] Harl. MS., 389 f., 464. Quoted Oman, *Henrietta Maria*, p. 40.

[2] C.R.S., I, 92 ff. The documents relating to this incident include a contemporary plan of Durham House.

the Watch'. Local inhabitants came 'in heaps' to Durham House 'with Bills and Clubs', and it seemed that a serious affray between the Frenchmen and Londoners was imminent. The Bishop of Durham himself came out and persuaded the Frenchmen to return to the house and the Englishmen to go away, so the Mass-hearers escaped without being arrested. Meanwhile others were leaving by the 'Water Gate, by 6, 8, 10, 12 Boatfuls at once'.

Such a public exhibition of the strength of the Catholics in London and the support they had from the French was a further irritant to the parliament, which met in February 1626. The main reason for the meagreness of the grant it made was, however, the king's continuing support of Buckingham. The Commons began proceedings for an impeachment of the favourite, so Charles dissolved his parliament in June.

Not only Buckingham but also the young queen were held responsible for the expensive masques and entertainments that in popular opinion accounted for the king's financial difficulties. The whole of the court's expenditure would in fact not have paid the cost of even the smallest of the ill-equipped expeditions sent out first against Spain, then against France, in pursuit of an erratic foreign policy. Charles's debts mounted; he levied forced loans and tried every expedient he could think of to raise money, but only angered his people without solving his problems. He was forced to summon another parliament, and the Commons seized their opportunity. In a Petition of Right they declared Charles's exactions, and the means he had taken to enforce them, to be illegal. The attack on Buckingham was renewed, but his assassination in August 1628 ended that cause of friction.

There could be no agreement between those who held that the king's power was strictly limited by law and a ruler who believed his prerogative to be a sacred trust. During a prorogation of parliament, Charles issued a declaration that the Articles of Religion were to be taken in their literal sense and no variation be made in the doctrine and discipline of the church. The Commons responded, when they met again in February 1629, by Resolutions on Religion, in which they complained of Romanist tendencies in the church, and 'an extraordinary growth of Popery' shown by 'frequent and public resort to Mass, in multitudes'. Another protest over customs duties led to the dissolution of parliament; in a declaration Charles said that he had ordered the laws against Papists to be enforced, but 'we must lay the fault where it is, in the subordinate officers and ministers in the country, by whose remissness Jesuits and Priests escape without apprehension.'

This was true, but as had been shown during the last four years, pressure from the central government did have a good deal of effect. John Southcote, D.D., the son of a Surrey landowner, kept a notebook in which, from 1623 to 1637, he summarized events of special importance.[1] In the autumn of 1625 he noted that special instructions had been given to the judges of assize at Reading 'to persecute Catholiques with all rigour', and pursuivants were commissioned to search the houses of Papists. In December, 'many priests were taken at London'; and in the spring of 1626 there were widespread prosecutions of Catholics. Though the priests were released to please the French ambassador, in August 1628 two men were publicly executed in Lancashire.

One was a priest, Edmund Arrowsmith, who was much respected. A justice was unwillingly forced to order him to be seized; when he was arrested he could have escaped if he had had a better horse, for many people in the district would have given him shelter. Even after arrest he might have avoided conviction, but he had the bad luck to be brought for trial before Sir Henry Yelverton, who came from a family largely Catholic and, according to a contemporary story, had been twitted by his colleagues, who said that 'he durst not hang a priest.' He was determined to prove that he could. His direction of the trial was such that Arrowsmith's condemnation was certain.

Local feeling was so strong that it was difficult to find any man willing to carry out the horrible rites of hanging, drawing and quartering. It was a felon, himself under sentence of death, who finally consented, on promise of his own release, a reward, and the clothes of the condemned man. A clergyman tried to persuade the priest to save his life by taking the oath of allegiance, but he refused, and bravely suffered his torments. The officials round the scaffold, and the jailers in Lancaster Castle, helped Catholics to collect relics of the dead man; fragments of his body, and cloth and straw soaked with his blood, were treasured: some still exist after 300 years.[2]

On the following day a local farmer, Richard Hurst, was hanged. He was a noted recusant, and had been arrested while he was ploughing. The farm servants attacked the pursuivants and a girl hit one of them with some tool; running away from her, the man fell and broke his leg, which became septic so that he died. Hurst was charged with murdering the man, and, in spite of the evidence, found guilty and condemned to death: that his real

---

[1] Printed in C.R.S., I, 97 ff.

[2] The full story is told in Myerscough, J. A., *A Procession of Lancashire Martyrs* (Glasgow, 1958), pp. 134 ff.

offence was his religion was made manifest when he was promised a reprieve if he would take the oath of allegiance, attend a church service, and hear a sermon. He would not accept these conditions, so he was dragged by the legs along the short rough path between the prison and the church where he lay with his fingers in his ears as a demonstration that he would not willingly listen to the service. When he was brought to the gallows, he teased the executioner for bungling the knotting of the rope, saying, 'Tom, I think I must come and help you.'[1]

It is possible that if Charles had known in time of these executions he would have prevented them, for there were no more for 11 years. This respite was the result of political rather than religious circumstances; but whatever its cause, it gave a welcome breathing-space to the Catholic priesthood and laity.

[1] Myerscough, J. A., op. cit., pp. 151 ff.

6

PEACE AND WAR 1629-60

'The King's Peace' is a name which has been given to the 11 years
when Charles ruled without summoning a Parliament. Now that
Buckingham was no longer there to spur him on to ambitious
enterprises, he withdrew from entanglements on the continent
and made peace with France and Spain. For the Catholics the rule
of a single man, who was susceptible to persuasion, was far
preferable to that of a government under which from time to time
their fate might be affected by a House of Commons containing
many of their bitterest enemies. Theoretically, it was still possible
for an absolute monarch to reverse the policy of the Tudors and
force a return to Rome upon the church in England. Few, if any,
of the Papists themselves really believed this, but to many of
the Puritans it did seem likely that by a steady modification of
the ritual of the services something far nearer to Rome than to
Geneva would become the national religion. Fear breeds hatred,
and every evidence that Catholicism remained the faith of a substantial minority in the country was likely to lead to a renewal of
persecution. Anti-Catholicism was not unlike anti-Semitism; it
was believed that as a body Papists were dangerous, led by
Jesuits, linked to Spain; any national calamity was apt to be
attributed to their machinations. As individuals they were
known, even to those who disliked their faith intensely, as no
better and no worse than their neighbours, quite harmless people
to meet socially or in business.

Charles's own attitude was on the whole tolerant. His personal
views were not unlike those of Elizabeth; he liked order, and
attempted with the help of Laud to bring about uniformity in
teaching and practice in the church. This of course prevented
any general relaxation of the laws against non-conformists,
whether Catholic or Protestant. The king's financial position also
affected his policy; although the drain of war had ended, his debts
amounted to over a million pounds, and his revenue from normal
sources did not suffice to meet even his reduced expenditure.
Some of the Catholics were prosecuted and paid the fines imposed,

or compounded for them, but a considerable number escaped. Others were willing to pay for licences granted by the king, giving them specific exemptions; many of these documents survive in family archives. For example, John Darrell of Calehill in Kent was in 1634 given leave to travel on the Continent, 'provided that he repaire not to the Citty of Rome'.[1] In the same year one of the family of Constable, of Everingham in Yorkshire, got exemption from the law that forbade Catholics to go more than five miles from their homes; he was not allowed, however, to visit London.[2] In 1638 Lady Elizabeth Stonor, whose home on the borders of Buckinghamshire and Oxfordshire was a constant refuge for priests, had failed to appear when she was summoned to Oxford for her recusancy. She secured an order to the magistrates that, 'she being a weake and sickly woman', all proceedings against her should cease and not be renewed without royal leave.[3] A similar benefit was given to Lord Petre in 1629;[4] this Essex family usually managed to be on good terms with the reigning monarch.

The comparative freedom from persecution enjoyed by the Catholics after 1629 may partly account for the development of intense strife among their clergy. A large number of their priests were chaplains in the households of families like the Petres and Stonors. Their position was sometimes awkward; their patrons, as they paid and lodged them, often expected them to help in other than purely spiritual work. Many of them acted as tutors to the children of the family; others were asked to assist in the business of the estate. The well-known Benedictine, Augustine Baker, who lived from 1575 to 1641, wrote his autobiography, in the third person. He had studied law in the Inns of Court before he became a Catholic, and as a priest used his legal knowledge to assist not only 'widdows, orphans and distressed persons' but also 'wealthy and greater personages'. When he was sent as chaplain to a certain gentleman, 'this man expected that he should dispach much of his seculer businesses for him; which he being backward to do', his patron complained that 'he was not a priest for his purpose'.[5]

Wealthy landowners resented any interference in their choice of chaplains and relations with them, so the laity were drawn into

---

[1] Darrell MSS., Kent Record Office, Maidstone C 17.

[2] Constable MSS., Ampleforth Abbey. (Contributed by Miss Akeroyd.)

[3] Stonor, R. J., *Stonor* (Newport, 1951), p. 272.

[4] Petre MSS., Essex Record Office, Q/SR 166/117.

[5] C.R.S., XXXIII, 100, 101.

an ecclesiastical conflict. There was something to be said on both sides when the Jesuits and some of the Benedictines objected to Bishop Smith's demand that they should come under his jurisdiction. To visit him, even to write to him, exposed them to danger and his very whereabouts were often unknown. The secular clergy shared this handicap, and they bitterly resented the pretensions of the regulars.[1] The Jesuits had direct access through their General to authorities in Rome, and to him Viscount Montague wrote in 1628, protesting at the way in which members of his society were treating the bishop. It was believed that they had been responsible for the proclamation of 1628 which declared him a traitor and offered £100 to the person who secured his arrest.

Appeals and counter-appeals went to Rome; it might take as much as five months before a letter from England reached the person for whom it was intended. Bishop Smith was in hiding; in a letter to the Cardinals at Rome he wrote in June 1631, 'I live shut up perpetually in one small bedroom, and can never allow myself to breathe fresh air; I am at the mercy of the plots of the heretics and of the harassing Regulars.' His room was in the French embassy; the king knew perfectly well where the proclaimed traitor lived, for he wrote asking the bishop to give Henrietta Maria permission to eat meat on fast days. Towards the end of August 1631 Smith left England; he could not, as things were, carry on the work for which he had been consecrated. The secular clergy petitioned for his return, and for the appointment of three additional bishops, but even after Smith died in 1655 their pleas were ignored. Fortunately the bishop had empowered the canons of his chapter to administer normal business during his absence, and this organization greatly strengthened the position of the secular priests.

The rivalry between the Jesuits and the seculars was also brought home to the laity when they performed a very popular devotional exercise. The Holy Well of St. Winifred in Flintshire had been for centuries a favourite place of pilgrimage, and all through penal times resort was made to the shrine by Catholics from all over the country. It was near enough to the estuary of the Dee for people to come from the Lancashire ports by sea, and yet some distance from Chester, the only city from which any force could be sent, but whose bishop had plenty to do in coping with his immense diocese. Here in 1581 the Jesuits had made a centre in the Star Inn; the secular clergy set up a rival establishment

[1] Hughes, P., *Rome and the Counter-Reformation in England*, gives a documented account of this melancholy story, pp. 347 ff.

in the Cross Keys. So many people came to pray at the well and seek cures for their diseases that probably both sets of clergy had their hands full: many of them, both seculars and Jesuits, were Welsh, and travelled round the country ministering to the local inhabitants.

In October 1626 the mayor of 'Poole' (Welshpool) in Montgomery wrote to the Privy Council that he was taking steps to check the pilgrimages. How ineffectual these were was shown by a report of an unusually large pilgrimage in 1629. Lord William Howard, the Earl of Shrewsbury, Lady Falkland, and 14 other knights and gentlemen were listed by name: the names of several priests were given, and the roll concluded with 'knights, ladies, gentlemen and gentlewomen of divers countries to ye number of fourteen or fifteen hundredth; and the general estimation about a hundred and fifty more priestes, the most of them well known what they were.'[1] Such a gathering was exceptional; the normal smaller pilgrimages went on, although in 1630 the mayor told the government that he was putting down unnecessary ale-houses, ordering all innkeepers to take the names and addresses of their lodgers, and keeping a watch on the well. He mentioned the possibility of walling up the well itself; that such an obvious means of stopping the demonstrations was not adopted shows how strong was the feeling in the neighbourhood about the famous shrine, and how unwilling were the local justices to interfere in the traditional veneration of the saint. Even during the Commonwealth visitors continued to come to Holywell, some from long distances; Sir Francis Throckmorton of Weston Underwood in Buckinghamshire was at the well in July 1657 and again in August 1658, and no precautions seem to have been needed to prevent detection.[2]

Such impunity was by no means general, even in areas like the north-east, where there were many Catholic gentry. In 1626 the castle in York was full of prisoners, chiefly ordinary criminals, but including two Jesuit priests, Father Morse and Father Robinson.[3] Morse had been disguised as an Italian, but when he was arrested he could not sustain the part; Father Robinson, who was captured on board ship before he could land at Newcastle, more successfully maintained the rôle of a Dutchman who could speak no English, but as he had theological books in his baggage, he too was arrested and imprisoned. He continued to pretend that he

[1] C.R.S., III, 105 ff.
[2] Barnard, E. A. B., *A Seventeenth Century Country Gentleman* (Cambridge, 1948), p. 47.
[3] Caraman, P., *Henry Morse* (1957), pp. 46 ff.

knew no English, so his activity was limited; but Henry Morse
moved about among the felons, praying for and with them, even
instructing and receiving some into his church. Among them were
a man and woman condemned to death for theft; when they were
hanged they created a sensation by professing themselves Catholic
and praying aloud. At the next assizes, strong protests were made
about the proselytizing efforts of the Jesuit, but the judge held
that it was good that criminals should die praying, even if their
piety had been taught them by a Papist. In 1630 Morse was
released and exiled; Father Robinson was condemned to execution, but was reprieved, remaining in prison for another 11 years.
As an old man, he used to tell a story of one of the Catholic felons.
John Bartendale was a strolling piper who had been convicted
and sentenced to be hanged—the usual penalty for any serious
crime. In March 1634 the sentence was carried out, and after he
had hung for three-quarters of an hour he was cut down and
hastily buried, not in a churchyard, but by the roadside. A passer-
by saw the newly dug ground heaving, and dug up the convict,
whose throat muscles, strengthened by years of piping, had
resisted the pressure of the rope. Bartendale went free, for it was
decided that as he had been executed and buried he was legally
dead.

In Yorkshire, too, there was a good example of the complica-
tions which occurred when a man of position changed his religion.
The Fairfaxes were a well-known family, with considerable estates;
the first Viscount Fairfax of Emly belonged to the Church of
England.[1] His eldest son Thomas travelled abroad, and on his
return he revealed that he had become a Catholic. He married a
Catholic wife, and when their first son was born, Viscount Fairfax
attempted to ensure that later generations should not be Papist
by creating a trust: at his death, the family property should be
administered by Protestants, his son being merely tenant, until
his grandson came of age. The Viscount also left the very large
sum of £1,200 for the child's education if he were reared by
Thomas Wentworth, who later became Earl of Strafford: otherwise, his second son, Henry Fairfax, who was not tainted with
Papistry, would inherit the money.

On the death of his father in 1636 Thomas succeeded to the
title, and his brother Henry went to Dublin to see Wentworth,
who was Lord Deputy in Ireland. Wentworth wrote to Thomas
Fairfax, saying that he was ready to educate the child and allowing him six months to fulfil the terms of the trust. When no move
was made, the Privy Council sent, in 1639, a letter demanding

[1] Aveling, H., article in *Recusant History*, Vol. IV, No. 2 (April, 1957).

that Viscount Fairfax should deliver the boy. This he refused to
do, pleading that the 'Lawe of nature gives the mother the
custody of her owne childe', and that the separation of the boy
from his younger brothers and sisters would harm all the children.
He kept his son, but had to let his brother Henry have the £1,200.
It is likely that the prominence in which the whole affair placed
Thomas led to his becoming the most heavily fined recusant in
Yorkshire, while many others escaped altogether, or got off more
lightly.

Catholics in London also got into a good deal of trouble, though
not many were arrested. Once Buckingham's influence had been
removed, Charles had fallen deeply in love with his little French
wife, and her intercession and her charity were often used to help
Papists. This was disconcerting to the many pursuivants, and to
the little companies of priest-catchers, who joined together to
obtain rewards. One of these groups had been formed in 1627 by
Francis Newton, a lawyer disbarred for unprofessional conduct.[1]
Mayo, an apostate priest, Cook, an official pursuivant, and others
were associated with him in searching for priests; they brought, so
they claimed, 37 before the authorities, but all of them were
discharged. They therefore changed their policy, and persuaded
priests and those who sheltered them to pay blackmail in money
and goods to prevent their arrest. This proved quite profitable;
Henrietta Maria bought back sets of vestments and eight watches
for the large sum of £200.

Charles himself was not concerned about the Papists. They were
no menace, even in Ireland, where Thomas Wentworth had
succeeded, by a merciless reform of the administration and a
shrewd economic policy, in turning a country which had been a
drain on the English treasury into a potential asset. Scotland was
now the danger point; the king had infuriated the nobility by a
wholesale resumption of lands which had been appropriated by
private persons from the crown and the church. When in 1633 he
was crowned at Holyrood, the ritual shocked the Presbyterians;
their intense dislike of what seemed to them Roman practices led
to violent opposition when in 1637 Charles attempted to enforce
the use of the Prayer Book in all churches. A Covenant was drawn
up and signed by thousands of Scots: they pledged themselves to
uphold 'true and reformed religion', and declared that the 'innovations' would lead to 'the re-establishing of the popish religion
and tyranny'. The document contained a long list of the erroneous
doctrines and practices of the pope, some of which, it was said,
were included in the service prescribed by Archbishop Laud. The

[1] Caraman, P., *Henry Morse*, pp. 116 ff.

General Assembly of the Scottish Church abolished not only the
Prayer Book but the whole episcopal system.

Both the Scots and King Charles firmly believed that they were
right; there was no room for compromise. The Covenanters began
to collect soldiers and arms, and Charles had to do the same.
Money was, as usual, lacking, so an extraordinary step was taken;
the queen appealed to the Catholics in England, who were in
theory as much rebels as were the Scots. Far from complaining,
they seized the opportunity of showing their loyalty to the crown.
The canons of the chapter and the superiors of the regular clergy
joined in drawing up an appeal to all Catholics to subscribe to a
fund; this was sent to all the priests, with a circular letter addressed
to the laity asking them 'to contribute cheerfully and bountifully
upon this occasion; which, as it is the first that ever we laboured
in of this kind, so we hope in God it will be the last'.[1]

The large sum of £14,000 was raised; in every county men of
position acted as treasurers. The priests themselves were asked
to collect from 'the servants and poorer sort of Catholics what
they conceive they may give, for gentlemen of quality cannot
so well speak to those persons as priests and their ghostly fathers
may'.

Three points of interest in the history of English Catholics are
illustrated by this collection. One is that, in spite of the legal fines
and confiscations, many Papists produced quite handsome contributions. Another is that in Lancashire, where the documents
concerning it have survived, lists were made of all the Mass
centres, with the names of the priests and the principal laymen;
whether this was exceptional we do not know, but when one recalls
the secrecy which was customary, the aliases used by the priests,
the concealment, when possible, of their religion by the laity, it is
astonishing that such dangerous information was committed to
writing. Thirdly, we learn that there were 78 priests in Lancashire
of whom 30 were seculars, 23 Benedictines and 25 Jesuits. Several
Lancashire families had close connections with the two orders: it
may be doubted whether similar lists for other counties would have
shown so high a proportion of regulars.

The gift made to Charles must have seemed very handsome to
the donors, but in relation to his needs it was trifling. Though the
militia was called up, the men were wholly untrained, and their
arms, which the parishes were supposed to have in store, were often
missing or of little use. Charles had to come to terms with the
Scots, but the treaty gave him only a breathing space; he could not
renounce his principles and abandon his authority over Scotland.

[1] Anstruther, G., article in *Recusant History*, IV, No. 1 (1957).

The English parliament was summoned in the summer of 1640, but rapidly dissolved before any money was voted. The king tried many expedients for raising funds, but, as had happened before, they provoked indignation and produced a quite inadequate amount. The sympathy shown for the Scottish Presbyterians by many of the leaders of the Commons made it certain that the next parliament, which met in November 1640, would prove equally intractable. One surrender after another was forced on the king, who even agreed to the attainder and execution of his ablest servant, Thomas Wentworth, Earl of Strafford.

Wentworth was dreaded by the Commons; in another case they were more merciful. John Goodman had been arrested and condemned to death as a priest. Charles reprieved him, and parliament protested. The king agreed to let the Commons decide whether the priest should die; Goodman himself petitioned that he should be executed, for he would 'esteem his blood well shed to cement the breach between your Majesty and his subjects'. His life was spared, but he was sent to prison, where five years later he died. Others were less fortunate; there was a rigorous searching out of priests, especially in London; between 1641 and 1646 Newgate was full of them. Twenty were executed; one of them, Father Lockwood, who was sentenced with another priest in York in 1642, was 87 years old; he had been working in England for 44 years. 'Since it was only with difficulty and loss of breath that he, being now almost worn out with age, could climb the ladder to the scaffold, he smiled at the people and said: "Who would not labour a little to reach heaven?" ' His preaching from the scaffold so moved the executioner that he ran away; when he was forced to come back, he tried to hang himself. But 'being won over by the persuasions of a certain harlot, from a humane man he became a most inhuman butcher, and dividing all the entrails of this martyr and his fellow sufferer into minute fragments, like a maniac he hurled them among the people'.[1] Henry Heath, a Franciscan, who died in 1643, had come to England almost, it seems, with the deliberate intention of being a martyr. He begged his way to London disguised as a sailor, having made no plans beforehand. There he was arrested as a vagrant: 'he had preserved in his hat a writing in which he expressed his intention of returning to England', and arguments in defence of his action and of the Catholic faith. He was of course tried and condemned.[2]

When these deaths occurred, the king was powerless to intervene. The final breach had come between Charles and the parliament.

[1] C.R.S., XI., 475. [2] C.R.S., XI., 478.

His attempt to impeach some leaders of his opponents in January 1642 led the Commons to issue an ordinance calling up the militia to protect the country against 'the bloody counsels of Papists and other ill-affected persons'. This invasion of the royal prerogative was the final straw; civil war was inevitable.

Ordinary people all over the country were unhappy and dismayed, for they were not ardent supporters of either king or Commons. Each of the contending groups could count on a number of loyal supporters—the king on the devoted members of the Church of England, on the Catholics, and on some of the landed gentry, particularly in the western and northern shires, while parliament had the backing of the Presbyterians and other Protestant non-conformists, of most of the merchants in London and other cities, and of some of the gentry, particularly in the eastern shires. Where to raise arms and men to use them was a problem for both parties. Many Englishmen had been serving in the forces of the European powers; as the confused struggle known as the Thirty Years War was drawing to a close, experienced soldiers were available for training the levies of reluctant peasants who were enrolled by both sides. Arms could be bought; the Dutch especially had large stocks available.

Henry Gage, of a noted recusant family, was a professional soldier. He had served with the Spanish forces, but in 1630 an English regiment was recruited and fought the Dutch in the Netherlands. He refused to fight in Germany, as this meant opposing members of the king's own family. As Henry Morse, the Jesuit who served as his chaplain after his banishment, said of him, he 'could not be won to do anything against his natural sovereign or inconsistent with the interest and honour of his nation'.[1] When the parliamentary agents began buying munitions in the Netherlands, Gage used his regiment in a number of raids, seizing the arms and sending what he could to Charles. Many of his men left him to join the royal army in England; he followed them, as did his chaplain. Both men died in 1645; Gage was killed in fighting near Oxford, and Morse was hanged at Tyburn.

All the English Catholics were royalist in sympathy, though by no means all of them—any more than their Protestant neighbours who shared their political views—actually joined the royal armies. The only notable difference between them and their fellow 'Cavaliers' was that the casualties of war affected them more severely. Many of the younger sons of the Papist families became priests; if the father of a family was killed, the line of succession to the estate was endangered. If a man left young children, they might be

[1] Caraman, P., *Henry Morse*, pp. 148 ff.

taken from his widow and brought up as Protestants, as happened to Mrs. Anderton of Clitheroe. Francis Morley, of Wennington Hall in Lancashire, escaped with his life, but, like many other royalists, left the country when the war was over. His wife had no news of him, and presumed that he was dead: she was persuaded to marry a Protestant, and Morley's sons were brought up in the religion of the man who believed himself to be their step-father. Morley came back, disguised; but when he found out what had happened, he did not interfere, but went back to France.[1]

Some of these royalists joined a regiment already raised for the king; others enlisted private forces of their own. Sometimes when a Papist was directly employed by Charles, objections were raised; the inhabitants of the Close in Salisbury protested when Sergeant-Major Innis was given charge of the fortification of the city, because he was, they wrote, 'of the Romish religion. . . . If so greate authoritie be placed in such a person, great discouragement maie arise to your religion.'[2] On the whole, however, there is little evidence of distrust of Catholics in the king's armies.

When gentlemen raised and equipped troops of their own, as was done by supporters of both sides, they felt that they had a right to use them as they thought best. The defence of their own lands meant much to them, so that a good deal of the fighting was of a local, even a personal, character. Small-scale actions took place round country houses; even when troops were sorely needed for the main armies, some commanders remained in their own district, and on both sides desertion was common if the impressed soldiers were taken far from their homes. Warfare was something personal; men who had been long acquainted might find themselves on opposite sides, and resume friendly relations as soon as the immediate battle was over.

The Arundells of Wiltshire are a good example of a Catholic family involved in the Civil War. Like the elder branch of the family at Lanherne in Cornwall,[3] they were persistent recusants; they had escaped heavy fines or confiscations, perhaps because their home, Wardour Castle, though in Wiltshire, was very near the borders of Dorset and Somerset. They were wealthy; James I had made Sir Thomas Arundell a baron, and his son, the second baron, had been able to give £500 to the collection made for Charles in 1639. In 1642 he raised a force for the king, commanding it himself, though he was 56 years old. His eldest son Henry joined the king's

---

[1] C.R.S., VI., 143, 255.
[2] Hist. MSS. Comm. Various, I (1901).
[3] See supra, p. 41.

main army; Lord Arundell kept his troop in the West. His wife was left in the castle with 25 men; in 1625 the house had been searched and sufficient equipment for 64 horsemen had been taken, so there was no great store of arms to attract marauders. The castle was not on any main route, and had no military importance, yet in 1643 a parliamentary force of over 1,000 men appeared to demand its surrender. Lady Arundell refused; her men lined the walls and the maids loaded muskets for them; but on 3 May a cannonade, and two mines which exploded in the vaults, forced the besieged to ask for terms. It was agreed that the ladies should go free, with the maids and six men-servants and all their clothing, and that an inventory should be made of all the furniture and no looting permitted. The treaty was immediately broken; immense and wanton damage was done, carved chimney-pieces smashed, pictures torn up, the deer in the park let loose, the fish-ponds destroyed, fine trees felled. Instead of being given safe conduct, Lady Arundell and her son's wife and children were taken to Shaftesbury, except for two of the boys who were removed to Dorchester, and the luggage was seized.

Colonel Ludlow was then sent to occupy the castle. Henry Arundell came with a small force, but had to withdraw; Ludlow found a hoard of money, plate and jewels hidden in the walls, and used the proceeds to prepare the castle for a siege. Lord Arundell had meantime been fighting near Bath; he was wounded, and died on 19 May. In spite of the sporadic fighting in the district, his body was brought back to Tisbury, near Wardour, where the Arundells were always buried. Henry, now Lord Arundell, and his uncle set about raising soldiers with the help of their friends and relations; later his uncle was accused of forcibly enlisting men and taking fodder and money from a farmer who had backed the parliament. A second long siege regained the castle for the Arundells; Ludlow resisted stoutly, but was starved out, having to kill his horses for food. After further damage to the building, the parliamentarians had to surrender. For the time the Arundells were victorious; but after the execution of King Charles, Henry decided to leave England for France.

The victorious parliament, after the defeat of Charles II at Worcester and his flight to France, was able to enforce the laws it had passed in July. The estates of the most distinguished royalists were confiscated, and parliamentary commissioners sent to take over the property of these 'delinquents'. The Arundells were on the list, but they were fortunate; another Catholic, Humphrey Weld of Lulworth Castle, bought the property and held it in trust for them. He had taken no part in the war, and so was not a marked man. The commissioners also investigated the case against Henry's uncle, but declared the charges 'frivolous'. When in December 1653 Cromwell became Protector, and order was restored, Henry Arundell returned. For years he had to live as best he could, moving from one of his smaller houses to another, for the castle was not fit for habitation.

In 1657 a further payment of £788 14s. 6d. was demanded, and Lord Arundell appealed to Cromwell in person. His petition was supported by his former antagonist, Edmund Ludlow. Henry wrote that Lieutenant-General Ludlow had already 'made appeal to the late Parliament, that your Petitioner was only engaged one summer in the first Warr, wherein he had the good fortune to preserve the life of the said Lieutenant-General with the hazard of his owne'. By his 'Early retreat from the Warre beyond the Seas he lost the benefit' of making terms, as others did, and because of his religion had not been allowed to compound for the fines imposed. Cromwell took the view that, as the Arundells had already paid £4,785 18s. 3d. no further sum should be levied. Like Ludlow, he was most friendly to this 'delinquent'; he is said[1] to have entertained him to dinner at Hampton Court, where they discussed various methods of farming. Henry was not a tranquil person; he got into trouble in 1653 for acting as second in a duel, but was released after being burned in the hand 'very favourably'.[2]

In proportion to their wealth, the Arundells did not suffer as much as did other Catholics. It was during and immediately after the war, before the setting up of a powerful government under Cromwell, that their religion, as distinct from their politics, led to their persecution. In Essex, where extreme Puritanism and Papistry existed side by side, the train-bands of Colchester in 1647 had attacked the house of a royalist, and afterwards 'some of the soldiers, country clowns and women, cried out that now they were met together' they should 'deal in the same manner with the Papists.' Several Catholic houses were broken into and pillaged, the mob 'miserably spoiling what they could not carry away'. At Crondon Park they had started tearing down hangings, stealing the silver and so forth when 'by chance a company of the Parliament volunteers coming to steal deer' frightened them away. Ingatestone Hall was saved, for Lady Petre was 'prodigally bountiful' to the poor of the village, helping them when they were ill; 'every Saturday night she divides the milk of twenty kine amongst those

[1] By Aubrey. Dick, O.L., *Life and Times of John Aubrey* (1949).
[2] The material used in the above section comes from the Arundell archives at Wardour Castle.

who have the least.' When about 100 men came and hammered at the great gates of the Hall, Lady Petre came out, with three of her young children, and told them she was a harmless widow. People from the village came to defend her, and a small payment of money sufficed to send the raiders away. Next day, a more official search of the house was made for arms; she freely showed the parliamentarians all the rooms, including the private chapel, which so disarmed them that they left without doing any damage. After this, she decided that it was wiser to go and live in a small house in the village.[1] Many other raids were made on farmers and other persons known to be Catholics, and quite poor people were robbed of their beasts and furniture.

Liverpool, like most of the principal ports, was seized by the parliamentarians early in the war. After Charles's defeat at Naseby in 1645, William Blundell, of Crosby, fled into Wales to escape arrest. His estate was sequestrated, but his wife succeeded in leasing some of the land and securing one-fifth of the property, half for herself and half for her children, whom she was ordered to bring up 'in the Protestant religion'. The eldest child was only six, so this condition could be evaded. Her husband returned, and, as he had feared, was sent to prison; in all, he served four terms of incarceration in Lancaster gaol. He kept in touch with various priests and other friends, writing obscure letters in which, he said, 'The sense dependeth on sundry private passages between the parties'. Not only the Blundells, but many other non-Catholics were impoverished by the war and its aftermath; famine and disease for a considerable time afflicted the country round Wigan and Liverpool.[2] Many Catholic houses were seized, though priests managed to hide nearby and continue their ministrations, in spite of the Act of Parliament of 1650 which offered cash rewards for their capture.

When the Protectorate was established, the laws against Papists remained unchanged, except that compulsory attendance at the parish church was no longer demanded. The oath of fealty to the new government was purely political in character, with no religious implications: a Catholic who took it foreswore his king but not his God. Although Cromwell could be ruthless, as he showed in Ireland, he was far more tolerant than the Presbyterians, and only two priests were executed between 1647 and 1660.

A member of the notoriously Papist family of Stonor was in 1653 given the important task of examining all the saltpetre dug

---

[1] MS. letter, now at Stonyhurst, and an unpublished *History of the Petre Family*, contributed by Canon B. C. Foley, Harlow, Essex.

[2] Blundell, M., *Cavalier* (London, 1933), pp. 17 ff.

up throughout England: his family had had to pay heavy fines, and Thomas Stonor must have been glad of the income.[1] Perhaps the Protector shared the view of Giant Pope that Bunyan later expressed in *The Pilgrim's Progress*—that by reason of age 'he is grown so crazy and stiff in his joints, that he can do little more than sit in his cave's mouth, grinning at the pilgrims as they go by'. The Church of England was the main object of attack; many parsons were dispossessed and replaced by Presbyterians or Independents; images and paintings that survived were in several places destroyed and defaced.

Numerous royalists followed Charles II into exile. In France and the Netherlands they lived, as so many Catholic recusants had done for years, on such money as they could take with them, or have smuggled out to them, or obtain from foreign sympathizers. The remarkable success of Cromwell's government, both at home and abroad, dismayed them, but they knew that the divergent factions in England were kept under control only by his strong personality, and that when he died he could have no successor. That Charles II would in the end regain his father's throne was taken for granted, and his supporters confidently expected to recover their confiscated lands and perhaps even the money they had lent to their king. The Catholic exiles hoped for even more, for Charles had many friends among them, and his mother's influence was constantly exercised in attempts to bring her sons into her church. In 1651, after his defeat at Worcester, the king had been greatly aided in his perilous flight by men experienced in smuggling priests in and out of the country. Charles was concealed in the 'priest's hole' at Moseley Hall in Staffordshire, and the Benedictine chaplain there aided him in his journey. This man, John Huddleston, came from the staunchly Catholic family of Sawston Hall, near Cambridge; a century earlier Mary Tudor had been given refuge by the Huddlestons from the enemies who tried to prevent her accession to the throne.

When in 1660 the long-awaited restoration of the king was arranged, the Declaration of Breda was part of the terms agreed on with General Monk. It promised a general pardon to the rebels who submitted, and a free parliament to settle the complicated problems raised by the many changes in ownership of land since 1649. The hopes of the Catholics seemed justified by the promise of 'a liberty to tender consciences, and that no man shall be disquieted or called in question for differences of opinion in matter of religion, which do not disturb the peace of the kingdom'. This was to be secured by an Act of Parliament.

[1] Stonor, R. J., *Stonor*, p. 276.

Many Catholics were in the cheering crowds that greeted Charles II when he returned to his kingdom in May. They confidently expected that the years of penal legislation and persecution were drawing to an end. It was not long before they found out how bitterly they had been mistaken.

7

TRIUMPH AND TERROR 1660–88

'Most mighty Soveraigne, Your roman-catholique subjects . . .
have thought this a convenient and reasonable tyme to cast themselves at the feete of your mercy for a repeale of those penal
statutes, under which they and their forefathers have long
groaned'. Sir John Arundell's petition to Charles II on behalf of
the Catholics of England went on to list a number of reasons why
this should be done. In their petition, the Dean and Chapter of the
secular clergy stated that they held 'that the pope hath no power,
directly or indirectly, to lay commands on the king's catholic
subjects in any thing belonging to civil and temporal matters'
and that it was 'impious, damnable and most unchristian', 'clearly
contrary to the word of God', to say that excommunicated princes
could be deposed or killed. The Benedictines also expressed their
'most unalterable fidelity, loyalty and sincerity'.[1]

Charles would have been perfectly willing to grant these requests
but it was the right of parliament to repeal laws. Henry, Lord
Arundell, presented a petition for the relief of the 'tender consciences' of Catholics in the House of Lords, when the Restoration
Parliament met in 1661, but it was soon apparent that, so far as
the church went, the new assembly had taken up the standpoint of
Charles I. Unity in church and state was essential; the demand for
liberty of conscience had led to rebellion and the abolition of
episcopacy. Revenge on the non-conformists, not reconciliation
with them, was the aim, and the Papists' loyalty did not justify
an exception being made in their favour.

One act after another was passed: they came to be known as the
Clarendon Code, since Edward Hyde, Earl of Clarendon, was the
king's most prominent adviser and a staunch churchman. In 1661
the Corporation Act[2] was passed: every member of a corporation,
the equivalent of a modern borough council, had to take the

---

[1] The full text of these petitions can be found in Petre, M.D., *The Ninth
Lord Petre* (London, 1928), pp. 73 ff.

[2] For the text of these Acts see Robertson, C. G., *Select Statutes and Documents*.

sacrament, and these corporations chose the majority of the members of parliament. Next year a new Act of Uniformity required not only the clergy but all schoolmasters to take an oath expressly admitting the validity of the rites and ceremonies so much disliked by the Puritans. About 1,200 of the parish clergy refused to swear; they had to leave their parishes, and were prohibited from opening schools, which would have been the obvious way for them to earn a living.

Further restrictions followed: the Conventicle Act forbade the assembly for non-conformist worship of more than five persons, and, as a single justice could deal with those who broke this law, they were practically deprived of the right of trial by jury. The Five Mile Act forbade any person who had preached in a conventicle, as the meeting-houses of dissenters were called, to come within five miles of any corporate town. This involved a forced exodus not only from London but from a large number of provincial towns, and therefore a complete disruption of the lives of those non-conformists who obeyed the law.

This legislation differed from earlier penal laws; it was an act of vengeance on the Puritans. But Catholics also suffered; they too came under the prohibitions and endured all the earlier laws as well. A Cheshire justice of the peace, Sir Peter Leicester, pointed this out to the grand jury of Nether-Knutsford in 1666. He said that 'Sectaries of all Sorts on the one hand and Papists on the other' were moles, working underground 'against the Peace and unity both of Church and State'. The new laws 'against the silly Quakers' extended to 'our old enemyes the Papists'; besides, 'there are sundry sharpe Lawes touchinge the Papists' still in force.[1]

At quarter sessions lists of local 'sectaries' were supposed to be regularly presented; like the returns which the bishops during the seventeenth and eighteenth centuries demanded from the parsons, they were often very imperfect, for no one liked to get his neighbour punished. This unwillingness to prosecute reduced the revenue of the king. Recusancy fines, if regularly levied, would have brought in a great deal of money, and Charles had debts to pay and was losing his popularity because he could not deal out the rewards so confidently expected by the old cavaliers, for his parliament was as niggardly as had been his father's. The heavy fine of £20 a month, or seizure of two-thirds of their land, was still due to be paid by persistent Papists. Evidence has been found that in Wiltshire presentments were actually altered; recusants were charged merely with having been absent from church for '3

[1] Halcrow, E. M., Ed., *Charges to the Grand Jury at Quarter Sessions, 1660–1677* (Chetham Society, Manchester, 1953), p. 44.

Sundayes last past', so that they could be forced to pay only three shillings for their default. It is highly probable that Wiltshire was not exceptional in this respect.

The commissioners of the Treasury made an attempt to rectify the negligence of the local authorities. A list was drawn up, county by county, of all the convicted recusants and presented to the Exchequer in 1671. It was noted that the nobility and 'considerable gentry' were almost entirely absent from the returns made; that many of the recusants were 'fanaticks', not Papists; and that the number of recusants in those counties which had reported no convictions might at least equal if not exceed those certified. Only half the counties had made returns of convictions; those which did not included Northumberland, Durham, Warwickshire, and others in which Papistry was firmly established. Of the 10,000 names in the list, over 5,000 came from Lancashire and nearly 2,000 from Yorkshire.[1] The calculation was made that if these people, who had actually been convicted, did in fact pay the £20 a month fine, with outstanding arrears, the total sum would come to between four and five million pounds, 'Which is more then all Recusants Nobility and Gentry in England are worth all together'. But, it was noted, most of those included in the actual convictions were hardly able to pay even one fine of £20. The conclusion was reached that 'Without question, a considerable summe might be raise by putting these laws in execution, but what disorder it might produce in his Majesties affairs is worthy consideration'.

From 1673 onwards the Treasury made repeated efforts to secure enforcement of the law: some money was collected, for part of the reward given to the Papist Humphrey Penderell for his help in the escape of Charles after the battle of Worcester in 1651 came from the recusancy fines. But the total was ridiculously small, and in 1680 the Privy Council stated that 'His Majesty finds that Papists of greatest note and quality, by the favour and connivance of their neighbours, or by the abuse of officers, have escaped unpunished . . . and those who have been returned have found means by secret conveyances of their Estates to protect them from any considerable forfeitures.' An attempt was made to improve the machinery of detection and the collection of fines. Under a Receiver-General the country was divided into areas, with receivers in each to ensure the presentment and punishment of recusants. This plan failed; heavy expenses were claimed, and though the officials were allowed eighteen pence in the pound on all moneys collected, this does not seem to have stimulated them to effective action. Indeed in 1684 the receivers were dismissed, and it was

[1] The list and comments are printed in C.R.S., VI, 76 ff.

reported that they had 'for the most part brought the king in debt to them, and not levied money enough to pay their charges'.[1]

The complaisance shown to the Catholics by local justices, and by their neighbours who served on juries, reflected the general attitude of the country gentry; it was the Protestant 'Commonwealth men' and the members of the newer sects who were the real enemies of church and state. 'Quakers' made up the bulk of the people presented in Cheshire for the Bucklow hundred.[2] Charles was a tolerant man, and was well aware of the need to diminish the bitter religious differences which had led, during the last 30 years, to the breakdown of normal government. He hoped by giving liberty to the 'sectaries' to win them over to the crown, as well as relieving the Papists whose loyalty was assured. In 1662 he had issued a Declaration of Indulgence, suspending the penal laws; this exercise of a disputed royal prerogative led to an outcry which forced him to withdraw it. A Bill of Indulgence was introduced and thrown out in the parliament of 1663.

Suspicion was aroused that the king and his brother were Papist in sympathy if not in fact. In 1662 Charles had married Catherine, a Portuguese princess; she brought him a great dowry, but unfortunately failed to give him the legitimate son he so badly needed. His youngest brother Henry, Duke of Gloucester, had died of smallpox four months after the triumphal return of the royal family, so the sole heir was James, Duke of York. The two brothers were very different; Charles was clever, witty, gay, lazy, and in most things unscrupulous; James was fanatically conscientious, austere and obstinate. Affection and loyalty led him in 1660 to marry Anne Hyde, the daughter of the Earl of Clarendon; she bore him two daughters, Mary and Anne, both reared in the Church of England. James had been attracted by Catholicism during his exile, and abandoned attendance at the services of the established church; his wife became a Catholic shortly before her death in 1671 and he followed her example the next year.

Once again politics and religion were intertwined, to the serious detriment of the English Papists. The majority of the men who sat in parliament were afraid lest the king should succeed in establishing a practically absolute monarchy, as Louis XIV had done in France. Now that the power of Spain was visibly declining, France began to take her place as the traditional enemy of England. In 1662 Charles had sold Dunkirk to Louis; it was useless and

[1] See Williams, J. A., *Some Sidelights on Recusancy Finance under Charles II* (*Dublin Review*, Autumn 1959, pp. 245 ff.). Material in the above section has been drawn from this article.

[2] Quarter Sessions Records. Contributed by Miss E. M. Halcrow.

expensive to hold, but its loss caused an outcry. Cromwell had been hated by many, but his seizure of a port across the channel had been hailed as a triumph. Soon afterwards, persecution of French Protestants drove them to seek refuge in England; by 1685 they were in much the same plight in France as Catholics were in England. The signing of a treaty between Louis and Charles in 1670 was therefore greatly disliked.

Clarendon had fallen from power and had been replaced by a group of five men, known as the Cabal. Only three of them were aware that in secret clauses in the treaty Charles had promised to become a Catholic in return for an income from Louis. The other two could not be kept wholly in the dark; they had strong suspicions if no exact knowledge. One of them was Anthony Ashley Cooper, an able and unscrupulous politician. He had joined the king at the outbreak of the civil war, but changed sides, and was one of the commissioners sent to arrange the restoration of the monarchy. In 1662 he had supported Charles II when the abortive Act of Toleration was before parliament, for he strongly sympathized with the Protestant non-conformists, and in 1672 he was made Lord Chancellor and Earl of Shaftesbury.

In that same year Charles made another effort to secure some religious toleration. It was badly timed, for his desperate financial position had led him in January 1672 to the 'Stop of the Exchequer'—an announcement that for 12 months the government would cease to make payments to its creditors. A few days later they were promised 6 per cent interest on the money withheld, but the upset to financiers and merchants was very great; the temporary relief the king secured led to a lasting lack of confidence in his government. In March Charles issued a declaration suspending the penal laws; the reason given was that it would allow the French refugees freedom of worship and eliminate the risk of secret and illegal conventicles. Protestant non-conformers would have full liberty; Catholics could hold services only in their own houses. If by this distinction he hoped to disarm suspicion, the king failed. Nor was his foreign policy a success; he joined France in a war with the Dutch, hoping to meet the cost by the capture of their trading vessels. The Duke of York was High Admiral; he had won a sea battle in an earlier war with the Netherlands, but now he was hampered by his orders to concentrate on seizing booty. There were no popular victories; expenses grew rapidly, so most unwillingly Charles had to summon a parliament.

In spite of Shaftesbury's efforts, before they would pass a money bill the Commons declared that penal statutes could be suspended only by parliament. On the advice of Louis XIV, Charles withdrew

HCE

his declaration. The triumphant Commons then passed the Test Act in March 1673. It not only made the taking of the sacrament obligatory for all holders of office, but added to the oath of supremacy a new declaration: 'I do declare that I do believe that there is not any transubstantiation in the sacrament of the Lord's Supper.' James had to resign his naval command. When he married an Italian princess, Mary of Modena, the belief that the brothers aimed at restoring Popery was strengthened. Shaftesbury was dismissed, and became a strong opponent of the king, organizing a party and conducting a press campaign.

It was still dangerous openly to attack the king, for fear of civil war lingered. The pope was an obvious target; he was a remote and mysterious personage, supported by cunning Jesuits and the hated King of France. In 1673 London was still making good the ravages caused by the Great Plague of 1665 and the Great Fire of 1666. The Papists were accused of responsibility for both these calamities, and pope-burning processions were organized in the city—excellent shows, ending in bonfires where effigies of the pope and his cardinals were thrown on to the flames. A particularly splendid one was arranged in 1677 for the anniversary of Queen Elizabeth's accession, 17 November. An onlooker gave a description. There were

> mighty bonfires and the burning of a most costly Pope, carried by four persons in divers habits, and the effigies of two devils whispering in his ears, his belly filled full of live cats who squawled most hideously as soon as they felt the fire: the common people saying all the while it was the language of the Pope and the Devil in a dialogue betwixt them. A tierce of claret was set out before the Temple Gate for the common people. Mr. Langhorne saith he is very confident the pageantry cost forty pounds.[1]

Those bonfires were not spontaneous outbreaks of popular feeling; they were expensive affairs paid for by the politicians.

In such an atmosphere the fantastic stories of Titus Oates's 'Popish Plot' found a credence which seemed extraordinary to reasonable men. Titus Oates was born in 1649; his father was Samuel Oates, a weaver, a rabid Anabaptist, who became chaplain in the regiment of Colonel Pride, the man whose 'purge' of the House of Commons in 1648 may possibly have prevented terms being made between the parliament and Charles I. In 1655 Oates was an active propagandist when discontented army officers tried to overturn

---

[1] Hatton, C., *Correspondence*, I, 157. Quoted by Furley, O. W., *The Pope-Burning Processions of the late 17th Century* (*History*, February 1959, p. 17).

Cromwell.[1] His son Titus[2] had had a scrappy education; his ignorance of Latin was frequently commented on. He went to Cambridge, but left in deep disgrace without taking a degree. Though he managed to get ordained, he could not obtain a settled living, for he antagonized all who came into contact with him. While he was in London in 1676 he was befriended by a comedian, Matthew Medburne, who was a Catholic, and this probably led to Oates's appointment as Protestant chaplain to the household of the Duke of Norfolk in 1677. He soon lost this position, as he had all his others, and fell into dire poverty. He knew many Catholics and their generosity to converts, especially parsons, so he persuaded a crazy priest to receive him into the Church of Rome. He next approached the Jesuits in London and asked to be admitted to their Society; they sent him to the Jesuit college in Valladolid. Here he behaved so outrageously that he was expelled and returned penniless to London.

He was given some help by Israel Tonge, a friend of his father Samuel Oates, and a notorious opponent of the Jesuits. It was very difficult for Tonge to get any information to support his attacks on the Society, and probably it was on his advice that Titus Oates now went to the Jesuit school at St. Omer in France, asking to be trained. He made a very poor impression on these Jesuits, who found him both ignorant and offensive; they would not admit him to the novitiate. After six months their patience was exhausted and he was expelled. He had gathered nothing of any value as propaganda against the Society, but he had picked up some idea of their organization and, above all, learned the names of many of their priests.

On his return to England he still frequented Catholic acquaintances and begged their help, for he was penniless; but at the same time he was in touch with Israel Tonge. Between them they drew up a narrative, in which Oates described his success in learning of an elaborate plot, organized by the Jesuits, for overthrowing Charles and establishing Catholic domination in England. A large French and Irish army was to be enrolled, and the names of prominent English Catholics were given as the designated holders of various offices. So ignorant and so stupid were the authors that the tale was full of inconsistencies and improbabilities. They tried in vain to interest Charles in their 'revelations', so in September 1678 they visited a London justice, Sir Edmund Berry Godfrey, and made formal depositions before him. Godfrey

[1] Woolrych, A. H., *Penruddock's Rising, 1655* (Hist. Assoc. 1955).
[2] Lane, J., *Titus Oates* (London, 1949). His story is told in detail in this book.

was murdered in mysterious circumstances; on hearing of the
justice's death Oates was reported to have said, 'That murder
happen'd well for me . . . my Plot had come to nothing without
it.'[1]

The political enemies of the king and the Duke of York were
quick to see their opportunity. Oates's narrative was laid before
the Privy Council, which listened to the tale with amazement.
Charles was persuaded to attend a second meeting, and asked
Oates questions on points of simple fact; the answers clearly
showed him to be a liar. The king then made a great mistake;
annoyed by the whole affair, he left the meeting; and instead of
adopting his view that Oates was a 'lying knave' the councillors,
from credulity or policy, accepted the story as a genuine revelation. The narrative was published, and was followed up by a
stream of pamphlets and newsletters organized by Shaftesbury and
his friends. These documents were spread all over the country,
rousing excitement and sometimes panic. Charles was taken aback;
he knew perfectly well that Oates was a perjurer, yet dared not
prosecute him lest the emotions so cleverly stimulated should be
turned directly against him and his brother.

Unprejudiced observers, such as John Evelyn, were dubious.
Oates, he wrote in his *Diary*, 'seemed to be a bold man' and 'everything he affirmed' was 'taken for gospel' by 'the Parliament now
growing corrupt'.[2] Men like Thomas Bruce, later Earl of Ailesbury,
looked on him as a 'vile fellow' and his evidence as 'no more than
the barking of a dog'.[3] Generally, however, emotion swamped
reason. Correspondence between the secretary of James's wife,
Edward Coleman, and people in France, in which he asked for
help for English Catholics, was seized and used to bolster up
Oates's fictions. For Oates and Tonge this was a time of wealth
and glory; Charles was forced to pay each of them £10 a week and
£2 for lodgings, as well as giving large sums to an adventurer
named Bedloe, who added his tales to theirs. To a man as short
of money as the king this must have been most galling. In addition,
considerable payments were made, also from secret service funds,
to those who searched for or informed against priests, and for 'costs'
of witnesses.[4]

For Catholics all over the country a time of terror followed
Oates's triumph. In Yorkshire 'the fearfull noyse of the pretended
Popish plot' 'put all in confusion, and no correspondence could be

[1] C.R.S., XLVII, 205. (Warner's History.)
[2] Evelyn, J., *Diary*, Everyman edition, Vol. II, p. 130.
[3] Cardigan, Earl of, *Life and Loyalties of Thomas Bruce* (1951), p. 46.
[4] *Camden Society*, Secret Services of Charles II and James II (1851).

kept'[1] by the priests who managed a fund for the support of the clergy. Several priests, not only from Yorkshire, fled the country. In Oxford there were demonstrations; the pope was burnt in effigy, and a great white cross, made of paper and sticks, burnt in St. Clement's. Houses were searched in and around Oxford, Oates himself going to Woodstock. One Catholic, George Holman, escaped arrest only because his brother, a Protestant, was a member of parliament. A large number of the leading Catholics were thrown into the Tower; even the Petre family in Essex did not escape—indeed, Lord Petre was particularly unfortunate. In the Petre MSS. is a copy of his letter to Charles, written in 1683 when he was a very sick man.[2] 'I haveing bin now above five yeares in prision & wt is more grievous to mee, Laine so long under a falls & injurious Calumny of a horrid plott', he feared he would die 'before I Could by a publicke tryall make my innocence appeare.' He absolutely denied the absurd story of Oates that a Spanish commission had been issued, making him a general in the army which was to invade England. He believed that 'ye sober part of mankind' were convinced that Oates was a liar, and declared that the Catholic Church had always condemned murder and armed rebellion. His plea was made in vain: he died in 1684 in the Tower.

The Papists confined there were at any rate safe from mob violence, although they were kept at their own expense and without a chance to defend themselves, until they were released in 1685. Exact figures for arrests are difficult to obtain; between 1678 and 1681 about 2,000 people in all were imprisoned, seven priests and five laymen were executed as traitors, and nine other priests simply on account of their priesthood. Five of them were Jesuits; when they were actually at Tyburn a pardon was offered them if they would give evidence that there really was a conspiracy. Among the Stonor MSS. in the archives of the Midland Area[3] are some contemporary printed broadsides containing an apparently accurate account of the 'Last speeches of the five notorious Traytors and Jesuits', as well as the denials of guilt made by Francis Johnson, a priest executed at Worcester.

Richard Langhorne, a well-known lawyer who had acted as solicitor for the Jesuits in England, was ordered to draw up a full list of their property in the country. This he did, but the total value was so small that it was worse than useless to their enemies.

[1] Unpublished MS. of the Yorkshire Clergy Fund, transcribed by Rev. Vincent Smith.
[2] Chelmsford Record Office, D/DP F 180.
[3] In Archbishop's House, Birmingham.

He was then offered his life and great rewards if he would support
Oates's stories. He refused to perjure himself, and was hanged
in 1679. Under a writ of the privy seal his estates were given to
the Earl of Longford and Christopher Hatton, in trust for his
widow and children. These two men clearly believed in the
lawyer's innocence. The publication of Langhorne's speeches
probably had little effect at the time, but must have caused those
who read them to doubt the justice of such condemnations and
to realize that Langhorne was right when he said, 'I take it to be
clear, that my Religion is the Sole Cause, which moved my
accusers to charge me' and 'could move my Jury to believe the
Evidence of such men'.[1]

Indeed the trials of people accused by Oates and Tonge and
Bedloe were a cruel mockery. The law was heavily weighted against
them, for no counsel was allowed to argue for the accused or to
cross-examine the witnesses in trials for treason; the man in the
dock was not even shown beforehand the indictment which
stated the precise crimes with which he was charged. A tradition
was already being built up in the English courts that the judge
himself should see to it that the prisoner's side of the story was
properly laid before the jury, but in these cases the judges were
determined to convict. Witnesses for the defence were over-awed
and even mishandled by the mobs surrounding the court, and were
terrified lest they too should be arrested.

William Howard, first Viscount Stafford, was a man of 66 and
ailing when he was accused of planning to be paymaster to the
hypothetical Catholic army. His trial began on 30 November in
Westminster Hall before the House of Peers; John Evelyn, among
very many others, was present. His view of Oates's evidence was
that 'such a man's testimony should not be taken against the life
of a dog', and that it was not likely that 'such piercing politicians
as the Jesuits should trust him with so high and dangerous secrets'.
In spite of the extreme improbability of Oates's story, Lord
Stafford was found guilty: Evelyn noted that 'he was not a man
beloved, especially of his own family',[2] and perhaps this had
something to do with his fate; he was beheaded.

The most sensational of the trials was that of Oliver Plunkett,
Archbishop of Armagh in Ireland.[3] The situation in Ireland in the
seventeenth century was radically different from that in England.
Frequently conquered but never subdued, the mass of the native
Irish remained Catholic, and they had been allowed to keep their

[1] Chelmsford Record Office, D/DY W 26.
[2] Evelyn, J., *Diary*, Everyman edition, Vol. II, p. 158.
[3] Curtayne, A., *The Trial of Oliver Plunkett* (1953).

own episcopal organization. Oates and Tonge and Shaftesbury were anxious to show that the Plot involved an Irish rebellion supported by French troops, which was one of the main points in the original 'revelations' of 1678. In the news-sheets written by Shaftesbury's employees constant references were made to the collection of arms in Ireland, but so far plans to produce evidence had miscarried. One story was that there were seditious letters concealed in the wall of a convent in Cork; unfortunately for the inventors of the plot, the man sent to 'find' these was delayed in Bristol on his way to Ireland, and the correspondence was discovered by a maid in a Bristol inn under the bolster of his bed, before he even set sail. A number of poverty-stricken Irishmen were brought over to act as witnesses against the archbishop, but they proved useless and had to be sent home again with good new clothes and money in their pockets.

Plunkett was selected as the best person to accuse because he was the head of the Roman Church in Ireland. He was first charged in Ireland, but there was no evidence against him, and the case was dropped. This was unfortunate for him, for he would have been acquitted. He was then transferred to England and lodged in the foul prison of Newgate. His plea that he ought to be tried in Ireland was ignored, and it was made practically impossible for him to bring over witnesses to testify for him. Sir George Jeffreys, later as a judge notorious for the 'Bloody Assize' of 1685, was the prosecutor, and the whole trial was a scandal. The end was certain; Plunkett was executed on 1 July 1681. Charles dared not intervene; the French ambassador reported that the king had said that 'his enemies were watching for him to make a false step'. Even those who were convinced of Plunkett's innocence played the coward; the Earl of Essex, who had known him when he was Viceroy in Ireland, asked for his pardon, saying that the witnesses against the archbishop were perjured. Charles asked, with justice, why he had not said so during the trial.

Plunkett was the last of the many Catholic clergy who were condemned to death in England for their religion, whatever the formal crime with which they were charged. Soon afterwards the persecution ended. The constant disorders, the trained bands of blackguards armed with 'Protestant flails' rather like the modern 'cosh', had sickened people, and Shaftesbury had failed to get a bill carried to exclude James from the throne. Parliament was dissolved in 1681; Shaftesbury himself was arrested, but the grand jury refused to send him for trial. Two years later he died in exile. But the fall of Titus Oates was not a rapid affair. Tonge died in 1680; Oates's income was first reduced and then stopped. In May

1685 he was tried and found guilt of perjury; he was forced to stand in the pillory and sentenced to imprisonment for life. When in 1689 he was released he had few friends; he joined the Baptists in 1701, having failed to get a living in the church; but they thought no better of him than had the Jesuits, and expelled him as a disorderly person and a hypocrite. In 1705 he died.

The Popish Plot was the last organized persecution of Englishmen for religious causes. Such Catholics as later suffered death were executed for their politics, even if it were their faith which had led to their action. The agitation against James had led to such excesses that a reaction set in; when his brother died in 1685 he was proclaimed king in the usual way, and when parliament met he was voted the same revenue as Charles II had received, with some slight additions.

In 1682 an attempt had been made to put forward James, Duke of Monmouth, Charles's beloved but illegitimate son, as heir to the crown. Now, in June 1685, the young man landed at Lyme Regis and was proclaimed king—as he was also a James, his followers were forced to call him King Monmouth. The rebellion was of very much the same type as the western rising of 1549 and the northern earls' rebellion of 1569. The appeal for support was, at any rate nominally, based on religion, and the organizers hoped for assistance from influential sympathizers. If neither this nor foreign aid was forthcoming, they were doomed, and in all of the risings the number of people willing to attempt to overthrow the existing government was limited to the inhabitants of a small area. James sent for his troops from Holland, who, superior in arms and discipline, scattered the ill-equipped and badly led rebels. Kirke, the general in command, was as cruel to his prisoners as had been the commanders of Edward VI and Elizabeth. Formal trials followed, conducted by Jeffreys; that this man should have been sent was a great error, for he had already shown his savagery at the trial of Oliver Plunkett. The 'Bloody Assizes 'of 1685 have become a familiar part of the English story, while the similar cruelties of the previous century are passed over. This is probably because in James II's time there was an active opposition party, which had been able to organize the 'Popish Plot' and could use the 'Bloody Assize' as valuable propaganda when the opportunity arose. News was now much more fully reported, and Jeffreys's abominable mockery of trials aroused strong feeling.

The accession of a Catholic king was an immense joy to his co-religionists. All over the country they proceeded, ignoring the law, to open old chapels and build new ones. Sycophantic courtiers found that the Church of Rome full well would fit their constitution; not many of them were as genuine converts as Lord Clifford, who had already become a Catholic during Charles II's reign, and adhered to his new faith when times changed. Loyal members of the Church of England were not at first alarmed; they were royalist by conviction and did not expect the awkward situation to last long. James was elderly, his wife was a sickly woman who had failed to produce a son, and his daughters were Protestant. But the king possessed all his father's obstinate belief in the Divine Right of Kings, and none at all of his brother's political acumen. He genuinely wanted toleration, but he set about obtaining it in the most foolish way.

Monmouth's rebellion had shown him how inadequate was the local militia, and he wanted a permanent army. He had given commissions to several Catholics, and in the test case of Godden v. Hales in June 1686 had secured a judgement that he had a right to dispense officers from fulfilling the terms of the Test Act. Whether he could have persuaded the parliament to repeal or modify the general penal laws is doubtful; that his decision to ask for the repeal of both the Test Act and the Habeas Corpus Act was unwise, is certain. If the Test Act were repealed, James could fill all important posts with Papists. The Habeas Corpus Act had been passed, largely through Shaftesbury's influence in 1679. It gave anyone detained in prison the right to apply, personally or through a friend, to any judge for the issue of the ancient writ of Habeas Corpus. The keeper of the jail was bound under penalty to bring the person concerned before the judge and show by what authority he was detained. Many obscurities, which had hampered prisoners kept without trial from obtaining this relief, were removed by this act. Its repeal would legalize the arbitrary arrest of James's opponents. Had the king asked instead for a wider but vaguer measure of toleration he might possibly have succeeded, but no parliament would surrender on these two points. James first prorogued and then dissolved parliament, although by so doing he lost a handsome grant.

He was determined to grant toleration, so, as the laws penalizing non-conformists were still on the statute book, in 1687 he issued a general Declaration of Indulgence. If he had confined himself to giving relief to individuals, he would have been on safe ground; his right to dispense laws in particular cases had been acknowledged by 11 out of 12 judges. Only 14 years had passed since Charles's similar declaration had been declared illegal by parliament, so it was playing straight into his enemies' hands for James to try the same plan. Under cover of his declaration he now tried to give Catholics posts in the universities. Like Queen Elizabeth, he sent commissions to Oxford and Cambridge, and like her found the colleges unwilling to accept his nominees. Circumstances were now very different, however, for Elizabeth had had the backing which James lacked, and men of ability and influence to assist her.

The Catholic king was far from recognizing that the 'Businesse of the Soveraign, is to choose good Councellors';[1] as was natural, many of his intimate friends were Catholics, whose faith had kept them from having any practical experience of politics, and others were time-servers who were 'converted' to please the king. A few sincere royalists, whose very adherence to the established church strengthened their loyalty to the crown, did their best to check the proselytizing ardour of their king and bring him to a sense of the realities of his situation. Among them was Thomas Bruce, who in 1685 sat in James's first parliament. He had been a gentleman of the bedchamber to Charles II, for whom he had a sincere affection, and he tried to organize a solid group of royalists in support of Charles's brother. Later, in 1685, he inherited the earldom of Ailesbury, and was given his former office at court by James. Thomas, though disliking the piety of his royal master, found him to be 'the most honest and sincere man I ever knew, a great and good Englishman. . . . He wanted for nothing but the talent of his royal brother.'[2] How badly James lacked that 'art called king craft' the earl soon discovered.

In 1687 the king decided to summon parliament, and, as a preliminary ordered the lords lieutenant of the shires to discover whether the leading gentry would support a bill repealing the penal laws. Lord Ailesbury was Lord Lieutenant for Bedfordshire and Huntingdonshire, and very much disliked being ordered to investigate the opinions of his neighbours. All the justices were to be asked three questions: 1. If chosen as a member of parliament, would they vote for the repeal of the penal laws? 2. Would they assist in the election of members who would be willing to do this? 3. Did they agree with the king's policy of liberty of conscience? When faced with this duty, Thomas Bruce thought of resigning his lieutenancy and his post at court, but decided 'to be silent and keep my place in Court as long as I could for to do good if possible',[3] and so prevent one of James's favourites from getting his offices.

As was to be expected, the replies to the first question were

---

[1] Hobbes, T., *Leviathan* (1651). Edition of 1909, Oxford, p. 270.

[2] Cardigan, *Thomas Bruce*, p. 110.

[3] Cardigan, op. cit., p. 116.

mainly negative or indecisive. In their answers to the second question, most of the country gentry expressed unwillingness to bring pressure to bear on their members, and some were bold enough to say that they would support only loyal Church of England men. Only the third question produced an affirmative answer. Toleration, yes, but only under the protection of the penal laws which debarred both Catholics and Protestant dissenters from full rights as citizens.

When James saw the responses he was furious, and dismissed all the deputy lieutenants, though, to his surprise, Thomas Earl of Ailesbury retained his office. Realizing that he had little hope of getting the law altered by parliament, James in 1688 re-issued his Declaration of Indulgence and, with an extraordinary lack of perception, ordered that all clergy should read it aloud in church. This instruction was widely ignored, and seven of the bishops sent the king a formal protest, saying, 'The Declaration being founded on such a dispensing power as may at pleasure sett aside all law, ecclesiastical or civill, appears to us illegal.'[1] James declared that he had been libelled, and ordered the prosecution of the seven bishops. Their defence was that their petition was privileged, as all citizens had a right to petition the king, and, after long and interesting legal arguments, on 30 June 1688 a jury found them not guilty. Widespread rejoicings followed; bonfires were lit as though for a great victory.

On 10 June the Queen had given birth to a son. This was a calamity for James's opponents, for now the next ruler would also be a Catholic. As in early days Catholics had turned to Spain, the Protestants now looked to Holland, for to William of Orange, husband of James's daughter Mary, an English alliance against France was vital. A group of influential Englishmen asked him to come over and restore the liberties of the country; precisely how this could be done was left vague. James knew what was afoot, but his preparations were inadequate. No one wanted another civil war; a great many people would almost certainly have supported him if he had, even at this late hour, summoned a parliament. His immediate friends expected him to raise a force to match William's and to ask Louis XIV for help. Indeed, when the Dutch fleet appeared in Torbay the Catholic chaplain of the Cary family of Tor Abbey thought it came from France, and summoned the household to sing a *Te Deum*.[2]

Although James was only 56, he was a sick man and surrounded by incompetent people who quarrelled with each other. Able

---

[1] Robertson, C., Grant. *Select Statutes*, etc., 2nd edition (1913), p. 392.
[2] Oliver, G., *Collections* (London, 1857), p. 21.

men like Churchill deserted him, and William's slow advance from the west was alarming. The king was urged to join his second daughter Anne at Nottingham; instead, he sent his wife and baby son to France. When he was persuaded to drive through London, he was hailed 'with loud acclamations beyond whatever was heard of.'[1] Yet when William demanded that his soldiers should take over guard duties at Whitehall, James dismissed his own men and on his son-in-law's suggestion left London for Rochester. On 2 December 1688 he told the Earl of Ailesbury that the Prince of Orange would not guarantee his safety, and said, 'If I do not retire, I shall certainly be sent to the Tower; and no King ever went out of that place but to his grave'.

Thus ignominiously ended the reign of the last Catholic king of England. His flight was followed by some anti-Papist demonstrations; in Exeter the 'Mass-house' was burnt down, but the priest got safely away. Three Catholic bishops were sent to the Tower, but were later released; there were no widespread searches, though many priests went into hiding or left the country for security. Convinced royalists, Protestant as well as Papist, joined the king in exile, for many of the Church of England disapproved of revolution. The bulk of the Catholic gentry, and of course all farmers and traders, waited quietly to see whether a new persecution would follow the revolution.

[1] Cardigan, op. cit., p. 146.

8

THE DAWN OF TOLERATION

Whether the brief reign of James II did more harm or good to his co-religionists is arguable. Certainly it revived anti-papal feeling and renewed the suspicion that Catholics must be opposed to the existing system in the state as well as in the church; on the other hand, their short period of comparative freedom had had a stimulating effect on both clergy and laity. A lasting gain was that a regular form of organization of their church was set up in England. For years the secular clergy had been asking for another bishop to be appointed, for though the chapter set up by Bishop Smith continued its work, it had no episcopal powers.

A highly critical list of the members of the chapter was drawn up by the President of Douay about 1667. Dr. Leybourne was himself a 'chapter man', but he and four others lived abroad, and some of the priests in England were old and ill. The most influential member was Thomas White, alias Blacklow, a man, said Leybourne, regarded 'as an oracle, though now he is gifted neither with judgement nor memory. The wicked old man lives in London'.[1] Controversy was raging, as it did before and for years after, round various proposals for the wording of a new oath of allegiance which could be taken by Catholics and would satisfy the government. The laity passionately desired to be free of the stigma of disloyalty; the theologians were anxious lest a definition should be accepted which diminished the spiritual power of the papacy. Blacklow was suspected of being unreliable on this point.

The priests of the chapter, and indeed most of the secular priests in the country, were very anxious that any new bishop should have the status of a bishop in ordinary, but such men were appointed as a rule only in countries where there existed a normal diocesan organization. They were also urgent—and this was a continuing demand—that he should be a secular priest, or 'clergy man'. The reasons for this were set out in a curious document, written about 1702. It was feared that a regular of any order would 'extend obedience almost to anything' demanded by his

[1] C.R.S., XI, 547.

superiors; that he would try to get his fellow monks appointed to the chapter, and so forth. Jealousies would arise, and he 'would never be obeyed by true-hearted Clergy men.'[1]

When James ascended the throne, the appointment of a bishop was possible, for the Roman authorities were always very unwilling to take such a step without the approval of a government. In 1685 John Leyburne (the name was spelt in varying ways), who was a nephew of the President of Douay, was consecrated Bishop of Adrumetum, another of the ancient sees which, like Chalcedon, existed only on paper. He therefore had the status of vicar apostolic, as had his two predecessors, and his successors until the restoration of the hierarchy in 1850. The 'Old Chapter', as it came to be known, gradually turned into a kind of benevolent society, and as such it still exists. The urgent need for a bishop's services was demonstrated when Leyburne on a visit to the northern shires admitted over 20,000 people to the sacrament of confirmation.[2]

It was perfectly plain that no one man could possibly guide and control the large number of Catholics, so in 1688 four districts were set up: the northern stretched from the Scottish border to a line drawn roughly from the Dee to the Humber; the western included all Wales and south-west England to the coast of Dorset. Thence the London district ran east; its northern boundary was peculiar, for it included all the home counties and Bedfordshire and Berkshire. The remainder of the country came into the midland district. Three more vicars apostolic, two secular priests and one Benedictine, were consecrated to take care of these huge areas. As time went on, extra bishops were appointed as their coadjutors.

James II promised £1,000 a year each to the bishops, but before they had begun work he had departed. Funds for their support were not easy to obtain; though several of the vicars apostolic were men of wealth, being members of great families, others lived in truly apostolic poverty. As late as 1809 Bishop Collingridge of the western district lived in two hired rooms and had no private chapel; during the greater part of his long life the famous Bishop Challoner moved from one modest lodging to another. Constant appeals were made to them by poor priests and layfolk; transport for their tours of their areas was costly, even if they enjoyed the hospitality of their flocks.

The secular clergy too had financial problems, especially when sickness or age fell upon them. Towards the end of the seventeenth

---

[1] Midland District Archives, Archbishop's House, Birmingham.
[2] Hemphill, B., *Early Vicars Apostolic* (London, 1954), p. 12.

century they began to organize schemes for mutual benefit, generally on a county basis. All members of the group paid what they could into a fund, solicited alms for it, and made bequests in their wills. A careful register was kept of the subscribers; three superiors and a treasurer were elected for three years at a stretch. Help was given from the fund to priests newly arrived in the county, to the sick, to the members in prison.

Regular meetings were held, often in an inn, and these served as opportunities to discuss pastoral problems. The obligation to keep the major feasts of the church as strictly as Sundays, and therefore to abstain from normal work on those days, was one which caused great difficulties to the laity. Were priests right to give 'dispensations' allowing farmers, for instance, to work on feast days? The feast of the Assumption falls on 15 August, and in 1686 at York a minute was made in the clergy fund's register to the effect that 'many of the more conscientious sort have suffered for not working on some holy days, when their corn has bin shaking, their hay layd at losse etc.'[1] Moreover, a farmer had to pay and feed his men on these feast days 'to sit still, or else they will go to others.'

Care was taken to limit the extent of each priest's area of activity and to prevent penitents from going to one confessor after another in hope of easier penance. Instruction of the 'common sort of people' was urged on members, who were also warned of the danger of getting involved in litigation, or giving scandal by drinking or gaming. Problems such as: Should the faithful be allowed to serve meat to Protestant guests and servants on Fridays? were discussed; the priests of Hampshire agreed in 1691 that they should not.[2]

Their fund, known as the Hampshire Hog, still exists, as indeed do several others of these mutual benefit societies. The records of their meetings are of great interest; they reveal many of the financial and spiritual problems of the English priests, and often show some aspect of their relationship with their flocks. Regular assemblies were, however, by no means always possible; political events often disrupted the labours of the priest and still more of the bishops. The Revolution Parliament of 1689, after passing the Bill of Rights which limited the prerogative of the monarch, prescribed new oaths of allegiance and supremacy; any person who refused to take them was liable to fine and imprisonment. Many non-Catholics, including five of the bishops who had been

[1] From the Register of the Yorkshire Fund, transcribed by the Rev. Vincent Smith of Lanchester.
[2] C.R.S., XLIII. 9 ff.

prosecuted for libel by James II, refused to swear, as did a large
number of the parish clergy. Having vowed fealty to one king,
however unwise he might have been, they could not now deny
him, for they would not accept the pretence that he had abdi-
cated. Papists could in no case have taken the oaths, which
denied the spiritual rights of the pope. Protestant non-conformists
were allowed to use a form of declaration agreeable to their
consciences, and by an Act of Toleration were exempted from
the penal laws and allowed to hold their own independent services.
Yet all the existing legislation against Catholics was still in force;
they were again banished from London and forbidden to possess
any arms or to own a horse worth more than £5. William suspended the Habeas Corpus Act, which his father-in-law had so
disliked, and was thus able to imprison any suspect without trial.
A good many Papists had their houses burnt, and in several places
not only priests but ordinary people went into hiding or left the
country.

There was, however, no repetition of the persecution of earlier
times, or even of the savage attacks of the Titus Oates period.
Most of the prisoners, including the bishops, were released after
a short time, or were acquitted when they were brought to trial.
William Blundell of Crosby, for example, suffered 'almost solely
by the insolence of private soldiers, who came without commission,
and without any officer or Constable, to search out houses' in
May 1689. One of his servants was robbed of 57s. and he himself
had his horses taken. Later he was imprisoned, but was brought
to trial after eight months and discharged. The Blundells had good
friends in Lancashire, which probably accounts for his being able
soon after his release to get a licence allowing him to have a good
horse. This did not prevent the seizure of the animal in 1692, but
it seems to have been returned. As in earlier times, the local
officials were not unfriendly; a group of informers hoped to make
their fortunes by charging Lancashire landowners with setting
land apart for 'superstitious uses', but failed to win their case;
another group of Papists charged at Manchester with conspiracy
were acquitted.[1]

At East Lulworth in Dorset the benevolence of the local vicar,
Joseph Tomes, to his patrons, the Catholic Welds, was shown on
Christmas Day, 1688, when he wrote to Lady Clare Weld, who was
in London.[2] 'Honourble Madam, God has been pleased to raise up
a friend of allmost an enemy mr Culliford, after haveing on ye
15th instant checked the Rable at Wareham (gatherd together by

1 Blundell, M., *Cavalier* (London, 1933), pp. 256, 264, 278.
2 MS. Box D 10, County Record Office, Dorchester.

a false allaram of the Irish) sent next day for Mr Willis . . . and afterwards for me, & proposed to me the searching of the Castle for Armes, which I willingly accepted, & desird certificat of it'. This certificate still exists in the Weld archives. 'The discourse of it, which he willingly sent abroad, has so far appeased the multitude, that I hope we are out of danger. I am very well assured if yr Ladyship would be pleased to live here, you might have p(ro)tection from all ye Gentlemen in ye Country.' Yet in 1690 William Willis, in charge at Lulworth, had to write to complain about 'false reports by evill persons'. As 'I cannot stir, above five miles, to make my complaynt', he asked two local justices 'to Issue out your warrant, against ye Authors of these false reports.'

The Welds were a peaceable family, highly respected; not all Papists got off so lightly. At Coughton Court in Worcestershire, for instance, on a day known as 'Running Thursday', the east wing of the house was destroyed by a mob from Alcester. The Throckmortons had made a new chapel there when the house was renovated after the Restoration. The 'allaram' of an Irish landing in England was ended by William's victory over James, which led to the loss of all political rights by the Irish Catholics, who formed the great majority of the population, and by the introduction into Ireland of all the English penal laws. As Sir Richard Lodge wrote, these laws 'seemed deliberately designed to degrade and irritate rather than to convert the sufferers. Their motive was greed rather than religious zeal'.[1] Until now, in spite of their sufferings under Elizabeth and Cromwell, the Irish clergy had been free as compared with their English brethren, and had occasionally been able to send a bishop over to England. Now they too were proscribed as enemies of the state. Ireland remained, though defeated, a foreign and a Papist land, and in later years events there were to influence directly the fate of Catholics in England.

Queen Mary's death in 1694 revived the hopes of the Jacobites: to forestall any immediate reaction, William had some leading Catholics arrested and charged with treason. Among them was Sir Thomas Clifton of Lytham Hall in Lancashire, a man of 66. Dutch soldiers were sent to arrest him, and he was lodged in the Tower; four months later he was tried at Manchester and acquitted, for there was no evidence against him.[2] A plot to assassinate William in 1696 led to a further wave of arrests of Papists. Thomas Blackburne was one of the most unfortunate; no evidence was ever brought against him, for he was never tried, but lay in Newgate Prison until his death over 53 years later.[3]

[1] Lodge, R. *Political History of England, 1660–1702* (London, 1910), p. 363.
[2] C.R.S., VI, 188.   [3] Ibid., p. 160.

There was nothing specifically Papist about the negotiations that were going on between Englishmen and the Stewarts 'over the water': a number of leading politicians were, as it were, taking out insurance policies in case there were a second Restoration. Too many were involved for there to be any widespread persecution, and this probably also accounts for the passing of the Trials of Treason Act in 1696, which did a good deal to prevent the shocking travesties of justice that had occurred in the past. The accused were now allowed the assistance of counsel and given the right to summon witnesses for the defence. A few years later they were also entitled to know, 10 days before the trial, the names of the witnesses for the prosecution, so they had some notion of the character of the evidence and a defence could be prepared.

The act was of great importance for the Catholics. It was still treason to be a priest or to hear Mass, and hitherto it had been practically impossible for an accused person to put up any effective defence. On the other hand, an act of 1696 barred all Papists from acting as barristers or solicitors, and four years later they were declared incapable of purchasing or inheriting land. This drastic prohibition was rarely enforced; the heirs of the Catholic gentry continued peacefully to inherit their family estates and property was still bought by Papists, though it was sometimes thought wise to use a friendly Protestant as an intermediary.

It had long been a principle of public finance that the Catholics should pay substantially for their obstinacy; the difficulty always was to find a satisfactory way of making them do so. Under the Commonwealth a new system of direct taxation had been evolved, a forerunner of the income tax which succeeded it. Most of the yield came from a levy on estimated revenue from land. Though this source of income could not be concealed, it frequently changed owners through sale, inheritance, or confiscation, so a calculation was made of the amount which each shire ought to produce and commissioners appointed to assess the tax due from each estate. To meet their expenses they were given one penny in each pound sent to the receiver for the county; he got 2d. and the collectors 3d. Such payments were not large enough to encourage efficiency; receivers often acted for several countries, and delayed sending the money to the Treasury for as long as possible.[1] Tenants paid the tax and deducted it from the rent they gave the landowner, as is still the custom with the tax on ground rents; but when a man farmed his own land its annual value was pure guess work. Land tax varied during the eighteenth century from 4s. to 1s. in the pound, according to the needs and policy of the government. The

[1] Ward, W. R., *English Land Tax in the Eighteenth Century* (1953).

money actually collected never balanced with the estimates; in 1711 and in 1716 it reached 44·66 per cent but in all other years the proportion was lower.

In 1692 it was ordained that Catholics should pay land tax at double the standard rate. It is difficult to discover whether this was, as had been intended, a serious burden on Papist landowners. Friendly commissioners could ignore the recusancy of a neighbour if he had not been formally convicted, or they could undervalue his estate. In March 1693 a letter to Sir James Simeon of Aston in Staffordshire reported that the commissioners had intended to charge the double rate on the whole of his property, but had been persuaded to levy it only on the demesne land.[1] In Kent, in 1780, Mr. Darrell of Calehill had to pay double tax on his share of the Little Chart estate,[2] but it is rare to find in receipts and accounts of estates a definite statement of the scale on which tax had been assessed. When Lady Arabella Howard sold land to a Protestant,[3] he secured a certificate that he would have to pay only £56 instead of £112. Such sales further complicated the collection of land tax.

That the Catholics as a whole were exceedingly wealthy was generally believed; the government was often urged to raise money from them to wipe out the new national debt, which the wars of William and of Anne had enormously increased since its foundation in 1693. In 1716 Sir Richard Steele delivered to the commissioners a paper by a Mr. Brooke, giving a description of the organization of Catholic priests in England, and referring to the 'vast treasures' needed to 'support so many and so great seminarys in Forreign parts, which is obvious are founded and maintained by English donations. . . . I'm sure I may venture to say they have vast sums in the Public Funds and Stocks'. This gentleman's communication was inspired by a claim he believed his wife to have on the estate of Catherine Winford, who in her will had bequeathed her only £20 and some trinkets. The executors rejected the demand, and he 'at that time being of that religion' was helped by the provincial of the Jesuits. He was thus enabled to discover that the bulk of the estate had been left to trustees with secret instructions, one of which was to make payments 'for educating youth at St. Omer's'. He suggested that heavy penalties should be imposed on all who undertook such a trust. Brooke's action resulted in the discovery of a codicil, which had not been submitted for probate,

[1] Contributed by Miss Holmes, County Archivist of Dorset.
[2] Darrell Archives, Kent Record Office, Maidstone. U 386 E 23/1-3.
[3] Wright, T., *History and Topography of the County of Essex* (1831), Vol. I, p. 612.

by which sums were left to various Catholic organizations and to a number of priests and other people.[1] If it had been possible to do as Brooke suggested, the blow to Papistry would have been heavy, but it was not practicable.

The ministers of Queen Anne had, naturally, kept a close watch on well-known Catholics, and especially on the bishops. Old Bishop Bonaventure Giffard, in the London district, was constantly threatened and in 1714 wrote that he had had to change his lodgings 14 times in five months.[2] When Anne died, a special eye was kept on Marlborough, which was known to be a centre of Jacobite activity; Ralph Allen, the postmaster of Bath, read the correspondence from the Marlborough area and reported the contents to the government.[3] This helped him greatly in his very prosperous career.

Theoretically, of course, all Papists were Jacobite for the same reasons that had led them to wish that Mary Stewart should be Queen of England. Lip service continued to be paid to the royal family in exile long after it was clear that there was no hope of a second Restoration. But the Catholics, like many of the Tory politicians, had some grounds for hope that Anne would support the succession of her nephew; that a complete foreigner in the unattractive person of George of Hanover should be king was unwelcome to practically everyone except the active Whig politicians.

The sheer incompetence of the Old Pretender and his advisers was responsible for the mistiming and bad organization of the rising of 1715. The Scottish force that crossed the border was ill armed and badly led. Several of the leading Catholic gentry had already been imprisoned in Carlisle; others, like Nicholas Blundell of Crosby, hid themselves from the local authorities—he actually got into the priest's hiding-place, 'a streat place for a fat man'.[4] When the Jacobite army reached Preston, a good many of the local Catholic gentry joined it, as well as several poor Papists and a barber and a joiner from Lancaster,[5] but there was no general uprising of the Catholics and Tory high churchmen such as had been anticipated. Perhaps if James himself had been present enthusiasm might have been kindled, but he did not arrive until a week after his supporters had been defeated and scattered at Preston.

[1] Payne, O., *Records of English Catholics* (London, 1889), pp. 106 ff.

[2] Hemphill, B., *Early Vicars Apostolic* (1954), p. 46.

[3] Williams, J. A., unpublished thesis on Catholics in Wiltshire.

[4] Blundell, M., *Blundell's Diary* (Liverpool, 1952), p. 151.

[5] Chetham Society, Vol. V (1845), *Journal of Peter Clarke*, pp. 90, 99.

They, too, had lost through their delay; an eye-witness ascribed their inactivity during a vital three days to the fact that "The Ladys in this towne, Preston, are so very beautyfull' that 'courting and ffeasting' occupied the officers. Quarrels broke out between the various leaders, some of whom were 'very unfit for such an important command'.[1] Two government forces were allowed to join, and attacked the Jacobites just as they were preparing to march. Their general surrendered, probably much to the relief of their opponents, for resistance could well have been prolonged. The greater part of the Scots and English evaded capture, but many leading Catholics were taken. Some were executed locally, others tried for treason in London, many imprisoned.

That several succeeded in escaping from their prisons perhaps indicates strong local sympathy. Thomas Riddell, of a well-known Northumberland family, escaped from Lancaster Castle, and John Talbot of Cartington, Northumberland, from Chester. He, like other fortunate people, got safely home; many others went abroad, as did a number of non-Papist politicians.

The vicar of Preston, Samuel Peploe, who had long been distressed by the number of Romanists in and around his parish, was very active in reporting the presence of priests and the names of those who harboured them. George I was pleased with what was told him of the vicar, and made a pun in his broken English, saying that he should 'Peep high', not peep low.[2] He was made Bishop of Chester when a vacancy occurred. But although a large number were imprisoned, several were released after a short time; even a priest, caught hiding in an oak tree, was kept only a few months in Lancaster Castle, and after spending two years abroad felt safe enough to escort two nuns to England in an attempt to secure the incomes they had received from the estate of the Earl of Derwentwater, which had been confiscated. A considerable number of those who had joined James's army were never indicted; in 1716 the constable of Myerscough reported that never 'was there any reputed pop. prts harboured within our sd towne that we know of', yet a convicted recusant farmer had Mass said regularly in his house.

The searches did, of course, lead to a considerable dislocation of normal Catholic life in Lancashire; a priest wrote, 'I scarce ever rest three nights in the same bed', and he once had to ride over 46 miles across the hills in a single day to escape arrest.[3] Many flocks were for a while left without a pastor; some chapels were closed after the confiscation of an estate. Yet the trouble was on the whole

---

[1] Ibid., pp. 107, 109. [2] C.R.S., XV, 316.
[3] C.R.S., XX, 37.

temporary; in one instance the vestments and plate of a chapel were seized in 1715 and again in 1718, yet it was re-opened in 1723, and two years later 580 people were confirmed there.

The lawyers had a busy time over the confiscated estates of those actually condemned, for many people had claims on them. In a few instances friends of the family secured them, as in earlier times, and held them in trust; but a considerable number of Jacobite Catholics were practically ruined. The whole picture was, however, very different from that of the sixteenth and seventeenth centuries. Colonel Oxburgh was one of the men who had surrendered at Preston, and who, like the famous young Earl of Derwentwater, was tried for treason and executed in 1716. His head was displayed on Temple Bar, and this, it was said, so revolted the citizens of London that many juries refused to convict men accused of treachery; one jury was reprimanded and dismissed by the judge and a new one summoned. This one duly found the prisoner guilty, as in fact he was, but he was later pardoned. In one case, the local parson gave evidence that John Dalton, a Lancashire man, was a peaceable Roman Catholic who had often drunk King George's health. Perhaps this is why he was not executed, though found guilty. Indeed, of 24 men condemned to death in July 1716, 22 were reprieved.[1]

Before the execution of Colonel Oxburgh, he delivered a declaration to the sheriffs, who were ordered to print it. It stated what were probably the sentiments of most of the Catholics who were Jacobites.

> I declare, for my own particular, that if King James the Third had been a Protestant, I should think myself obliged to pay him the same Duty, and do him the same service, as if a Catholic; nor do I know of any Catholic that is not of the same Principle: For I never could find that either by the Laws of God, or the Ancient Constitution of the Nation, Difference of Religion in the Prince, made any Change in the Allegiance of the Subject.[1]

In 1716 all Papists were required, shire by shire, to register their lands. It must have been a galling and fairly costly business for those who owned land in several areas, and had either to go to each centre to sign or pay a lawyer to act for them. With this information at their disposal, the government was able—or should have been—to see that due taxes and fines were paid; but once more the lack of a Civil Service prevented this. After the conspiracy of the high-church Bishop Atterbury in 1722 a special

[1] Chetham Society, V, (1845), pp. 221 ff.
[2] Ibid., p. 219.

levy was ordered on all non-jurors of one-quarter of the capital value of their land; a sum of £100,000 was fixed for the whole of England, and the allocation for each shire announced. In practice, it was only the Catholics who were asked to pay. Assessments varied greatly; the North Riding of Yorkshire was to produce £5,685 10s., Cornwall only £371 6s. 1¼d. Margaret Weld of Lulworth copied out the list; sums were worked out to one-eighth of a penny —Norwich, for instance, was to produce £54 18s. 3⅜d. She petitioned against the assessment of her son's estate, pointing out that it was charged with salaries for three local parsons and other fixed payments, and that rents had fallen since the registration.[1] Naturally everyone avoided payment if he could and the result was that the collection of the levy took several years and brought in only about two-thirds of what had been expected. Yet it was a serious drain on many Catholics, as well as humiliating, and perhaps it had a share in the abandonment—sometimes only temporary—of their traditional religion by some of the Catholic nobility.

For the next 20 years things went quietly for the Papists. Defoe made a Tour of England in 1724; when describing Winchester he referred quite casually to

> a piece of an old monastery undemolish'd, and which is still preserv'd to the religion, being the residence of some private Roman Catholic gentlemen, where they have an oratory, and, as they say, live still according to the rules of St. Benedict. This building is call'd Hide-House; and as they live very usefully and, to the highest degree, obliging among their neighbours, they meet with no obstruction or disturbance from any body.[2]

Winchester was a strong Catholic centre, and some of the local clergy were not at all happy about it. Fourteen parishes in the deanery of Winchester reported Papists in the visitation return of 1725, and the parson of St. Peter Chesil declared that though none in his parish were of 'considerable note or substance', they and others 'receive weekly or monthly contributions' from rich Catholics. 'I find a predominant spirit of Popery among many of my parishioners which urges me the more strenuously to confute their errours in almost all discourses . . . Yet I am abused, insulted and persecuted by the prevailing Party of Rich Papists & their correspondents who instigate the common people to revile me in the street.'[3]

[1] Weld MSS., D 10, Dorset Record Office.
[2] Defoe, D., *A Tour through England and Wales*, Everyman edition, Vol. I, p.186.
[3] C.R.S., XLII, 124.

When in 1743 England went to war with France, Charles Edward
believed that there was a chance to regain the throne for his
father. A renewal of Jacobite propaganda among the Catholics
was, on the whole, feared and disliked by the vicars apostolic.
Though they continued formally to address the Stewarts as their
sovereigns,[1] they were convinced that nothing but harm could come
to the Catholics from an attempt to upset the Hanoverians by
French aid, yet without such aid the plan must fail. In 1743 a
priest was removed by his bishop from Egton in Yorkshire for
engaging in Jacobite propaganda.[2] Very few of the leading gentry
were willing to run risks for a cause which they frequently drank
to. When the rising actually began in 1745 the Duchess of Norfolk
wrote that she prayed God 'that this wicked rebellion may soon
be suppressed, lest it hurt the poor Roman Catholics'.[3] She and
the Duke were, however, close friends of the Prince of Wales:
the future George III was actually born in their house, where his
parents were staying during one of their frequent quarrels with
King George II.

The failure of the Rebellion of 1745 was not quite so disastrous
to the 'poor Roman Catholics' as might have been expected.
Once more they were ordered to leave London; the chapels of all
the embassies except the Bavarian were closed. In Lancashire
some of the Papist squires had their houses burnt, several chapels
were destroyed, and many priests and prominent laymen arrested.
In Northumberland it was reported that the Catholic gentry
had been asked to promise not to support the Pretender; as
they would not pledge themselves, 'its thought they be imprisoned.'[4]

Those who actually took part in the rising and were captured
were executed, transported or imprisoned. One melancholy case
was that of Edward Clavering and his wife. While he was in
prison in York Castle he was married, on 9 June 1746, to Elizabeth
Grant by another prisoner, Father Monox Hervey, alias J. Rivett,
who noted in his private register: 'N.B. This marriage made a
great Noise, & J R, alias M H, was mightily blamed; but It was
done ad Melius Bonum, in order to prevent Sin: . . . sin att all

[1] E.g., in 1760 Bishop Hornyold addressed Charles as King and asked his
support in requesting a Coadjutor. Midland District Archives, Archbishop's
House, Birmingham. MS. A 143 A.

[2] T. Liddell, of Egton Bridge. From notes of the late W. G. Ward, in the
possession of Mr. Bennison, Borrowby, Thirsk.

[3] Quoted Burton, E. H., *Life of Challoner* (London, 1909), Vol. I, p. 237.

[4] C.R.S., XIV, 383.

times should be, If possible, Prevented'.[1] The pair did not long enjoy wedded bliss; on 1 November Clavering was executed, and in the following April his widow was transported as a felon to America with several rebels.

Father Hervey had been arrested at Ugthorpe on 11 December 1745 along with the priest who had replaced the ardent Jacobite at Egton Bridge, after 'playing hide and seek' and being 'denyd shelter'. After a year his companion was released, but Hervey was finally brought to trial in March 1747. There was no evidence that he had taken any share in the Jacobite rising, but that he was a priest was amply proved: some of the depositions are in the Record Office. One man, a weaver, to whom the priest had been particularly generous, gave a full description of his saying Mass and administering the sacraments. Hervey himself admitted that he was a priest and kept a school; Elizabeth Clavering told of her marriage. In spite of all this he was acquitted, though under bond to leave Yorkshire.

Many other priests and layfolk were acquitted by sympathetic juries, but still a great deal of suffering was inflicted on harmless people. The Five Mile Act, which had been ignored, was now sometimes enforced, to the great inconvenience of people like a clockmaker of Stokesley, who wrote to Monox Hervey a month before the priest's arrest to inquire about the condition of the chapel clock at Ugthorpe and explain that he could not travel over to see it. He went on to ask for £5 or £6 'if you Possibly can', for 'our Neighbouring Gentlemen are So malicious against Catholicks that Where I Use'd to get much Buisiness is at Prisant Jntirely turn'd out and where I have Bills due instead of having them Answer'd, Meets with no other Return but the Vilest Redicule'.[2]

Those of higher social rank also found that the rebellion had given an opportunity to those who wished them ill. At Poole there was a 'discovery' of a plot in a letter dated 22 September 1745. After suggesting that plans were afoot to release the prisoners at Plymouth, it went on, 'I thoft proper to wish you Joye of our Sweep in the North and if our Naibours Should land Westward I hope you are ready to assist with what you mensioned in your last but I faire ye Whinds has prevented them'. It was expected that this would lead to serious trouble for the Weld family, as it certainly would have done in earlier times, but when the local justices sent the missive to the lord lieutenant, Lord Shaftesbury, he declared it 'Malicious and Improbable'. Edward Weld was summoned to London and immediately discharged, but thought

[1] C.R.S., XIV, 341. [2] C.R.S., XIV, 384.

it wise to conform with a law which he had been breaking. He wrote to the justices to thank them for their unanimous opinion in his favour, and went on to tell them, 'I have sent my coach horses to Mr fframpton's stables that I may not be any ways obnoxious to the Governmt and I faithfully promise you that I will always remain quiet and peaceable.' He also offered a reward of £40 for the discovery of the author of 'that vile piece of forgery'.

Frampton wrote to him not long after, saying that he ought to have his horses back: 'as you are the only Resident Roman Catholick in the county of any fortune its likely there will never be any order about them.' This view was shared by 'all the gentlemen' in the neighbourhood, and Frampton was able to report that Lord Shaftesbury thought 'you might have your horses whenever you please'.[1] The Welds were indeed quiet folk, and greatly respected, but it was also the case that in the mid-eighteenth century the general feeling was opposed to anything like religious persecution.

Though some parsons dutifully reported the names of Papists in their parishes, several of them considered that the real menace to the church lay in other directions than Rome. In 1706 the return to the Bishop of London for Chiswick gave the names of three Papists, adding that one, Sir Richard Beeling, is 'quiet and peaceable in his behaviour.' The parson went on to add that he wished that similar watch could be kept on 'those who are of such Prophane Principles, as to own themselves of no Religion, or of such ill Lives and Loose morals as to become a Scandal to all.'[2] In Oxfordshire, in 1738, Somerton 'has always been remarkable for a great many Papists, which I suppose proceeds from most of the Inhabitants being Tennants to Mr Fermour a Roman Cathk. gentlm. who lives at Tusmore.' John Watson, the parson, added, 'I have formerly been advis'd by my superiours not to be troublesome to ye Roman Catholicks so long as they live quietly and peaceably, and get no ground amongst us. The Protestants and Papists by long living together in ye same Parrish are so blended and united together, having for several years married one among the other, that shou'd we put ye laws in execution against ye Papists, I am afraid that instead of bringing them over to the Church, it would be a certain means of driving some of our own people away.'[3]

The Rev. William Cole wrote in his Blecheley Diary on 21

---

[1] Weld of Lulworth MSS., Box D 10, Dorset County Record Office.
[2] Visitation Returns, London. Box 9800, I CSR 68, Guildhall, London.
[3] Oxfordshire Record Society (1957). Visitation Returns, 1738, pp. 135, 137.

August 1767 that the Bishop of Lincoln wanted a list of Papists.

> Why don't the Bps enquire after the Growth of Dissenters of multi-
> farious Denominations? After Atheists, Deists and Libertines, surely
> these are more dangerous to our Constitution & Christianity in
> General than the Papists, whose Tenets are Submission to Govern-
> ment & Order. Great Pity it is the factious Element against them is
> not true, & that they actually did encrease, that they might be a
> Ballance against them.[1]

By no means all of the parish clergy shared these views. In
1706 the parson at Mountnessing in Essex suffered greatly from
the power of the Petre family. He stated that there were 30 or
40 Papists in his parish, of which Lord Petre was patron; one Horne
a farmer with three sons, was particularly obnoxious to him. He
'is a very impident fellow giving ill language when I demand what
is my due & calls me names & 'twas he or one of his sons I am
confident yt wrote upon the church wall He yt preacheth here is
a rogue & a dog. My church is surrounded with 'em so yt I am
almost afraid to goe through their grounds towards night to
inter a corpse.'[2]

In 1737 the Rector of Whitby wrote to the precentor at York to
complain of the growth of Popery and the situation at Egton
Bridge in particular. There was 'a sort of compromise; for (as
Mr Robinson ye curate assures me) ye Papists have a particular
Part of ye Church yard assign'd 'em for ye burial of their dead.
And they are married, baptiz'd and interr'd without his knowing
anything of ye matter 'till afterwards yt they come to pay his
fees.' Yet 'our Friends are so tender in speaking out, when seriously
call'd upon, that it is extremely difficult to convict 'em legally.'[3]
The Robinsons, father and son, were in charge at Egton for many
years; the local landowner, Cary Elwes, tried to help by attempting
to prevent his tenants from marrying Papists, but failed. In
1753 he wrote to the archbishop for help in 'suppressing so Growing a Calamity. Out of 136 Tenants near a Third are Papists.'
Jonathan Robinson reported that Elwes had 'left orders immediately to discharge any one of his Tenants either man or woman
that shal for ye Future suffer themselves to be seduced to ye Ch.
of Rome.'[4] But York was a long way off, and there was little
the archbishop could do without effective help from the local
gentry.

[1] Cole, Rev. William, *Blecheley Diary*, Ed. Stokes (1931), p. 253.
[2] Diocese of London. Certificates as to Papists. MS. 9800, Guildhall Library.
[3] Ward, W. G., unpublished history, op. cit.
[4] Bishopthorpe Archives, Borthwick Institute, York. Bundle 5, No. 237.

The open practice of Popery troubled the Bishop of Winchester in 1759. He wrote to a member of the government about a house with a large chapel, which he said had cost £1,200 or more; a priest had built it at Havant on land leased from the bishop himself. He had no legal means of evicting his tenant, but thought the government ought to take some action. 'All the Papists in & about Portsmouth, & all who come from abroad, or go abroad from thence, make no secret of going to this Chapel. . . . Every Thing possible to be known by Enemies in these parts may be known in France, from Langston Harbour, in a few Hours.'[1] Catholics had used the creeks on the Hampshire and Sussex coasts for furtive journeys in the sixteenth and seventeenth centuries, but they were certainly not going to act as spies for France in 1759. There is no record that any steps were taken in this or in other cases where state aid was invoked by anxious clerics.

Another worried man was the incumbent of St. Peter's parish in Marlborough. In 1767 he reported to his bishop that Mass was being said in the house of a Mrs. Hide. 'I see a poor silly yeoman with three or four others . . . constantly attending the House, not only on Sunday mornings, but on other days which they esteem equally or rather more worthy of their worship, viz: Thomas a Beckett, the assumption, and the rest of them.' A woollen draper, 'a vigorous bigot', a cabinet maker and others were among those who are 'such bitter enemies of our Happy Constitution in Church and State'.[2]

There is ample evidence that both the clergy who feared and those who tolerated Catholicism knew perfectly well that the laws were not likely to be enforced, and that in the mid-eighteenth century Papists formed a permanent element in English society, recognized if not approved. A toleration based on indifference rather than on charity prevailed; religious controversy continued, but with far less bitterness and without the political overtones of the seventeenth century. The interposition of the reign of 'Good Queen Anne' between that of the unpopular Dutch William and that of German George had reduced the sense of tension in domestic politics. The rising of 1715 had displayed the weakness of the Jacobites; that the king was a foreigner was not important now that parliament met every year. The age of reason had come; enthusiasm was unfashionable; standards of living were rising as new methods and new markets offered

[1] C.R.S., XLIV, 145.

[2] 1767 Recusant Returns, Salisbury, transcribed by J. A. Williams.

larger rewards in agriculture and trade. The law was enforced by judges who, since the Act of Settlement of 1701, were secure from arbitrary dismissal by politicians. That the heavy penalties still in force would be laid on Catholics was unlikely, if they remained inconspicuous.

9

THE ROAD TO FREEDOM

In 1753 an Act of Parliament was passed which very seriously embarrassed both lay Catholics and their priests. It was not intended to do so; what was galling was that when the marriage law was being reformed they were wholly ignored. Such a reform was badly needed, as the Catholics would have been the first to admit. Marriages in England were performed in the parish churches only after the publication of banns and the issue of a licence, which involved a certain amount of publicity. These precautions were not required for weddings in private chapels, and there was nothing to prevent any ordained man from opening a chapel and marrying people without any preliminary notice. Such a person actually advertised in 1744 that he would, for the fee of £1 1s., unite couples 'at any hour till four in the afternoon'.[1] The results of this form of trade were shocking; men and women were entrapped into secret unions that might not even be valid, for many sham parsons took advantage of the situation. Proof of clandestine marriages was difficult, so confusion arose over inheritance of property, and bigamy was easy. There was no escape by divorce for a deceived wife or husband: a complicated and costly action in the ecclesiastical courts might possibly be successful, or a private Act of Parliament, even more expensive to obtain, could declare the marriage void.

Catholics had always been married by their own priests according to the rites of Rome in their own chapels, and these ceremonies had been recognized by the courts in spite of the statutes. That 'seminary priests and Jesuits' were properly ordained was tacitly accepted; a priest who decided to join the Church of England merely had to preach a sermon of recantation when appointed to a living. But the Marriage Act of 1753 declared null and void any marriage performed in England or Wales which was not celebrated according to the ritual of the established church, after the publication of banns and the granting of a licence.

[1] *Daily Post*, quoted by Burn, J. S., *The Fleet Registers* (London, 1833).

Quakers and Jews were exempt, but not other dissenters. Attendance at an Anglican ceremony for such a purpose did not seriously weigh on the conscience of most Protestant non-conformists, but for the Catholics it was a denial of their faith. For them, marriage was a sacrament with a deeply religious significance. The Council of Trent in 1562 had laid down that 'English Catholics may not be present at the prayers of heretics without grave sin'.[1] To take an intimate part in a Protestant service was therefore to deny the very principle for which their ancestors had suffered and died. Even had the vicars apostolic been closely in touch with English politicians, and aware of the difficulties which the act would create, it is doubtful if they could have gained exemption for Catholics. No government would have risked, in 1753, being accused of favouring Popery; they might ignore the penal code in practice, but openly to grant to Papists a privilege of this kind would probably have endangered the passage of the act.

Now any priest who carried out a marriage ceremony was breaking the law of the land; any couple who married in the parish church broke the law of Rome. Bishop Challoner and other vicars apostolic appealed to Rome for guidance, but, as so often happened, preoccupation with other problems and ignorance of the situation in England prevented their obtaining a satisfactory ruling. The obvious plan was for Catholics to attend two ceremonies, the one which they thought really mattered before their own priest, the other a legal formality in the parish church. Arguments went on, sometimes with bitterness, about the right order of the two weddings. Should sacramental marriage come first and the legal form follow, or should the order be reversed?

The bishops, anxious to preserve the less well-instructed of their people from thinking that the Anglican ceremony was adequate, and that it was proper for them to attend a church service, wanted the Catholic ceremony to take precedence in time as well as in estimation, as happened when Robert Worden, a Lancashire linen weaver, was married by a priest on 15 May 1765 and went next day to the parish church.[2] Bishop Stonor wrote in 1755 of 'parsons who have been very civil, excused them from kneeling, sometimes permitted them to walk about the church during the prayers' of the marriage service.[3] But when the bishop's directions were followed, both the priest and the couple he married were technically breaking the law, and strong opposition to the plan was made by the laity. Charles Butler, an able and pugnacious

[1] Quoted Burton, E. H., *Challoner* (London, 1909), Vol. I, p. 344.
[2] C.R.S., XXIII, p. 87 (note).
[3] MS. letter in Midland District Archives.

lawyer, strongly resented anything like dictation by the bishops in such an important affair. In 1806 he wrote to Bishop Milner, with whom he was on very bad terms, saying that by enforcing this policy he 'compelled his Clergy to a general commission of an act of felony'.[1] In fact most Catholics did take the safer course, and the Anglican service preceded the Roman, although there is evidence that many Catholics never attended the parish church at all, and were content with a rite which to them was wholly valid, though in the eyes of the law null and void.[2] It was not until 1836 that marriage in a Catholic or Dissenting chapel, in the presence of a registrar, was recognized as valid in law.

Apart from the serious problems raised by the Marriage Act, priests were at intervals during the century reminded that they were still under the ban of the law. Wolverhampton was one of several places which at different times were nicknamed 'Little Rome' because of the numbers of known Catholics there. There was a 'chapel house' which was supported to some extent by rents from four small houses, nominally owned by a trustee. The vigorous priest in charge, Thomas Brockholes, had a harassing experience in 1729. He had made many converts among the ordinary people of the town, and in 1727 had received a comb-maker, Phineas Phillips, and his wife into the church. They were in financial difficulties, and Mrs. Phillips applied to the priest for loans—amounting in all to £2 5s.—to pay off debts and prevent her husband from being sued. They did not pay their creditors, or repay the priest, and eventually Phillips was arrested. His wife appealed again to Father Brockholes, who 'layed hold of the occasion to reprehend her for having carried malicious and false tales between two famillys in the town, by which she had set them (who before were friends) at variance . . . till finding out her tricks, they made a complaint to Mr. Brockholes.' He told her that 'this kind of tale-bearing was acting the Devil's part', and that those who copy him in this life must share his fate in the next.

The gossip was furious, and when her husband was released they left off attendance at the chapel and 'wrote a lot of peevish letters some of which were much better penned than he was able to do'. On Christmas night, 1728, Phillips turned up at the chapel with some Protestants, who were 'desired to go out, as being of another

---

[1] MS. letter in Midland District Archives, op. cit., MS. A 1082.

[2] Mr. J. A. Williams, by comparing Catholic and parish records, has shown that this was the case in Wiltshire. Similar work in other areas is needed before any general conclusion can be drawn. For labouring folk the cost of a double ceremony would be of importance, and they had no property for the 'illegitimate' children to inherit.

persuasion'. He and his wife then went to the parish church and 'if not before, at least afterwards, acted under the direction of Parson Cradock.'

The parson had, not unnaturally, been disturbed at losing members of his parish to popery. Early in 1729 he seized a chance of action. An apprentice to one Skirt, a Presbyterian baker, decided to become a Catholic. Skirt, who normally never attended the parish church, forced the boy to come with him to a service, but the lad slipped out and went to Mass instead. Mr. Craddock then got Skirt and Phillips to make a deposition in which Phillips and his wife swore that Brockholes had bribed them to turn Papist, had said all Protestants were damned, and—this was pure fiction, not mere distortion—had told them to burn their Bibles.

When Brockholes heard that the parson had been to the Bishop of Lichfield to lay a complaint against him, and that a local justice was issuing a warrant against him for 'seducing people to Popery', he hastily left the town. Phillips then tried in vain to get money from a Catholic tradesman, saying that he did not want to swear an information against the priest. On Sunday, 2 May, two men arrived from London and searched the Mass-house, but found it deserted and the priest absent, so they went away. A few weeks later another priest came to say Mass, and Mrs. Phillips made a commotion at the chapel door. This annoyed local sympathizers, and when on 17 June Mrs. Phillips went to buy herbs from a Protestant gardener, and boasted of having driven the priest from the town, he 'grabbing back his herbs and flinging to her the brass he had received, swore he would have none of her cursed money'. The noise attracted a 'number of little boys and girls who calling her priest-catcher huzza'd about her'. She went to the parsonage, with the shouting children running around her.

Mr. Craddock was very angry, and called on the schoolmaster to whip the children severely. He also sent for soldiers to 'deffend her; and they were weak enough to do it without the knowledge of their officers'. Here he made a bad mistake, for any intervention by the military in local affairs was greatly resented. Phillips went to a magistrate and persuaded him to grant a warrant for the arrest of over 20 people who, he swore, had stood in their doorways laughing at him and his wife and insulting them. When next day they were brought before Justice Gough, he indicated that he thought the Phillips to blame for 'bustles and disturbances'. No action was taken against the accused; two of them had not even been in the town on that day.

It was reported that the justice rebuked the parson; 'as to Cradock he writt to him last night a very rough letter and tould

Kce

him that if their town was to be govern'd by parsons and redcoats' he would throw up his commission. So the affair ended, but Brockholes decided that he had better go away for good, lest the troubles should be renewed.[1] Disturbances of this kind occurred occasionally, reminding Catholics that the penal laws still stood on the statute book.

In 1764 and 1765 there was some renewal of persecution. In part it came from people who, like Parson Craddock, believed and feared that Catholicism was increasing. But most was due to the realization by unscrupulous men that the act of 1699 offered a reward of £100 to anyone who brought about the successful prosecution of a priest. The *Universal Museum* of 1767 stated that four 'Mass houses' had been closed in London between 6 February and 27 March, and in many Catholic chapels Mass was celebrated behind locked doors and only known members of the congregation were admitted.

The arrest of priests seldom, however, led to the infliction of the legal penalty. Help was now available for them: one well-known firm of lawyers undertook the defence of no fewer than 20 priests, mostly free of charge. When a condemnation did occur, it aroused feelings of disgust rather than triumph. Such a case was that of an Irishman, J. B. Maloney. A man called Payne got him arrested and tried at Croydon for 'administering the sacrament of the Lord's Supper to divers persons, after the manner of the Church of Rome'. Maloney was found guilty, and Payne got the £100 reward. The sentence was life imprisonment, although after four years the priest was released and banished. Bishop Challoner wrote a testimonial for him to Catholics abroad as 'an exile for Christ'.[2]

This success led Payne to hope for more. He brought four more priests to trial in the court of King's Bench, but here the story was different. Lord Mansfield demanded absolute proof that the charged men had been ordained as priests; he was not content with evidence that they had performed rites. Such a point had seldom been raised in court before,[3] even in Maloney's case; as the evidence lay in the seminaries of Europe it was not forthcoming. The Lord Chief Justice in his summing up spoke disdainfully of Payne, and the verdict of 'not guilty' was assured. Once again Payne tried to get £100 by accusing a bishop, James Talbot, who assisted and succeeded Bishop Challoner. The evidence was so unsatisfactory

[1] The letters in which this story is told are in the Midland District Archives, (A 70 and subsequent numbers), Archbishop's House, Birmingham.

[2] Burton, E. H., *Challoner*, op. cit., Vol. II, p. 158.

[3] See infra, p. 195.

that the prosecutor dropped the case. A greater contrast can hardly be imagined than between the conduct of the lawyers and judges in Plunkett's case in 1681 and that in Talbot's in 1771. No longer was hearsay and corrupt evidence permitted; the strictest of legal proof was demanded, to such a point that the chances of a successful prosecution were negligible.

There was a widespread atmosphere of religious tolerance, and a consciousness that the penal laws were not worthy of a civilized country. Charles Edward, though he did not die until 1788, had ceased to be a menace; three popes in succession had refused to acknowledge him as King of England. The accession of George III in 1760 was as popular as had been that of Anne in 1702; he was the first Hanoverian who could truly boast of being English. The difficulties of the Jesuit order raised no triumphant outcry, even though it had been and was again to be a Protestant bogy. In 1767 Parson Cole wrote in his diary, 'the Jesuits entirely banished out of Spain & its Dominions. A sad Prospect'.[1] To the average Englishman the official disbanding of the Society in 1773 made no difference at all.

That this complaisance towards Papists would have had any practical result without some outside stimulus may be doubted. The spur came from America, where the long-standing difficulties of the colonies had led to open rebellion. In 1775 troops were needed, and two possible sources of man-power were Ireland and the Catholic clans of Scotland. From 1759 Irishmen had been enrolled as private soldiers, though this was not technically legal, as they did not take the oath. To rectify the situation, in 1774 the Irish Parliament passed an act which allowed 'His Majesty's subjects of whatsoever persuasion to testify their allegiance to him'. The new oath was so worded that only the temporal power of the pope was denied as an article of faith. For years the Catholics had wanted a chance to abjure in public the unpatriotic character attributed to them; in 1723 Alexander Pope had written that he wanted to declare 'even upon oath how different I am from what a reputed Papist is'.[2]

In 1777 it was decided that it would now be safe to use the Catholic highlanders in Scotland as soldiers. Bishop Hay, one of the two vicars apostolic in Scotland, did not think it prudent to ask for a complete repeal of the penal laws; he suggested that the saying and hearing of Mass should no longer be illegal; that the laws which forbade Catholics to buy or inherit land should be

[1] Cole, W., *Blecheley Diary* (London, 1931), p. 205.
[2] Quoted Stapleton, B., *Post-Reformation Catholic Missions in Oxfordshire* (London, 1906), p. 180.

repealed; and that they should be allowed to take an oath similar to that administered in Ireland. He came to London to discuss these points with George's ministers.

That English Catholics should share in any relief granted to the Scots was obviously logical. The acknowledged leader of the English Catholic clergy was Bishop Challoner, but he was an old man and very much afraid that the peace which his flock enjoyed in practice might be upset by a violent anti-popery movement if the law were altered. The direction of negotiations therefore fell into the hands of the laity. There were a number of able Catholic lawyers who acted as conveyancers, the only type of legal activity they were permitted to exercise.[1] One of them, William Sheldon, got into touch with some of the best-known wealthy Catholic landowners. They had for years been galled by the act of 1699 which led to all sorts of subterfuges whenever they bought or inherited land, and they were anxious to show that they were fully as patriotic and loyal as their neighbours. Sheldon got a group of them together, and it was decided to petition the king, negotiating directly with the government and not letting the bishops interfere; they even refused to let Bishop Hay join their meeting to give them the benefit of his experience.

A petition was available that had been drawn up by Edmund Burke in 1764. His strong sense of justice made him favour the emancipation of Catholics as well as of Americans or any other group suffering from injustice. The petition was signed by nine peers and 163 other gentlemen. So well was it received that a bill was drafted to secure the repeal of the act of 1699, with its rewards for informers and denial of rights of inheritance: the relief to be given would apply only to those who took an oath of loyalty. Bishop Challoner would much have preferred a general recognition of the right of Catholics to practise their religion in private, but the committee pushed on rapidly with its plan.

John Dunning, perhaps the best-known lawyer of his day in the House of Commons, was asked to introduce the bill. It was reported[2] that he refused because he found that it gave little relief to the clergy. To a later generation it does seem strange that men who professed to speak for all Catholics in England appeared in fact to be chiefly concerned with their own interest as landowners. Some Catholics, too, disliked the way in which the initiative had been taken by a few laymen and the bishops largely ignored. For the men of the committee, however, it may be said that the moment was opportune and should be seized without delay, and

[1] See infra, Chapter 13.
[2] Burton, E. H., *Challoner*, Vol. II, p. 202.

that their arguments would be sympathetically heard by a parliament in which the landed interest was supreme, but which might be afraid to grant a wider toleration.

The Roman Catholic Relief Act of 1778 was passed with little opposition. The Catholic committee had asked only for the repeal of the act of 1699, which made Catholic priests and schoolmasters subject to life imprisonment, promised rewards to those who secured their conviction, and prohibited Papists from inheriting or purchasing land. The earlier penal laws still stood; priests were still traitors. The benefits of the new act applied only to those who took an oath of loyalty to the crown. The terms of this oath had been agreed on by the lay committee before being shown to the bishops; Bishop Challoner doubted whether Rome would wholly approve them, but he realized that if the oath became law the papal authorities would probably accept it, as indeed they did. It was rather lengthy: those who took it had to swear to bear true allegiance to George III; to abjure 'Charles III' (Prince Charlie) and any other claimant to the throne; to declare that it was unlawful to depose or murder a prince, that the pope had no civil jurisdiction in England, and that no one had power to release them from their oath. Henceforward prayers for the king were said in every Catholic chapel; at last Catholics were recognized as loyal Englishmen, and priests and laymen hastened to take the oath.

Slight as the relief was, except for the landowners, it was sufficient to rouse, as the bishops had feared, an anti-popery movement. Though the Protestant dissenters had fewer legal disabilities than the Catholics, they, much more than the Anglican clergy, hated popery with something of the venom of the seventeenth century. A Protestant association was formed, and in November 1779 elected as its president Lord George Gordon, a younger son of the Duke of Gordon. He was ambitious to play a part in politics; he had tried to secure a seat near Inverness, 'nursing' the constituency by playing bagpipes and giving balls, and declaiming against popery. The sitting member of parliament bought off his possible opponent by giving him the nomination for a 'pocket borough', Ludgershall in Wiltshire, where he was duly elected in 1774. He caused amusement rather than admiration in the House of Commons by his many eccentricities; there is no doubt that he was at any rate half crazy. Such a condition seems to be no disadvantage to an agitator; emotion, not reason, sways crowds, and Lord George's fierce attacks on the pope when he addressed mass meetings were most effective. So strongly held was the idea that any concession to popery was dangerous and evil

that a man of the calibre of John Wesley published in January
1780 a pamphlet in which he spoke of the 'purple power of Rome
advancing by hasty strides to overspread this once more happy
nation'.[1]

Trouble had already begun when Wesley's fiery words appeared.
In Scotland in 1779, when the Relief Bill for Scots Catholics had
been introduced into parliament, riots broke out in Edinburgh
and other towns; Catholic chapels and houses were burnt and
plundered, the local authorities doing nothing to stop the
destruction. The General Assembly of the Church of Scotland
demanded that none of the penal laws should be repealed. In
England streams of pamphlets were poured out and sermons
preached; fantastic stories, recalling the days of Titus Oates, were
circulated. Twenty thousand Jesuits were said to be waiting in
Surrey to blow up the banks of the Thames and flood London;
others were plotting the assassination of George III.

On 4 January 1780 the Protestant association presented to
parliament a petition for the repeal of the act of 1778; but Lord
George Gordon behaved so very oddly in the House of Commons
that no one took him seriously. He decided to get up a monster
petition, and called for a meeting in St. George's Fields on 2 June.
An enormous crowd collected; sincere fanatics were joined by the
riff-raff of London, and the riots began. Catholics and those
believed to be friendly to them were attacked, but the violence
spread wider: not only Catholic chapels, including those in foreign
embassies, were pillaged, but prisons were broken into, shops
looted, and a distillery set on fire, causing immense damage and
many deaths. The Archbishop of York and other bishops were
assaulted, as were many members of parliament. Law-abiding
people stood by helplessly, for though there were troops available,
no magistrate dared publicly to read the proclamation that would
allow them to act. Lord Petre's house in Park Lane was set on
fire; the conflagration was watched by a baronet, in company
with a Protestant clergyman called Warren. The mob seized on
the parson, saying he was a priest in disguise and that they would
throw him into the flames; Sir George Mannock, S.J., swore that
he knew well that he was a Protestant, and saved him.[2]

Not until 8 June were forces sent to restore order, and then it
was George III himself who intervened by issuing a proclamation.
Once the troops came into action the mobs were quickly scattered,
but at a great cost of lives. The official figures were that 285
people had been shot or died of their wounds, but very many

[1] Burton, E. H., *Challoner*, Vol. II, p. 224.
[2] Foley, B., article in *Brentwood Diocesan Year Book* (1958).

more had died, often trampled to death by the maddened crowds. The majority of prisoners taken were young boys and girls; 21 of them were executed, but most of the ringleaders had evaded arrest.

Bishop Challoner and the other clergy escaped; Challoner found refuge in the Finchley house of his friend the well-to-do draper Mawhood. Catholics all over the country were alarmed when they heard of the London riots, but there was no outbreak of persecution in the provinces. The only serious trouble was in Bath, where, it was reported, four of the London rioters went in a post coach and four. There a new Catholic chapel had recently been built and was due to be opened in a few days. It, together with the house occupied by the vicar apostolic, was destroyed, and with them all the records of the western district. The Benedictine priest in charge sued the town in 1781 for its failure to protect property, and obtained £3,734 damages.[1]

Yet though they suffered no personal harm, Catholics in the provinces were greatly agitated. Letters from London to Wardour Castle told terrible stories of the damage done and 'many Lives Lost, as is said the Marshall Law is now to take place'. C. Carpue wrote this to Mr. Clinton, the chaplain at Wardour, on 8 June; warning was also received from well-wishers, so troops were sent from Salisbury and the Catholics got the desired 'Martial Law'. In Bristol too the Catholic chapel was guarded by the militia.[2] There, in September 1780, Edmund Burke presented himself for re-election to parliament, and felt it necessary to defend his vote for the Catholic Relief Bill. As he had spoken for the American colonies to the electors of Bristol in 1774, 1775 and 1777, so in 1780 he spoke for the Catholics.[3] The penal laws he described as 'cruel outrages', and suggested that the English Reformation would not be fully complete until they were repealed. The act of 1699 had, he said, 'condemned to beggary and to ignorance in their native land' the whole body of Catholics. The judges of England were unwilling to enforce the law as it stood; recent trials had shown how abhorrent it was to decent people. As for the Catholics themselves, they 'consist mostly of our best manufacturers', and if they had got no relief they would have been driven to emigrate to Flanders 'by the bigotry of a free country in an enlightened age'. This point was doubtless aimed at the merchants who feared competition from the Netherlands. The bill, said

[1] Oliver, G., *Collections*, op. cit., p. 57.

[2] Letters in Weld MSS., Box D 10, County Record Office, Dorchester.

[3] Burke, E., *Works* (World's Classics edition, London, 1906), Vol. III, pp. 20 ff.

Burke, was good and necessary, but imperfect. 'To revise the whole body of the penal statutes was conceived to be an object too big for the time.' The Catholics' address to the king 'in the hour of our dismay' showed 'that all the subjects of England had cast off all foreign views and connexions'; their discipline and courage had been proved by their forbearance from violence during the riots in London. They ought to have received 'the thanks of both houses of parliament'. The repeal of all penal laws against them was, he indicated, long overdue.

Three days later Burke publicly withdrew his candidature. He found that the city was 'in a state of miserable distraction' and that he would probably fail. It can hardly be doubted that his frank and open defence of the Catholic cause had lost him support. Bristol's attitude was not unique, and accounts for the extremely slow progress of that total emancipation which the liberal philosophers felt to be necessary for the good repute of their country.

The group of Catholic gentry who had prepared the way for the act of 1778 had reason to feel triumphant, but were anxious that the road to full emancipation, of which the first stage had now been constructed, should be pushed on farther. The original committee dissolved itself in 1782, but immediately a new one was formed with 10 members 'to manage the public affairs of the Catholics of this Kingdom'. Another very able lawyer, Charles Butler, was the secretary, and the character of this committee was typical of the eighteenth century. That the bulk of the Catholic population consisted of merchants, tradesmen, craftsmen and labourers was wholly ignored; only the 'respectable' landowners and their tenants counted. That the bishops had any right to direct policy they firmly denied, drawing a sharp line between religion and politics in a sphere where they were inextricably mixed. They wanted to demonstrate that English Catholics were not 'slavishly dependent on their ecclesiastical superiors',[1] and their passionate loyalty to England made them wish for as slight a tie as possible with Rome.

In 1788 Lord Petre and two others had a conference with William Pitt, the Prime Minister, who asked for further reassurance that the pope could not dispense Catholics from their oath of loyalty. At this time the dogma of the infallibility of the pope when defining the faith had not been promulgated, and the fact that the heir of St. Peter was a temporal prince as well as Head of the Church led to much confusion and obscurity. After receiving assurances from six Catholic universities that the pope could not dispense anyone from a solemn oath which he had the

[1] Petre, M. D., *The Ninth Lord Petre* (London, 1928), p. 272.

right to take, and that he had no power over temporal sovereigns not of his flock, the committee drew up a protestation stating their beliefs. This was a long quasi-theological document, drawn up by laymen; many of its phrases were open to misunderstanding. The infallibility of the pope was denied, and the general tone of the statements suggested that in some way English Catholics were rather different from those on the Continent.

It was unfortunate that since Challoner's death in 1781 no other bishop had gained a comparable influence and independence. In 1788 two of the vicars apostolic were brothers, James and Thomas Talbot, members of a prominent and wealthy Catholic family. Matthew Gibson, in the north, was the son of a Durham landowner; in the west, Walmesley was a Benedictine monk, and therefore regarded with suspicion by some of the secular priests. After long hesitation, all four signed the protestation, but they were by no means unanimous in their attitude to the committee; only the Talbots were really sympathetic to men whose point of view they well understood. Two hundred and forty priests and 1,500 laymen also signed the document.

With this support behind them, the men of the committee pressed the government of the day to accept a further bill for the relief of Catholics. At this critical time, two of the vicars apostolic died: James Talbot of the London area in January 1790 and Matthew Gibson in May. It was clear that the fate of the negotiations might well be affected by the views and character of the men who replaced them, and very unedifying disputes and intrigues appeared among both the clergy and the prominent laymen. The method by which the new bishops would be appointed came sharply into prominence. For some time past, the custom had been for the other vicars apostolic to forward proposals to Rome, frequently after consulting the clergy of the vicariate and paying heed to any letter of advice that might have been left by the late bishop: but their suggestions could be ignored. Often the bishop who had served as coadjutor to the deceased vicar apostolic was nominated, but in 1790 Gibson left a letter in which he specifically rejected his coadjutor as a suitable successor.[1]

A large number of the priests in England wished that, even though they had no cathedrals, chapters of canons could be set up to elect bishops, or at least to send nominations to Rome. The laymen of the committee took a different view; they thought that they ought to have some influence in the choice of men who, whether they wished it or not, were bound to play some part in

---

[1] The correspondence of Robert Bannister, now at St. Joseph's College, Upholland, near Wigan, illuminates the situation in the north.

the delicate negotiations with English politicians which must
precede any further emancipation of Catholics. Suspicion of the
pope and of foreign influences at the Vatican was rife and must be
diminished. The great landowners were known and trusted by their
Protestant counterparts: if they had some say in the choice of
their spiritual leaders, the British government would be reassured.
Mr. John Throckmorton wrote pamphlets, Lord Petre wrote letters;
a deputation to Rome from the committee was planned.

The clergy joined in the debate, dividing, as did their parishioners, into two parties, those who opposed the committee and
those, whom they nicknamed the 'Oathites', who supported it.
Feeling ran high, especially in the north; Bishop Matthew Gibson
had lived at Stella Hall, near Durham, the home of his family,
where he was not very accessible to his priests, and there was
also some jealousy between the priests of Yorkshire and of Lancashire. In the end, after the authorities in Rome had been
bombarded by letters and petitions from England, William
Gibson, brother of the late bishop, was appointed vicar apostolic
for the north, and John Douglass for London.

The new bishops sided with Bishop Walmesley in objecting
strongly to certain points in a bill put forward by the committee.
Its production had been delayed, for Charles James Fox had
introduced a motion into the House of Commons for the removal of
all disabilities from all dissenters. When this was rejected, an
amended bill for Catholic relief was brought in. The first draft
contained an oath which seemed to deny even the spiritual power
of the pope in England, as well as limiting the proposed benefits
to 'Protesting Catholic Dissenters'—that is, the people who had
taken the oath of 1778. This peculiar phrase was strongly disliked
by the bishops, as was the oath itself, and though Bishop Talbot
supported the committee, the three others issued an encyclical
letter condemning the new oath. After a meeting with Bishops
Douglass and Gibson which led to nothing, the committee produced a counter-manifesto. Both the bishops and the committee
were expressing their views to such members of the cabinet as
would hear them, and every member of the House of Commons
received a statement of the bishops' arguments on the oath and
the limitations proposed for relief.

This statement was written by John Milner, a priest of lowly
birth, widely read, extremely orthodox in his views, immensely
courageous and obstinate, outspoken to the point of rudeness.
He looked on the men of the committee almost as heretics, and
pointed out, with justice, that they in no way represented the
great mass of the Catholics of England. It was probably owing

to his efforts that the 'Protesting Catholic Dissenters' disappeared from the bill; but it was Samuel Horsley, the Bishop of St David's, who in the House of Lords got the offending oath removed and replaced by the one in the Irish act of 1774. With these emendations, the bill was passed, to the intense joy of the ordinary Catholics and to the great relief of the bishops. Unfortunately, the long and bitter controversies that had preceded it led to a lasting antagonism between Charles Butler, by far the ablest of the men of the committee, and John Milner, the turbulent priest, which, especially after Milner was made a bishop in 1803, prevented harmony among those who at last enjoyed a considerable measure of freedom in the practice of their religion.

10

THE FINAL STRUGGLE

The act of 1791 opened a considerable stretch of the Catholics' road to freedom. For over 200 years the saying and hearing of Mass had been prohibited under penalty of death; now it was permitted, though not expressly by name. Safeguards were still imposed, lest Catholicism should step too boldly into the open; services could be held only in registered chapels, and not more than five people could attend worship together in a private house. The objectionable oaths demanded from lawyers were abolished, as was the double land tax; deeds and wills of Papists need no longer be specially enrolled. Odd prohibitions which had long ceased to be enforced were also repealed; Catholics could now legally enter the City of Westminster and approach the presence of the king. The rejoicing that followed the passing of the act was widespread; the committee's last duty before it was wound up was to pass a vote of thanks to Charles Butler, who was also given a well-earned £1,000, to his clerk, to Lord Petre and to Mr. Clifford. No word of praise was uttered for the bishops, although they had done much to secure the final passage of the bill in a satisfactory form. That a collection taken at the last meeting raised £1,560, to make up the deficit on the accounts, indicates the wealth of the members.

Much had been gained, but much was still lacking. The oath demanded from voters and from members of both Houses of Parliament was still one that no Catholic could take, for it explicitly denied the doctrine of transubstantiation. One of the penalties of their religion that the landowners found most galling was their exclusion from any share in the political life of the country. They could not hold any office, or even a commission in the armed forces, and the Marriage Act still obliged them to break the law of the land or of their church. In 1792 therefore the victors of 1791 formed a new association to continue the work they had begun. It no longer claimed to represent the whole Catholic body, but was a private club. Its name—the Cisalpine Club—was significant. In times past the word had been used to signify the

Roman side of the Alpine barrier, and Ultramontane the regions beyond; but the passage of years had reversed the meaning. To Charles Butler the name signified the school of theology which denied any secular power to the pope beyond his own frontiers, and held that even in spiritual matters he was subject to a General Council;[1] the Transalpine or Ultramontane school accepted the infallibility of the pope and his right to rule in spiritual, though not in temporal, matters. Among the original members of the club was a priest, a protégé of Lord Petre, who had been deprived of his faculties: it was clear that the association was not likely to be meekly obedient to the bishops. Lord Clifford refused to join, and so did Thomas Weld of Lulworth. The Cisalpine Club survived until 1830, but only in its first years did it give rise to controversy.

Lord Petre had been the leading spirit in the Catholic committee, and in the club he remained prominent. He was proud and pugnacious. He had become a Freemason, and was Grand Master of the English Freemasons in 1772; although in 1738 and again in 1751 Catholics had been prohibited from joining the order, these bulls—like all other papal documents—could not be published in England, so Lord Petre held that they were not binding on him. There was no moral objection to the principles and practices of the Freemasons; it was their imposition of a binding oath of secrecy that led to the papal prohibition, and this in its turn led to the strongly anti-clerical bias in continental Freemasonry. Lord Petre remained a Catholic, but was frequently quarrelling with the bishops; those who agreed with him and detested John Milner believed that in England the laity ought to have some recognized part in matters ecclesiastical. Milner's own elevation to the episcopate in 1803 strengthened the wish of the association to have some control over the hierarchy. The more conservative Catholics strongly opposed the idea that laymen should intervene in the choice of bishops; among the archives of Thomas Weld of Lulworth is an amusing skit on the committee's propaganda on this point. It is a 'Petition' addressed to the committee by the 'Ladies, Widows, Wives and Spinsters; Housekeepers, Cooks, Housemaids and other Female Persons' protesting that their rights had been ignored, that they ought 'to vote in the approaching election of bishops' and even to 'elect deaconesses for ordination'.[2] As the idea that women should exercise any political power was then held only by extreme revolutionaries, the satire was double-edged.

[1] In his *Historical Memories*, quoted in Petre, M., *The Ninth Lord Petre*, p. 301.
[2] *The Month*, February 1960, contains the text of this 'Petition'.

There is no doubt that Lord Petre and his friends were right in believing that opinion among English political thinkers was on their side; but they underestimated the persistent opposition of George III. He was on terms of intimate friendship with many Catholics, including both Lord Petre and Thomas Weld,[1] but he believed that the oath he had taken at his coronation to 'maintain the Protestant reformed religion' and the 'settlement of the Church of England and Ireland' prohibited him from ending the union of church and state by allowing Catholics political rights. Even more disadvantageous than the sentiment of the monarch were the events in Ireland, and on the continent, that followed the Relief Act of 1791.

In that year the parliament in Dublin, composed wholly of Protestants, rejected a petition for the abolition of the penal laws. Next year, Irish Catholics were granted the relief already given to the English, but the situation of the two groups was very different. The English Papists formed a small minority; the Irish were the great majority of the people. Agitation, very skilfully led, secured for Ireland in 1793 a peculiar constitutional compromise: Catholic '40s. freeholders' were allowed to vote, but not to sit as members of parliament. It might have been thought that to have a vote, but to be unable to use it in favour of his natural representative, would have been of little use to an Irishman, especially in a land where politics were notoriously corrupt. That this was not the case was shown by a marked change in the attitude of the Irish House of Commons; members now had to win over, or buy, the votes of a considerable number of Catholics.

The outbreak of war between England and revolutionary France in 1793 affected the Papists in different ways. The government became absorbed in waging a war which turned out to be far longer and more serious than had been expected. French ideas as well as French armies were dreaded; as a result any suggestion of reform was frowned on lest, as in France, it should be the first step towards revolution. Opposition of any kind was unpatriotic. In 1795 a proposal to give full political rights to Irish Catholics was rejected, and revolution broke out. The semi-independence of Ireland was thought to be dangerous, and in 1801 heavy bribery was used to induce the Irish Parliament to pass an Act of Union which ended its own existence. Henceforth there would be only one body of law-makers at Westminster. The Irish Catholics had been led to expect that one result of this surrender would be their emancipation, but George III utterly

[1] See infra, pp. 211–12.

refused to allow Papists to be members even of a parliament in which they would be a small minority. There was little hope, therefore, that English Catholics would be given the right to vote.

The English government did, however, prove a friend to the French Catholics who fled from persecution to seek safety across the Channel. At first, only a few of the 'aristos' came over; the majority of the French Royalists went to other countries. But when after the execution of Louis XVI the party in power proclaimed the Religion of Reason, and a reign of terror began, priests and nuns escaped as best they could. The old English convents and seminaries and schools had to be abandoned; their inhabitants joined the stream of French refugees who arrived, often penniless, on the shores of England.

At first, some degree of secrecy seems to have been necessary for the safe removal of the emigrants from France; there is an indication of this in a letter from E. Phillips, in Calais, dated 4 March 1793, stating that he had received 'three black mares belonging to Thos. Weld Esq. I promise to take due care of them on condition of being paid two crowns per week for each mare and I will carefully provide for the transportation of the said mares into England.'[1] The tone of this letter so closely resembles the correspondence of the days of persecution that it seems probable that the 'mares' were in fact nuns. Later, not only the English, but hundreds of French, priests and nuns fled across the Channel; the problem of finding food and shelter for them absorbed the energies and the spare money of English Catholics for some time. Those fortunate enough to have country houses which they used only occasionally handed them over to religious communities, as Sir Edward Smythe did when he gave the Benedictines from Douay a house at Acton Burnell. Many schools and seminaries had connections with English families; their relatives and their former pupils came to their aid. Thomas Weld gave his house at Stonyhurst in Lancashire to the Jesuits from Liége; at Lulworth he built a special dwelling on some waste ground for a group of Trappist monks, where they could live by cultivating the soil.

As a rule, the non-Catholics were sympathetic, but this particular act of charity aroused the wrath of an anti-Papist, probably a local parson. He published anonymously a long poem, in which Weld, called 'Numa', is described watching a dramatic landing by a number of monks; he recognizes that they are chanting

the songs and symphonies that we
Sing on our high and solemn festivals

[1] This letter, and the poem later referred to, are in the Weld archives at Dorset Record Office, Dorchester,

> When by the holy dictates of our Church
> We d—— all heretics.

The poet goes on to accuse 'Numa' and the monks of turning the people of 'Lulo' into Papists; a footnote adds, 'among whom is the parish clerk'. The massacre of St. Bartholomew and other wicked deeds of the Papists are recounted, and the verses end with an exhortation:

> Scorn not the danger, but in time prevent it.

Weld wrote a carefully drafted letter to the Bishop of Bristol, protesting against these 'most Gross, false and insulting charges', explaining what he had done for the Trappists, and pointing out that their vow of silence prevented them from proselytizing even if they so wished. The bishop soothed him by replying that his action about the monks 'sounds laudable', and that at a meeting of the archbishops and bishops all had agreed in 'lamenting that you should have suffered any causeless uneasiness'. The Trappists stayed in peace at Lulworth until they went back to France in 1817.

Bigotry of this type was rare, and could usually be ignored. Domestic opposition was more difficult to circumvent. In Paris lived six English 'Blue Nuns', all that remained of the staff of a school which had been highly esteemed by Catholic parents. They were expelled in 1800, and went to Sir William Jerningham for shelter; his wife had been their pupil and his niece their abbess. They had very little money and, as Lady Jerningham wrote to her daughter Lady Bedingfield, they were dressed like beggars except for one who had her proper habit. Though they kept quietly out of the way, Sir William did not much like having a convent in his London home. His wife tried in vain to find someone who would lend them a house in the country, or let it to them for a trifle, so the only way she could rid herself of her guests was to send them to 'Cossey', Costessy near Norwich, Sir William's country seat. Lady Bedingfield was urged by her mother, 'I beg you will endeavour to put your Father in a good mind about them, about their being in Norwich if necessary', for 'Your poor Father has been a little impatient about them'. It was suggested that if Sir Richard Bedingfield invited one of them, who was elderly and ill, to stay with him, 'it will put them in fashion with your Father'. Meantime, Lady Jerningham was busy collecting money for the nuns. In the end, she persuaded her husband to let them stay at 'Cossey' until a house was found for them in Norwich.[1]

Other convents were settled at Winchester, where a flourishing

[1] Castle, E., ed., *Jerningham Letters*, Vol. I, pp. 373 ff.

school for girls was established; at Amesbury, where nuns from
Louvain stayed for nine years, and were much missed by the
local people when they moved away to Spettisbury; at Stapehill,
near Wimborne, where Lord Arundell gave a house to a Cistercian
convent; and so on in many other places.[1] By 1817 most of the
French religious communities had returned to their own land;
the English schools and seminaries remained and flourished on
their native soil. Even the English College at Rome had to be
abandoned when Napoleon's armies occupied the city. It was
greatly damaged; tombs were broken open, and when in 1817 its
former inhabitants returned, one of their tasks was to collect
and re-inter the bones confusedly scattered on the ground. It
took much hard work and expense to restore the college for the
use of English priests-to-be.

Secular priests from France also arrived, in numbers far too
great for the Catholic community to cope with. In Gosport alone
there were over 250;[2] the government gave them a disused prison
for their lodging and a small weekly allowance for food. The
building was far too small; from 8 to 16 men were crammed into
each little room. Many of them were transferred to Winchester,
where a large number of French priests lived in the King's house,
but in 1796 this was needed for troops. A mansion in Thame and
an old inn in Reading were then taken over by the priests; by
December 1797, there were 252 in the inn and another 104 in
rooms outside it.[3] When in 1802, most of them were able to go
back to France, as Napoleon had come to terms with the pope,
they must have been overjoyed. In several other English towns
there were refugee priests; even as far away as Durham, where
the local clergy accepted them as entitled to benefit from their
fund.[4]

This influx of refugee priests was of considerable service to the
English Catholics. They had been driven out by the national enemy,
and so aroused strong sympathy; their standards of piety and of
behaviour were on the whole high, for only men of conscience
had abandoned their country rather than accept the domination
of the state over the church. Several of them learned enough
English to be able to come to the help of over-burdened clergy,
and they showed great energy in their work. At Portsea an
optimistic priest had built a new chapel, and two houses behind
which it was partially concealed; this cost so much that the
buildings were heavily mortgaged, and the bishop thought that
they might have to be abandoned, as 'The present inhabitants

[1] C.R.S., XLIII, 127.   [2] C.R.S., XLIX, 4.   [3] C.R.S., XXXII, 122.
[4] MS. account of the Durham Clergy Fund, by Rev. Vincent Smith.

LCE

cannot find ways and means of paying the interest of the mortgage and maintaining the priest'. The Abbé Delarue took it over; he taught French to the naval officers, whose gifts he devoted to the support of the church. He served it for 21 years, during 12 of which he also looked after the congregation at Gosport, and not only preserved their chapel for the Catholics but helped them by his popularity in the town.[1] In another Hampshire parish, Sopley, near Christchurch, Frenchmen took charge when the priest died in 1802; he had hurt his foot during his long walks from Christchurch, blood poisoning set in, and he did not survive the amputation of his foot. The mission was in difficulties, since after the death of its principal benefactor there was no regular financial help. One of the *émigré* priests appealed so successfully for funds that a new chapel and priest's house could be built.[2] In Plymouth, also, a refugee priest established a permanent church, after saying Mass for some time in a room over the stables of the George Inn in Devonport.[3]

This building of chapels was going on all over England. Congregations were enlarged, in some areas, by the Irishmen whose names begin to appear in the registers kept by the emancipated parish clergy. In several places a chapel in a mansion had been used by all the local Catholics; some patrons did not wish to register their own oratories as public chapels, and, as no more than five people could attend a service in a private house, a new place of worship had to be provided. Often a group of Catholics would not only build a chapel, but undertake the responsibility of maintaining a priest. The 'sale of work' and other devices for raising funds appeared; the coppers of the labourers were collected. At Ugthorpe in Yorkshire money was raised by installing seats in the chapel; the wealthier members of the congregation bought benches and paid rent for them, from 2*s.* a year for each seat in the front five benches down to 1*s.* a year for a whole bench at the back, one being reserved for 'ye poor strangers' free of charge.[4]

For ordinary Catholics all over England, the early nineteenth century was a time of relaxation from strain and hope for the future. However, divisions remained to worry the bishops. The old quarrel between the secular priests and the Jesuits seemed to have died down when the society was formally disbanded in 1773. At that time, there were about 120 Jesuits working in England, and they were in charge of the English College at Rome, as well as of the schools and seminaries which they themselves had founded. Informal arrangements were made for most of

[1] C.R.S., XLIX, Pt. II, 5 and 6.   [2] C.R.S., XLIII, 94, 97.
[3] Oliver, G., *Collections*, p. 26.   [4] Parish accounts at Ugthorpe.

them to remain in their accustomed work; in England, Bishop Challoner treated them with the utmost sympathy, allowing them, as secular priests, still to keep in touch with each other. At length, in 1814, Pope Pius VII re-established the order, with the proviso that it must obtain explicit permission from the government of every country in which it proposed to operate. It was perhaps because they feared a renewal of ancient feuds that the English bishops would not urge their own government to recognize the society in England, or perhaps because they knew the irrational fear that the very word 'Jesuit' provoked. Until 1829 the priests of the society had to carry on nominally as seculars, and even after 1829 they were singled out from the other orders.

The activities of the politically minded gentry were also an anxiety to the vicars apostolic. In 1800 Lord Petre again brought to public notice the disabilities still endured by Catholics, by claiming that as a peer of the realm he had a right to send letters free of charge by franking them with his signature. He brought an action against the Postmaster-General for 7d. which had been charged on one of his letters; he lost his case, for it was held that the privilege appertained only to members of parliament, and, since he would not take the oath, he was not a member of the House of Lords.[1] Next year, this doughty fighter died, and attempts were made to reconcile the varying groups of Catholics; Lady Jerningham, in March 1805, wrote that Bishop Milner had 'dined here yesterday with Lord Clifford and they were really Hand and Glove, which I enjoyed'. A number of sympathizers continued to raise the 'Catholic question' in parliament, but, as Lady Jerningham sadly wrote, 'the silly majority of Numbers carried the day'.[2]

In 1807 a Catholic Board was formed to organize the agitation. It was still a predominantly lay body; Sir William Jerningham's brother Edward, a lawyer and a man of letters, was the secretary. He did his best to bring about harmony between the gentry and their spiritual fathers; in 1809 his sister-in-law wrote: 'Thanks were voted yesterday to the *dear Secretary* for the Conciliatory Pains he had taken'. But there was no way of overcoming the radical differences between the views of Milner and of the lay members of the board, and in 1810 'Edward is in a dreadful Warfare with Bishop Milner'.[3] A bill introduced in 1813 would have placed the bishops in England and Ireland very much under lay control. A commission of laymen would guarantee the loyalty of the

[1] Petre, op. cit., p. 318. [2] *Jerningham Letters*, Vol. 1, p. 268.
[3] Ibid., pp. 363, 366.

bishops; the government would have the right to veto the appointment of any individual to the episcopate, and to examine all communications from Rome. The men who thought that they themselves would be the advisers to the government considered these proposals harmless, and believed that Rome could be persuaded to accept them; they did not realize what might be involved if a party less favourable to the Catholics were in power. The independence of the church in England would be greatly diminished if it appeared to be controlled by a handful of aristocrats, and the degree of power which the state would exercise might well involve the sacrifice of the principles for which Sir Thomas More had died. The bishops, supported by their Irish brethren, helped to get the bill rejected. The only victory of the Catholics was the passage of a bill in 1817 which withdrew the barriers that had in law prohibited Catholics from holding commissions in the armed forces. In fact, there were already many officers who had never taken the oath demanded. To the disappointment of the Papists, the Prince Regent, both as deputy for his father and as king himself after the death of the aged George III in 1820, strongly opposed Catholic relief in any form although he had been a friend of Fox, the consistent supporter of the Papists' claims. He had married a Catholic, Mrs. Fitzherbert, in 1785; but as this union would have barred his right of succession to the throne, he publicly denied the fact, and married in 1795 Caroline of Brunswick, who proved a most unsatisfactory consort. After they separated, he resumed his relations with the woman who, in the eyes of Rome, was his lawful wife; but her influence in no way moderated his determination not to agree to the granting of political rights to her co-religionists.

The Irish Catholics who held freehold land worth 40s. a year kept the right to vote which they had gained before the Act of Union, but had lost the influence they had successfully used in the Irish Parliament. Like their brothers in England, they petitioned in vain; after 1807 no politician who was favourable to Catholic claims was given ministerial office. The Union aggravated rather than diminished the economic evils from which the island suffered; there was no coal for steam power to attract industrialists to set up factories, even though there was an ample supply of cheap labour. A rapidly increasing population attempted to live by cultivating small plots of land; the people became listless and dispirited, until the man appeared who, whatever his faults, earned the proud name of 'The Liberator' of the Catholics of England as well as those of Ireland.

Daniel O'Connell was born in 1775; he was well educated, partly

abroad, and became a barrister in Dublin. The violence that cul-
minated in the revolution of 1798 seemed to him not only hateful
but foolish; yet he was as determined as any of its leaders to win
independence not only for the Catholics but also for Ireland.
His brilliant defence of men charged with crimes gained him not
only a great reputation but a considerable income; he often
secured verdicts of 'not guilty' by a combination of oratory,
destructive cross-examination, and an exploitation of deficiencies
in the law. He joined the Irish Catholic Association, which was
refounded in 1806 to gain full rights for the Catholics and the
repeal of the Act of Union, using petitions, not violence, as its
means. At first a small body, by 1810 it had attracted enough
members to form a central committee to draft and present petitions
and to ventilate the grievances of the Irish. This alarmed the
English government, which declared the association illegal; but
local associations evaded the law until the formation of a National
Board led to a further suppression in 1814.

The many efforts to get Catholic relief bills through parliament
all foundered on two rocks—the persistent anti-popery of the king
and many leading politicians, and the unwillingness of the
Catholic hierarchy to accept the 'Veto', the popular name for the
controls which the government proposed. In 1821 and 1822 there
was distress amounting to famine in large tracts of Ireland; despair
led to violence, violence to coercion. In 1823 O'Connell was one
of 47 men who each subscribed a guinea a year to a new Catholic
Association; from this small start sprang the organization that was
to defeat the powerful English government. O'Connell produced
the brilliant scheme by which the natural leaders of the Irish
peasantry, their parish priests, were asked to collect a penny a
month from each active member of their flocks and send the money
to a central fund. This plan of the 'Catholic Rent' was welcomed
with enthusiasm; by 1825 the collections came to over £1,000 every
week. Probably some people paid more than 1s. a year, but the
subscribers must have numbered at least two million. From the
fund were paid the costs of the defence of every Catholic brought
before a court, and the expenses involved in holding meetings all
over the island.

The government was alarmed; O'Connell was arrested and
charged with sedition, but no adequate evidence could be brought
against him. The Catholic Association was declared illegal. Another
relief bill was passed by the House of Commons, but thrown out
by the Lords, where the Duke of York, the heir to the throne,
spoke violently against any concessions to Popery. The association was reorganized as a charitable society, with another name,

and at the general election of 1826 entered the political field. At Waterford and Louth candidates supported by the Catholics opposed the government's nominees; the priests from their pulpits urged those who had the vote to use it, with such success that at Waterford Lord George Beresford, a member of one of the great Protestant families which had ruled Ireland for generations, withdrew from the contest. O'Connell could not prevent a good deal of disorder and rioting, but the Secretary for Ireland dared not use the troops—too many of the soldiers were Catholics.

In 1828, at a by-election, O'Connell himself stood for County Clare. He secured over 2,000 votes, his opponent less than 1,000. The embarrassed sheriff had to make the peculiar return that O'Connell had the majority, but had declared himself a Catholic. The victor made no attempt to claim his seat; if he appeared and was declared unable to sit, as he did not take the oath, a new election could be held; as it was, the government was helpless. The cabinet had intended to give a peerage to the member for Galway; as this would have meant another by-election, they had to postpone the grant. O'Connell's triumph led to a decrease in violence and to an immense number of peaceful demonstrations; over 2,000 local meetings of the association were held on a single day. Wellington feared that prosecution and repression would lead to civil war in Ireland; he was already harassed by the demands of Englishmen for parliamentary reform, and on the continent the storm clouds which heralded the revolutions of 1830 were gathering. For long he and his cabinet hesitated to pacify Ireland by granting Catholic emancipation; various 'safeguards' were contemplated, but abandoned as impracticable. It was indeed necessary to give way if the Union were to be maintained.

George IV, almost as insane as his father had been, gave his ministers much trouble before he assented to an act which, by granting full political rights to dissenters, would end the nominal integration of church and state. Petitions poured in as soon as it was known that Wellington was planning emancipation: some were favourable, but most were hostile. Little towns expressed their views; at Abingdon in Berkshire, 700 people signed a petition against further concessions to Roman Catholics.[1] Members of the royal family, most of the bishops, and a great many peers shared this view. Only the personal prestige of Wellington and Peel carried the Roman Catholic Emancipation Act through both Houses. Its passage was slightly eased by the introduction of two other bills: one gave the Lord Lieutenant of Ireland power

---

[1] Townsend, J., *News of a Country Town* (Oxford, 1914), p. 172.

to suppress any association which he thought seditious; the other raised the property qualification for the freeholder's franchise in Ireland from 40*s.* to £10, so that the majority of the Catholic peasants lost their votes. Even so, Lord Winchilsea accused the Duke of Wellington of 'insidious designs for the infringement of our liberties, and the introduction of Popery into every department of the State'. Wellington challenged him to a duel; fortunately, on the field both men came to their senses and fired into the air.

The act of 1829, although it gave the long-sought political rights, still contained clauses which made a distinction between Catholics and other citizens. They could now vote and sit in either House of Parliament, but had to take an oath 'not to disturb or weaken the protestant religion' and yet again to deny that the pope had any political rights in England. They could hold offices in local or national government, except those of Lord Chancellor, Lord Keeper, or Lord Lieutenant of Ireland. Not unnaturally, they were forbidden to join in any election to any body connected with the church or with organizations, such as the universities, which were held to be an integral part of the ecclesiastical system. Jesuits and members of other religious orders had to be specially registered, and recruitment to the orders was prohibited; any person who joined one in England was subject to banishment. Nuns were excepted from these regulations: they were considered harmless.

Seven years later the repeal of the Marriage Act allowed Catholic chapels to be licensed for marriages; in 1850 a normal Catholic hierarchy was restored, the bishops taking their titles from places like Birmingham and Salford. Other restrictions were removed or ignored, but not until 1926 did the last traces of penal legislation vanish from the statute book.

It appears that some of the leading Catholic gentry rather regretted that it was a pugnacious, rampageous Irishman who was really responsible for the grant of their political liberties. At any rate, when O'Connell applied for membership of a Catholic club, he was blackballed. The government, perhaps naturally, showed its dislike of him by not admitting him as King's Counsel, though the silk gown was given to other Irish lawyers who had been associated with him. In fact, it might have been said that his victory had won more for the English than for the Irish, for to them freedom meant freedom from the tithes which they had to pay to an alien church and the restoration of their own independent institutions. For the English Catholic layman, the only serious handicap still imposed on account of his religion was his exclusion

from the universities, where until 1854 religious tests excluded
all dissenters, Catholic or Protestant. Young men did go on, as
they had before, living in a university town and studying under
college tutors, yet unable to be undergraduates, much less to
take a degree. Some colleges were friendly; in 1822 Henry Jerningham planned to go to Magdalene College, Cambridge, where
the Master 'did not require any attendance at the Chapel. Sir
Rd. Acton belonged to it, and his Brother, who has a vocation to
be a priest is there yet'.[1] In 1827 two young Cambridge men
became Catholics; both had been influenced by the interest in
things medieval which was a feature of the Romantic Revival
in England. One, Ambrose Phillipps, had been attracted by a
French refugee priest who taught French in his school. He wanted
beauty and richness in church, and tried to get his local parson
to wear a cope and have a cross on the communion table; the
Bishop of Peterborough ordered the removal of the cross. From his
school at Edgbaston he went to a Catholic chapel in Birmingham
and asked if he could see the vestments. The priest had little of
beauty to show, but soon afterwards the boy wrote to him asking
him to meet him at the cottage of an old Irishwoman and receive
him into the church. After convincing himself of the lad's knowledge of Catholic doctrine and the sincerity of his intention, the
priest agreed. In spite of his family's efforts, some months later
he was conditionally baptized. In 1826 he went to Trinity College,
Cambridge; there he met a man a good deal his senior, Kenelm
Digby. He too was a romantic, who as a boy had amused himself
with sham tournaments. In his foreign travels he had been both
surprised and attracted by Catholic services, but it was his study of
theology that led him to ask to be instructed by a priest. Unlike
Phillipps, he had difficulty in finding one who would undertake
the task, but at last he succeeded. Phillipps and Digby showed
their devotion to their new faith by riding 50 miles every Sunday
to and from Ware to hear Mass. Gradually over the years more
and more men of ability followed them, to be part of the 'Second
Spring' of Catholicism in England.[2]

The opposition aroused by the act of 1829 was strengthened
by such defections, especially by that of Newman in 1845. The
result was a social antagonism to Catholicism far greater than had
existed in penal days; the immigration of Irish labourers, often
causing trouble to local authorities, made matters worse. It would
probably be true to say that, far from integrating them more
closely into English society, the freedom won by the Catholics

[1] *Jerningham Letters*, Vol. II, p. 226.
[2] Gwynn, D., *The Second Spring* (1944), pp. 15 ff.

resulted in a separation from their neighbours. It took many years for the old prejudices to break down, and in certain aspects they remain.

Yet 1829 was a genuine victory. Catholics were no longer an alien body in their native land. Sooner or later, as the old conception of 'one state, one church' withered away, emancipation was bound to come; in 1858 the Jews were at length given full political rights. That emancipation came when it did was an unforeseen result of the Act of Union with Ireland; whatever harm that act caused in English as well as Irish politics, it is clear that it was owing to an Irishman that in 1829 the Catholics of England gained the freedom to be truly Catholic and wholly English—a freedom for which they had prayed for 270 years.

11

THE EDUCATION OF CATHOLICS

Some of the 300 grammar schools that existed in the early six-teenth century had survived the raids made on their endowments when monastic and chantry lands were confiscated;[1] some were re-established and new schools were founded in the late sixteenth century. The sons of the gentry sometimes attended a local school, but if their parents were wealthy, they were taught at home by a tutor. They went on to Oxford or Cambridge or, as in earlier times, became members of the household of a great landowner. Their sisters stayed at home, or were sent to live with friends or relations to learn the ways of polite society. Special masters taught music and dancing to both boys and girls.

In Elizabeth's reign the education of the next generation of Catholics did not present a peculiar problem, save that as time went on fewer boys could go to the universities. Priests took refuge as tutors, and seminarists arriving from the continent found the teaching of music a useful cover for their religious activities. Thomas Woodhouse, a 'Marian' priest, and R. Crockett, a Cam-bridge man, who were both executed in 1580, had been acting as schoolmasters. G. Lingan, another 'old' priest, was said to go from one Papist house to another 'under colour of teaching the vir-ginals'.[2] In spite of the law, chaplains continued to supervise the education of the children of their patrons. Laymen also found security in this way; John Gerard the Jesuit found a convert called Line, who had been arrested in 1586 but released, teaching Latin and the art of playing the harp in a Catholic family.[3] Such men usually held a lowly position in the household: in 1670 when a tutor was being sought his wage was to be £5 a year; he was to eat with the servants and supervise the children's toilet.[4]

Often, especially when the family tutor was a man of ability, a small school was formed for boys of the district. Swithin Wells

[1] Leach, A. F., *The Schools of Medieval England* (1915), pp. 219 ff.
[2] Jessopp, A., *One Generation of a Norfolk House* (1879), p. 17.
[3] Gerard, John, *Autobiography* (London, 1951), p. 83.
[4] Blundell, M., *Cavalier* (London, 1933), p. 83.

who played a prominent part in the protective organization for receiving and helping priests,[1] was in the 1570s a member of the household of the Earl of Southampton, and ran a school for the neighbourhood.[2] He was often in trouble; when the prisons were filled at the time of Babington's plot in 1586 he was arrested, and though released was prosecuted the next year for receiving Catholic books from abroad. At last in 1591 a priest was found in his house in Holborn in the very act of saying Mass. Wells was not present, but when his wife was arrested he gave himself up to save her, and was executed the same year.[3]

Small local schools continued to exist, and, as persecution diminished, increased in number and reputation. William Eyston, of an influential family at East Hendred, had a school in Oxford in 1602;[4] in the middle of the seventeenth century the Jesuits had a boarding school at Stanley Grange in Derbyshire, the house of their patroness Anne Vaux. School books marked 'Stanley Grange' are still to be found in the library of the Jesuit school of Mount St. Mary.[5] In Lancashire a boarding school was established at Fernyhalgh in 1651; this was carried on until 1760, and in the early eighteenth century, when it was managed by Dame Alice Harrison, it had a high reputation. About 1680 seven sisters, the Misses Dalton, had a boys' school at Yealand, Lancashire. There were several schools in London; five were known by the government to exist in Yorkshire in the seventeenth century, and a considerable number of Papist schools was reported to the bishops when they made their visitation inquiries in the eighteenth century.

These schools, depending as they did on a single teacher, were often short-lived and were of varied quality. Some were run by men of high standing; R. Reeves, the Master of Magdalen College School, a friend of Anthony à Wood, became a Catholic and had to resign in 1673. He joined the Benedictines as a lay brother, and, after a temporary restoration to his old post, in 1687 opened a school in the Cotswold village of Bourton-on-the-Water. Here he was arrested on suspicion of being a priest, but, as this was not the case, he was released. He continued teaching in various places until his death in London in 1693; his boast was that of his pupils 60 had become Protestant ministers and 40 Catholic priests.[6]

[1] Supra, p. 30.
[2] Devlin, C., *Life of Southwell* (London, 1956), p. 14.
[3] Ibid., p. 238.
[4] Humphreys, A. L., *East Hendred* (London, 1923), p. 112.
[5] Anstruther, G., *Vaux of Harrowden* (Newport, 1953), p. 462.
[6] Stapleton, B., *Post-Reformation Catholic Missions* (1906), p. 222.

Another scholarly man, named Hudson, had a school at Kidling-
ton, near Oxford; Thomas Hearne, the antiquary, bought books
for him.[1] A Catholic school at Milford in Hampshire figured in
a law case in Chancery that went on from 1732 to 1735. There
was a proposal to found a new school there; objections were raised
that two already existed, but it was declared that one was managed
by a 'notorious sot' and the other was Romanist. No comment was
made on its quality.[2]

The seminaries on the continent required a high standard of
education, and especially a knowledge of Latin, from aspirants to
the priesthood. In Douay, at the end of the sixteenth and begin-
ning of the seventeenth century, there were several houses of
English priests and nuns; the Jesuits opened a boys' school there
to prepare their postulants for higher studies. As the supply of
men from the universities dried up, boys began to come to the
college, which Cardinal Allen had founded at Douay,[3] too young
and too ill-educated for theological training. These lads were
sent to the Jesuit school; they lived in their own college and
marched to school in double file, speaking only if necessary, and
then in Latin or French; never in English lest they should be
overheard by spies, from whom there was constant danger. When
the boys went for walks for exercise ponds and rivers were avoided,
lest the lads should break away for a swim.

Discipline had to be very strict. As the college was supported
by alms from England and the continent, no shadow of scandal
could be tolerated. Unsatisfactory pupils could—and did—turn
informer, letting the English government know in advance when
priests were coming over. Yet to expel them was not simple; they
had to return to England, not only illegally but in disgrace, or
else seek work abroad. Sometimes they stayed in the town; in
1602 two of them went to live in an inn kept by the college cook,
and were arrested by the town police for brawling. After Cardinal
Allen's death, some of his successors found it hard to maintain
the standards of enthusiasm and learning which he had set.
When in 1602 the pope gave leave to English Benedictines to go
to England as missionaries, some of the men left to join them.
Others rebelled against the rules; Edmund Hopwood was expelled
in 1606 for his 'excessively manifest spirit of contention' and
especially the 'abusive and calumnious address' which he publicly
delivered instead of the 'pious exhortation' he should have given.[4]

In 1612, after a visitation, there was a change of president,
and in 1619 the college started its own school. There had for some

[1] Stapleton, B., *Post-Reformation Catholic Missions* (1906), p. 222
[2] C.R.S., XLIII, 92.   [3] See supra, p. 19.   [4] C.R.S., X, 344.

years been friction between the Jesuits' own pupils and the—so to speak—day-boys. Allen's college had as its chief recreation the performance of plays; in 1619 a comedy by William Drury was presented in public in the open air—in January! After a quarrel involving one of the actors, who was said to have roused 'the envy of all the scholars of the Jesuits',[1] the boys were withdrawn and the college started classes for its own juniors. Thus the school of Douay, as distinct from the seminary, began. At the end of the seventeenth century valuable assistance was given by Lady Mary Yate, who agreed to give £1,000, or an annual income of £42, to the president on condition that Greek was taught throughout the school.[2] Most of the boys who attended this school returned to their homes in England, and with varying fortunes it persisted until the French Revolution and the wars which followed it drove Englishmen back to their native land.

The removal of the boys in 1619 led, not unnaturally, to strained relations between the Jesuits and the college, reflecting and strengthening the divisions already apparent in England. The Society of Jesus had already, in 1592, established a house at St. Omer, known in England by the code name of Flamsteed. Here in 1624 a school was opened and this became one of the most popular of the continental schools for English boys. The Benedictines too had a school in Douay, and there were several others of less renown in the Low Countries.

The decision whether to send a boy abroad or to have him taught at home, or in whatever English school was available, was often a very difficult one for a parent to make. Gilbert Langley, a London goldsmith[3] in the early eighteenth century, was not content with his son's education either in a local school or at Charterhouse. The boy himself said later that in the English schools they 'run through all the Classick Authors' before the pupils were 'sufficiently grounded in the first Rudiments of Learning'. His father, 'being fully persuaded of the almost universal error and corruption in our English schools, resolv'd to send him over to the Benedictine monks at Douay'. His wife opposed him; she preferred 'the Presence of her son in Ignorance', so the plan fell through until 'Providence, as a peculiar mark of its Favour, was pleased to take her away'. 'No sooner was Mamma dead' than in 1721 the boy was sent to St. Gregory's School in Douay; this school is now established at Downside Abbey.

Young Gilbert Langley wrote long letters to his father. He had

---

[1] C.R.S., X, 380.   [2] Midland District Archives, A 1271.
[3] See Birt, Dom H., *Downside* (London, 1902), passim.

the humiliation of having to go back to Latin Grammar and Caesar, which he considered 'a plain proof of the vanity of some of our *English* schools'. The description he gave of his daily life would probably have applied to that of most English boys in one of the schools abroad. Like the Charterhouse scholars in England, the pupils wore gowns. They were divided into classes according to their ability and knowledge, which were tested every month as well as in full examination three times a year. Latin was a familiar tongue, for no other language was permitted to the boys for daily use. Gilbert noted that in the dormitories each boy 'has his Bed a-part', which was not usual. There was a recreation room known as the Calefactory, which suggests that it alone was heated; but even there fires were lit in the two grates only in the evening, and the fuel was strictly rationed, so some 'young Sparks' used to steal wood. The boys' food seems to have been good and ample: bread and butter for breakfast, boiled meat and broth at midday, and roast meat and salad at night, half a pound of meat being allowed to each boy at each meal, with unlimited bread and beer.

The time-table was rigorous. All rose at 5 a.m., and were supposed to study until 7.30, when they washed and had breakfast. Classes were held from 8 a.m. to 11, and again from 2 p.m. to 4.30, with half an hour for play in the large yard. The rest of the day was for private study. But the accounts of the school show that the lads had a billiard table in their Calefactory, that they performed plays, went skating and fishing, and played football, as well as marbles and other games. There was a house in the country to which they went for a change of air; there they kept pets and went for walks.

Dancing, fencing and music lessons were provided, so a boy went home equipped for normal social life. Before he returned, he might be sent on a tour of Europe, as was many another wealthy young Englishman; but the Papist often had a priest as his guardian and tutor. Tommy Haggerston had been idle at school at St. Omer, and in 1740 his uncle, Sir Marmaduke Constable of Everingham, reported to his father, Sir Carnaby Haggerston, that he ought to be placed in charge of a tutor who must 'above all endeavour to bring him to a love of reading, at least English and French'.[1] He also advised that Tommy's younger brothers should be sent to a school in Durham, as a boy from there was 'very forward'; but in fact they went to a well-known school in Hampshire.

A Jesuit priest was chosen as Tommy's tutor. He had to be

[1] Transcript of Constable MSS. at Ampleforth Abbey.

fitted out with suitable clothes, including handkerchiefs, a sword and boots. His salary, and the expenses of himself and his pupil, were estimated at £300 a year in all. Two years later the boy was reported by his uncle to have made great improvement, and he seems to have settled well enough into English society when he came home, aged 23, in 1745.

One anxiety that haunted parents who sent their children abroad was that they might come home foreigners. Cuthbert Constable, of Burton Constable, wrote triumphantly to a friend in 1742[1] that his son had come home 'pretty expert I believe in his exercises and whats useful and expected of a Gentleman. . . . For all he has been some years in France yet he'll stand up and argue for his own country as warmly and as solidly as one that has Liv'd & been bred 30 years in England.' Yet the fear that boys would become 'foreign' was referred to in 1769 by Thomas Weld, who wrote from Bruges to his brother, 'What would you say if I had forgot my English? however I have not entirely but I Can assure you I speak french much better than I do English[2].' That Thomas retained a thoroughly English character he showed in later life, when he played an important part in the struggles over Catholic emancipation.[3]

This method of education was, of course, available only for the sons of wealthy men. Many of the smaller landowners and merchants had difficulty in getting their children properly taught. It was not only the Papists who found the usual schools, closely connected with the established church, unsatisfactory on both religious and educational grounds. Several 'Academies' were established in the eighteenth century by Protestant dissenters, and their standards of learning were often much higher than those of the grammar schools. Priests often ran schools, but they had other duties, and their training was predominantly theological; moreover, they might be unacquainted with the customs of polite society.[4]

Several Catholic schools for boys were therefore founded in England from the time of James II onwards. The Commissioners for Forfeited Estates reported in 1716 that in Yorkshire there were 'two famous Popish schools, endowed with land to ye value of £200 per annum and upwards'.[5] One was at Osmotherly, the other at Egton, near Whitby. In 1724 an account was given in

[1] MSS. 146, Box 310, East Riding Record Office, Beverley.
[2] MS. Letter in Weld Archives, Dorset County Record Office.
[3] See supra, p. 141.
[4] Hemphill, B., *Early Vicars Apostolic* (London, 1953), pp. 96 ff.
[5] Payne, O., *Records of the English Catholics* (London, 1889), p. 153.

the Exeter newspaper, *The Post Master or Loyal Mercury*,[1] which in its sensational distortion of facts is equal to the best efforts of the 'yellow' press of today. A Catholic seminary, it says, had been '*by accident* discovered' near Wimborne. "'Twas found out by some gentlemen that were hunting, who came upon them before they were aware, and surprised some of the youths that were walking at a distance from the house. . . . There were about *sixty rooms in it, handsomely fitted up, which are all underground*; so that nothing but a bit of a farmhouse appears.' The house was, in fact, all that there was; the extraordinary subterranean mansion existed only in the imagination of the reporter. The 'seminary' was a small school, run by a Mrs. Stafford and maintained by the Jesuits who were patronized by the Arundells of Wardour.

Near Winchester was a larger school which had been founded in the reign of James II and was established at Twyford. Alexander Pope was educated there. In the 1725 visitation returns for Winchester diocese it was referred to as 'a supposed Papist school consisting of about 20 boarders',[2] with a master and an usher who were in fact priests. It was probably never large, but had an excellent reputation. The panic felt by many Catholics after the rising of 1745 led to its being closed. Bishop Challoner replaced it in 1749 by founding a new school in Hertfordshire, at Stanton Lordship,[3] a great house where Lord Aston had kept an establishment of over 100 persons. Here pupils were taken from an early age; the rules were strict but humane. Time was allowed for play, and the boys had their own little gardens. The beating of a boy was reserved for rare and serious occasions.[4] In 1769 the school moved to Old Hall, where it survives as St. Edmund's College, Ware.

In 1763 another important school was opened at Sedgley Park, near Wolverhampton. A covered waggon brought the first dozen or so of pupils from a small school which had been started near Newcastle-under-Lyme the previous year. Questions were asked in the House of Lords about the grant of a lease of the mansion by Lord Ward for such a purpose; he defended his action by praising the school, and the matter was allowed to drop.[5] By 1770 there were 100 boys, and a large number of well-known men were pupils there, including the actor John Kemble. This school, too, survives under the name of St. Wilfred's.

By the late eighteenth century many Papist schools flourished.

[1] Oliver, G., *Collections* (London, 1857), p. 41.   [2] C.R.S., XLII, 124.
[3] Burton, E., *Challoner* (London, 1909), Vol. I, pp. 290 ff.
[4] The rules are printed in Ward, *History of St. Edmund's College*.
[5] Burton, op. cit., Vol. II, pp. 35 ff.

Some were 'Charity' or 'Poor' schools, like that in Lincoln's Inn Fields, or the one managed by the Jesuits in Bristol. At Stratford in Essex a French refugee priest, the Abbé Chevrollais, was very active in his care for the poor; his name gave the local authorites a good deal of trouble—they spelt it Cheveller or Shiverly or even Schevelle. In 1816 his appeal for help brought in enough subscriptions, some of 6d. a week, for him to open a charity school where poor boys were taught to read and write; one for girls followed three years later. Evening and Sunday schools were opened in 1819.[1]

There were many little schools in villages; several are mentioned in parsons' returns of Papists. These generally lasted only a few years, as they depended on the presence of a priest willing and able to undertake the teaching. Some of these parish schools continued for years, but only in rare cases have their records survived. One such school, which still exists, was begun in 1734 at Ugthorpe, in the moors of East Yorkshire a few miles from Whitby.

This lonely village has a persistent record as a centre of Catholics; many of the priests who landed on the coast near Whitby took refuge with the Radcliffes at Ugthorpe Old Hall or with neighbouring farmers. Some years ago a subsidiary chapel was found in the garrets of a farm, with the priest's vestments laid out ready for Mass; doubtless he had had to hide and was unable to return. One local priest, Nicholas Postgate, was a victim of Titus Oates's plot; he was executed at York after serving in his home district with outstanding devotion. Papists were generally tolerated, however. Another priest in 1708 was arrested while actually saying Mass; he was after a while released, and when in 1719 he died, the local parson recorded him in his register of deaths as 'Mr. John Danby, a priest of the Church of Rome.'[2]

In 1734 Ugthorpe's priest was Monox Hervey, a convert from Suffolk; his unusual Christian name, and the alias of Rivett that he used, were both taken from his mother's family. He was an active and intelligent man; a number of the notes he made on his work in Oxfordshire, Yorkshire, and on the Welsh borders survive, with his racy comments. During the rising of 1745 he was betrayed by a man he had befriended, was arrested, tried and imprisoned in York Castle. After two years he was released on condition that he left Yorkshire; this he was very willing to do. He made a catalogue of the hardships suffered by priests at Ugthorpe, ending

[1] *Essex Recusant* (1959), Vol. I, No. 2. Pub. 'Little Haylands', Chigwell.
[2] Ward, W. G., unpublished MS. in the possession of Mr. Bennison, of Borrowby, Thirsk.

MCE

with the words, 'From the Moors in Yorkshire Good Lord deliver us'.[1] He left behind him in Ugthorpe a permanent memorial of his energy; the school he founded in 1734 was maintained by the priests who followed him.

Perhaps the existence of the school partly accounts for the continuous support given to their church by the people of Ugthorpe. In 1776 a list of the principal families was made; it contained 119 names, many of which are still represented in the registers of today. That they valued the education given their children was shown in 1802 when they decided to put the school on a permanent footing. Three acres of land and some houses were presented, their rents to be used for providing an income for a teacher, ten pounds a year 'for a schoolmaster teaching ye whole year'. If the priest chose, he could undertake the work; if not, he could 'discard' at will any teacher whom he thought unsuitable. The master had to teach 'all ye poor Cath. & Protest. who are not able to pay . . . *gratis* in consideration of ye said salary'.

It was not easy to find a schoolmaster: the one appointed in 1805 was not a Catholic, and there was doubt about his qualifications. But he promised 'to become a Cath.': and 'to keep ye school in good order', and produced evidence as to his character and experience. The accounts show that he had a house and garden free of rent, and was given as 'encouragement' for teaching the poor, free of charge, sums varying from 4s. 6d. in 1808 to £2 5s. 4d. in 1809. Care had to be taken lest the giving of a fixed salary should entitle the schoolmaster to a legal settlement in the parish, so that he had a claim on the poor rate '& thus ye Priest would be continually exposed to get ye ill will of ye Parish & be in a manner forced to keep ye same schoolmaster'. It was therefore arranged in 1812 that his salary should be £9 19s., which brought him below the limit allowed, and that he should pay 1s. a year rent for his house. Presumably he also got fees from parents who could afford to pay.

There were, no doubt, many such schools, especially in country districts where Catholicism was strong, and in large towns where they would not be conspicuous. The humble parentage of many priests shows that it was not only the children of the gentry who received an education both in the principles and practice of their religion and the normal curriculum of schools of the time. Often some charitable squire would pay the fees, either at an English school or overseas, for a promising boy who thought he had a vocation for the priesthood. Except for men entering the priesthood, or training as doctors or lawyers, education ended with

[1] Monox Hervey's notes and some of his correspondence are printed in C.R.S., XIV, 313 ff. See also supra, p. 120.

school days. In this Papists did not suffer much as compared with their social equals, for the universities of the eighteenth century were by no means places of learning for the average man. Sometimes, indeed, Catholics went to live in Oxford or Cambridge for social, as much as for academic, training. Sir Francis Throckmorton was the only surviving son of Sir Robert, a wealthy landowner of Coughton Court, Warwickshire, and Weston Underwood in Buckinghamshire.[1] In 1653, when he was 13, James Smyth was appointed as his 'steward'; he not only had charge of his master's purse, but seems to some extent to have acted as his tutor. When Francis was 14, the two of them went to live in Cambridge. The boy was young enough to want a top and a whip for it, but old enough to lose money at cards. 'Mr Bagley that passed as my master's tutor' was in orders and attached to King's College; presumably he directed the studies of the lad, who was on sufficiently friendly terms with the university authorities to entertain one of the proctors. Dancing and fencing lessons were taken as well. Three years in all were spent in Cambridge, broken into by trips to London and to friends in different places; Oxford was also visited, but only for a short time.

This plan of being in, but not of, a university continued; if the authorities were friendly, a Catholic might get as much instruction as an ordinary undergraduate. He could never proceed to a degree, for that involved an oath which no Papist could take.

Catholic parents were concerned about the education of their daughters, as well as of their sons. A steady stream of young women crossed the seas, and houses of English nuns were opened, chiefly in France and the Netherlands. Schools were established by many of these convents; several of their pupils became nuns, and English girls also joined convents already founded. But as time went on, more and more young ladies came merely to receive the education they needed to take a fitting place in society.

A remarkable woman, Mary Ward, who was born in 1585 and died in 1645, became greatly concerned that the future mothers of Catholics should be intellectually equipped, and that the children of the poor should receive some education. She conceived the bold idea of founding a new order for women, less trammelled by ancient custom than the existing orders. She greatly admired the work of the Jesuits, whose organization made them available for whatever work in whatever place their superior believed could best serve the church. With seven companions, she went in 1609 to St. Omer, and so, in spirit if not formally, began the Institute of the Blessed Virgin.

[1] Barnard, E. A. B., *A Seventeenth Century Country Gentleman* (Cambridge, 1948).

The idea of an order of women following the Rule of St. Ignatius rather than that of St. Benedict, not bounded by the walls of a convent but moving about the world, was revolutionary. The 'English ladies', as they were called, showed remarkable courage and devotion, and attracted many recruits. After years of mis-understanding and opposition, the persistence of Mary Ward led to permission from the pope to carry on her work. Her two cardinal points were that the members of the Institute should not be bound by the strict rules of enclosure, and should owe obedience to their own superior, and to the local superiors whom she might appoint, instead of to the local bishop. It was not until 1703 that Clement XI, saying, 'Let women govern women', gave full sanction to the new foundation.[1]

After establishing a house in Liége, Mary Ward returned to England in 1617, where she and her sister were forced to dress as ladies of fashion in order to avoid arrest. One friend, a Protestant, said of her, 'Except the Mother of God, there never was such a woman'; but Abbot, the Archbishop of Canterbury, thought that 'she did more harm than six Jesuits'. Other women joined her, and when she was arrested her friends were sufficiently influential to obtain her release. She returned to the continent, where her ideas proved so popular that she had to set up several more houses. Schools for poor children were opened, and various works of charity carried on.

Some of the 'Mothers' were sent to England, to instruct girls when opportunity offered, and give aid to the sick and the poor. The Jesuits helped them as much as they could, and this led to the disapproval of the secular clergy. The President of Douay College in his report to the nuncio in 1622 showed clearly his dislike of the 'English ladies'. People, he said, were 'scandalized by such boldness in women', and would not believe that they were really members of a religious community, as their life was 'exactly like that of lay people'.[2]

The schools opened by the Institute were as a rule successful; in fact the standard in Latin exercises at the school in Monaco was so exceptionally high as to arouse the suspicions of the shrewd foundress. She feared 'these subtill wenches hadde some help at home to make their theames', as she wrote in 1627 to Mother Bedingfield. That the standard should be high was however her constant demand; 'any public display yf done yt must be so

[1] Material for this section comes from various Lives of Mary Ward, and from the Archives of the Bar Convent, York, by kind permission of the Superior.
[2] C.R.S., X, 398.

performed as better cannot be and may serve to prevail against bacbiters and scornfull enimies'. Yet such academic success was not her principal aim; she longed to 'have common schools in the great citty of London, wch will never be without [a] miracle'.

By 1686 the members of the Institute in England had found a benefactor in Sir Thomas Gascoigne. Acting through a merchant, Edward Topham, he secured a site just outside Micklegate Bar, one of the gates of York, where the 'Ladies' built a house. They also had a school at Hammersmith. In 1699 Bishop Talbot wrote to the pope, commending the 'communities of noble virgins in York and Hammersmith . . . which take upon themselves the education of young ladies, form their manners and instil into their tender hearts every Christian virtue'. This testimonial no doubt aided the granting of formal recognition in 1703. Many girls were educated at the Bar Convent school as pensioners (or boarders); by 1709 there were 43 of them, coming mainly from the northern counties, but some from considerable distances. Non-Catholics too sent their daughters, and by the late eighteenth century parents and friends were being entertained in style. The hairdresser cut and curled the girls' hair, but only three of them had their coiffure powdered. Then a performance was given, and the time and worry this cost the nuns is reflected in a note written on 29 July 1775. 'Mr Bedingfield brought the Ode he had composed for Suprs Jubilee, to be taught those Young Ladies who were to repeat it. He kept Mrs Dillon and self almost 2 hours talking about it.' When on 8 September the celebration of Superior's Jubilee actually took place, 'Mr B highly pleased with the Young Ladies manner of delivering it'. After the ode came a song, accompanied by pipes. 'It pleas'd highly well done Pensioners', and 'after they had all drank Wine and eat Cake they sallied forth into the garden here the music waited for them, there they danced.'

The success of the school had not been won without difficulty. In 1694/5 the Mother Superior was arrested and imprisoned in the Ousebridge gaol. She appealed to the Archbishop of York: 'your Grace is so full of mercie and pitty that you can't but think a prison must go hard with me who want but 2 years of 80 yeare old besides being so weak and infirm. . . . We have carried ourselves . . . quiet and civily and alwayes under great submissiveness to the Lord Mair and Aldermen'. She was released, but in 1696 a mob threatened to attack the convent. Suddenly it dispersed; the nuns were kneeling in prayer inside the doors when, as eye-witnesses declared, St. Michael the Archangel appeared as a man on a white horse, and terrified the crowd into flight. No further trouble of a serious nature occurred, and later accounts show that people in the locality thought very highly of the school, as they do today.

The other house of the Institute, established at Hammersmith, also developed into a successful school. The two foundations kept in touch with each other, but with some difficulty. Letters survive which show that a code was used for security, but, unlike the codes of earlier days, which used a merchant's terms to conceal dangerous words, this one seems designed rather to arouse than to avert suspicion. Nuns were 'shepherdesses', the chaplain a 'Bagg' or a 'smith', the bishop a 'myth', mischief-makers 'sparrows'—which makes the letters read oddly. Under such conditions, it is not strange that the two foundations at York and Hammersmith separated. Mother Cecily Cornwallis, who was in charge, placed the Hammersmith house under a rule of obedience to the bishop, which was contrary to the constitution of the Institute. Scarcely had this been done when in 1703 papal approval of the order was granted; but the community preferred to remain under the bishop. Cordial relations between York and Hammersmith persisted, but the two foundations were now distinct.

It is not surprising that the superior at Hammersmith wanted direct support, for during the Popish Plot troubles the house had been searched: the chaplain hid in the shrubbery and so escaped. The nuns left for a while, and quietly returned, but they had to do their shopping and other errands after dark. So respected were they that non-Catholics sent their girls to the nuns even though this might lead to their becoming Papists: one chaplain reported that 'not a year passed but I received some twelve pupils of the school into the church'. There was therefore no secrecy about the existence of the convent; in 1705 the local parson reported to the Bishop of London,[1] 'That House is reported to be as full of Papists as it can hold. I have no means to know ye Number of them. They have a private Back door in ye Lane, for their priests and ye Papists of ye Place to go unobserved.' As an identical report was sent the next year, it seems that the bishop was not unduly worried.

Both local girls and boarders attended the school: a daughter of Sir Richard Arundell was there in 1718 and there is a letter in the Wardour archives from an indignant woman apothecary, who wrote that the superior at Hammersmith had 'deprived me of serving yr Dear Child Miss Molly in ye Measles . . . upon no other Pretence but that she always makes use of ye Apothecary in Town.' One's sympathies are on the whole with the superior; if every boarder had had a private apothecary attending her in illness, life would have become very complicated.

In 1780, during the Gordon Riots, local tradespeople sheltered

[1] Guildhall Library, London, MS. Box 9800, 1 CSR 68. Dioc. Lond.

the nuns, and their work went on. In 1810 Lady Jerningham, writing about the education of a friend's children, described the school as very good.[1] There were other Catholic girls' schools in and around London; a Mr. and Mrs. Hughes had one at Hackney which moved to Greenwich in 1769. A wealthy merchant sent his daughter there as a weekly boarder.[2] However, most of the girls from the really rich families still went to the convent schools on the continent. It is an interesting sidelight on Roman Catholic practice in the seventeenth and eighteenth centuries that so many people ran these risks, and incurred the very heavy expense involved.

In 1658 William Blundell of Crosby Hall, Lancashire, was keen on the proper education of his daughters, of whom he had 10. He borrowed money from his brother-in-law to send two of them to Bruges; one intended to be a nun, but the other was sent 'for her breeding'.[3] He himself wrote 'An Exercise for the Children to embolden them in speaking', part of which had to be recited by three of them, aged four, seven and nine. In 1665 two more of the girls went to Bruges. The same plan was followed by his grandson, Nicholas Blundell, who had himself been educated at St. Omer. When his elder daughter Mally was 10 she was sent to a school in Liverpool where the charge for a boarder was 5s. a week, plus 5s. a month for dancing lessons.[4] Apparently this was not a success, for she came home after four months. In 1716, in spite of the difficulties caused by the Jacobite rising, which had driven Nicholas Blundell abroad, his wife brought their two daughters over to Ghent, where they were placed in a Benedictine convent. There they remained for six years.

As journeys were costly, the girls rarely came home during their school days, and the best way of keeping in touch with them was by visits from parents or friends. While Sir Marmaduke Constable was concerning himself with arrangements for Tommy Haggerston,[5] he was also making plans for Sir Carnaby's three daughters. He urged that they should not come home; 'they are the best natured sensible and virtuous children I ever mett with', but the school they were in at St. Omer 'is not sufficient. . . . I do not propose here to qualifie your daughters as if you had designed them for Court ladies . . . I wou'd have them only learn such qualifications as are merely necessarie for women of their birth'. Not only their

[1] Castle, E., *Jerningham Letters* (London, 1896), Vol. I, p. 369.
[2] C.R.S., L. (Mawhood Diary), pp. 26, 31.
[3] Blundell, M., *Cavalier* (London, 1933), pp. 73, 45, 110.
[4] Blundell, M., *Blundell's Diary* (Liverpool, 1952), p. 146.
[5] Supra, p. 158.

learning but their wardrobes needed attention: 'they like to have ruined themselves by wearing their stayes too long.' The cost of what he considered to be the bare necessaries did, however, somewhat dismay their uncle.

In the end, the eldest girl was sent to school in Paris. The second had made up her mind to become a nun; the youngest, who was rather backward in her studies, was put under the care of her aunt, a Benedictine nun. Fees for a girl in a good school were about £100 a year, so it was important that the money should be wisely spent, and that when a girl came back to England she should be fit to take her place in local society. Music, dancing and deportment were best acquired in the great cities, so Paris and Brussels were the favourite centres for the fashionable schools.

How well they succeeded is illustrated at the end of the century by the Jerningham correspondence, and by the delightful pictures of life in a convent school drawn by Charlotte Jerningham, some of which are with the Petre archives at Ingatestone and Chelmsford.[1] When full social emancipation came, the Catholic ladies played a prominent part at the court of George III and in fashionable society; and all through the years the women of the house were, as in all other great country mansions, managing servants, laying in stores, organizing entertainment. The only marked difference between the Catholics and other young ladies was that the education of girls in convents increased the likelihood of their becoming nuns, and so saved parents from some of the troubles attendant on the marrying of their daughters.

[1] See Frontispiece, which shows her arrival at the Blue Nuns' School.

12

ORDINARY PEOPLE

It is never easy to get information about the workers who formed the majority of the population in times past. They wrote few letters, they rarely made wills; it is generally only in parish registers or in the records of the courts that their names survive. The ecclesiastical legislation of Elizabeth and her successors produced additional sources of information, as those who did not attend church could be prosecuted and the bishops made special inquiries from time to time, ordering all incumbents of parishes to report on the Catholic and other dissenters in their area. It is often difficult to know whether the recusants reported were Papist or 'fanatic' unless some other evidence exists. After 1660 the returns to the bishops usually distinguished the two groups, but these are not all available and those that are often contain vague or imperfect information. For instance, John Bulger, a mason, was mentioned by the parson of Cardinham in Cornwall as 'not to be found in my list, as it is presum'd he is taken proper notice of in the List of the parish of St. Mawgan, where He is properly a Resident', but St. Mawgan parish returned that it contained no Papist.[1] In earlier days it is likely that these returns were deliberately imperfect, for parsons might well wish not to get people into trouble, or else to conceal their own failure to win them over to the church. Many lists gave merely a rough number of families; others contained entries such as that from Borley in Essex in 1706, where the names of one man and seven women were given, 'most of them very ancient and very poore';[2] some gave full details including the occupation of the recusants.

The aim of the government in securing this information was predominantly financial, so it is not surprising that those who could not possibly pay the fine of £20 a month were often ignored. To bring them to justice involved labour and expense without

---

[1] Exeter Returns, 1767. Devon County Record Office, Exeter.

[2] London Returns, 1706. Guildhall Library. MS. Box 9800.

any corresponding advantage. Yet in the lists of convicted recusants many humble people were included, so we have slightly
more information about Papist workers than about their neighbours who dutifully went to church. How many they were, at any
given date, it is not possible to say. One may state with confidence
that the majority would have been the labourers, servants, and
small farmers on or near the estates of the Catholic landowners who maintained priests in their homes; when a squire
conformed, or sold the estate, or left no direct heir, the chapel
was usually closed, and, deprived of the ministrations of a priest,
the villagers would gradually abandon their religion. There
are examples of a chapel continuing after a Catholic household
came to an end, and of long walks to the nearest 'Mass-house',
or wearisome rides undertaken by a priest to visit scattered
cottages. Normally, however, the removal of a Catholic landowner meant the end of Catholicism in his immediate neighbourhood.

At times of crisis, when a close watch was being kept on possible
centres of trouble, the central government took more interest
in reports from the parishes. In 1745 the parish clerk of Stour
Provost, a village in Dorset not far from Shaftesbury and the
Catholic centre of Wardour Castle, reported that the Papists
were 'behaving themselves very insolently'. Lord Shaftesbury
asked a local justice to take the evidence of Gilbert Coward, the
informer, on oath. This was done on 20 December 1745, and the
clerk's story is an example of the way in which private grievances
could lie behind accusations which in earlier times might have
had very serious consequences.

In his sworn deposition, the parish clerk stated that Thomas
Pike, a carpenter who was known to be a Papist, had owed him
'eighteen pence for beer, ever since Easter last, and that on the
fifth of October last, as he was going home after winding up the
Church Clock, he accidentally met the sd. Thos. Pike at Mary
Melyard's, a little Alehouse, when he was something in Liquor'.
Pike declared that, as Coward had asked him in public to pay his
debt, he 'would now never pay him, and at the same time did
strike at him, but missing his blow fell down', whereupon the
clerk 'kiked him in the Breech'. Pike got up and said; 'Thee hast
the keys of the Church in thy hands, but thou shalt not keep
them above a month longer'. 'This,' admitted Coward, 'was all
the Disturbance'. No wonder that Lord Shaftesbury reported
to the Duke of Newcastle that 'the thing turns out to be a mere
trifle', especially as the clerk also stated that there were 14 or 15
Catholic families in the parish, 'all labouring people, but they

have made no disturbance, nor made use of no insolent language towards his Majesty or any of his Protestant subjects'.[1]

If they did cause any 'disturbance' Papists like any one else might appear before the justices, and if they were very poor they would come before the churchwardens in search of relief. A Catholic, Nicholas Blundell of Crosby, was elected a church-warden of Sefton in 1714;[2] other Papists may possibly have held this office where there were many of their co-religionists. Most of the assistance given to the Catholic poor came from people of their own faith, a fact sometimes noted by the parsons in their reports. In 1738 at Banbury the vicar stated that among the six to seven hundred families in his parish 'Nine or ten of the Families men-tioned . . . are most of them Papists, all exceeding poor, under the Influence of Mr Holman a very great contiguous Papist.'[3] A surprising number of the parishes in the diocese of Oxford reported one or two Papists, frequently women, of 'low' or 'mean' rank. At Swincombe there was 'a poor wid. supported by the Alms of the Parish', presumably the poor rate. In Essex, in 1706, at Foxearth one man was 'actually receiving help from the over-seers'.[4] The churchwardens therefore seem to have accepted responsibility for the poor even if they were recusant.

Some information about these humbler Catholics may be obtained from the records kept by the priests who served them. Until the calmer times of the eighteenth century few priests dared to keep any sort of register of their administration of the sacra-ments, though a few scrappy notes have survived. Of the later registers, many have been lost, and of those that survive several are very imperfect, but sometimes the priests entered the occu-pations of the people whom they married and buried and whose children they baptized. In Gosport, and other places near the naval bases, towards the end of the eighteenth century these congre-gations were joined by Irish immigrants. The priest at Gosport was mystified by names such as Murphy, Connolly, and Sullivan; they were entered as Merfey, Kanelly, and Silyvan or Sylaven.[5] Some Irish priests accompanied this advance guard of the con-siderable force of Irish labourers who came to England in the nineteenth century.

[1] P.R.O., S.P. Dom. Geo. II, 36/78, No. 13. Transcribed by Mr. J. A. Williams.

[2] Blundell, M., *Blundell's Diary*, p. 127.

[3] Oxfordshire Record Soc. 1957, p. 14. William Holman of Warkworth was the 'very great Papist'.

[4] London Diocese returns, 1706. Reproduced in *Essex Recusant*, Vol. 2, No. 1, 1960, p. 20.

[5] C.R.S., XLIX, Gosport Register.

In spite of legislation to prevent mobility of labour, country people with energy were migrating to the towns, and Catholics were no exception. In the 1671 list of convicted recusants,[1] the Lancashire returns included 38 websters[2] and 13 weavers, so there were Papists in the expanding textile industry. There were also 21 tailors, 20 blacksmiths, 18 'servants' (a heading which could include apprentices as well as domestics) shoemakers, butchers, coopers—in fact representatives of almost every craft. Some of the men entered as of a lowly occupation were in fact people of substance; Thomas Kay, of Warrington, was entered as a 'husbandman' but was a glover and had a thriving business. Richard Martincroft, of Manchester, who had been described as a joiner in 1626, left a son who by 1682 was entered as a 'gentleman'.

More information is available about the substantial merchants and manufacturers who flourished in many provincial towns. Several of them built chapels and supported priests; their relations with their fellows were affected only when the need arose for them to take an oath which disturbed their consciences. In York several Papists were freemen of the city; in 1735 there were apparently no less than 21 of them,[3] some of whom held office as chamberlain. The 'upholder', or upholsterer, Richard Farrar was Lord Mayor in 1755 and 1769, although he was registered as a Papist. In 1742 Edward Wallis, one of a well-established Catholic family in York, was elected a councillor in spite of his religion; in 1773 he was given a diploma by the Royal College of Physicians for an essay on the use of chemical preparations in medicine, and in 1781 the city of York awarded him a 'silver prize medallion for judiciously planning and effectively promoting a navigation between York and London', so he must have been a man of parts. Another Catholic was made director of the York dispensary in 1804, and, as soon as the 1829 act made it possible, Seth Agar, a merchant and grocer, became a councillor and the Hon. Edward Petre of the famous Essex family became sheriff and Lord Mayor elect.[4] It seems that their religion had made little difference to the standing of these citizens among their fellows.

In Newcastle-on-Tyne in 1636 a Catholic, William Jenison, was an alderman; he was almost certainly a 'boothman', that is a

[1] C.R.S., VI., 75 ff.

[2] Originally a feminine of webber or weaver, but in the list the word is used for men.

[3] C.R.S., Vol. IV, 368 ff.

[4] Contributed by Miss Akeroyd from the files of the *Yorkshire Courant*, the *York Gazette* and the *Yorkshire Herald*.

corn merchant, of the Company of Merchant Adventurers.[1] The
Common Council granted him the large annual pension of £40
in return for his resigning his position as alderman in favour of
John Marley. Marley became mayor, and was knighted; when in
1644 the Scots crossed the border, he held the castle for the king
until he was forced to surrender. The council then came under
the influence of the parliament; Marley was deprived of his office
and Jenison of his pension. In 1653 those who turned Papist
were prohibited from becoming freemen; this regulation was
carried only after long debate and apparently did not apply to
freemen who were already Catholics. In 1661 Sir John Marley
regained his position as mayor; there is no record of a restoration
of Jenison's £40 a year, though a William Jenison was made a
freeman in 1655.

The coal trade was rapidly expanding, and Catholics took their
share. In the development of the mines of the Forest of Dean two
recusants, Sir Basil Brooke of Madeley and Sir John Winter, were
active in the intrigues that went on between 1627 and 1634 to
secure leases and concessions. Winter, an ironmaster, was able to
offer an advance payment of £8,000 to secure a lease at £4,000 a
year.[2] In the north one of the Papist Grococks of Kippax, Yorkshire, was *Magister Carbonarum*—a master coalman.[3] The Silvertop
family were landowners in Minster Acres; 'Mr George, born 1704,
from being Ld Widdrington's pit-man, set up for himself and
made an immense fortune.'[4] The importation of mahogany and
other timber enriched the family of Chaloner, of Speke and
Garstang in Lancashire. Along the valleys of the Tyne and the
Mersey overseas trade was flourishing, and many Catholics shared
in the prosperity.

Probably more permanent were the profits of those engaged in
the skilled trades and manufactures. There were several Lancashire
Catholics making watches and clocks, another expanding industry.
One of the Booths of Warrington was entered in the 1671 list as
a husbandman; in fact he was the inventor of the 'repeating'
watch.[5] The Roskells of Garstang were well known for their
craft as well as for their faith; they appear in recusant rolls from
1591, and their skill was record in a local ballad:[6]

> And there lies little Garstang
> With houses all o' thatch,

[1] Contributed by Miss Halcrow from the Journal Book of the Common
Council of Newcastle.
[2] Hammersley, G., article on Forest Laws in *History*, XLV, 15 June 1960.
[3] C.R.S., VI, 185.   [4] C.R.S., IV, 253.
[5] Ibid., 224.   [6] Ibid., 205.

That gave arise to Roskells all
And patent lever watch.

Such men as these had considerable wealth, as did the jewellers, silversmiths and goldsmiths, whom we find in different parts of England.

Men who used gold as the raw material of their trade often developed, at the end of the seventeenth century, into dealers in money, receiving deposits and making loans. Many Catholics were bankers in the eighteenth century, like the Arrowsmiths at Preston, one of whom had been executed as a Jesuit in 1628;[1] the Roskells were connected with this family. The Worswicks founded a bank in Lancaster which developed into the Lancaster Banking Company; this did so well that one of its cashiers, James Whiteside, was rich enough to found a chantry in a new church built in 1859.[2] Yet another Papist banker was John Coulston of Hawkshead.[3] These country bankers were normally engaged in purely local business; their loans helped in the development of the Mersey overseas trade in slaves and other merchandise, and in the rapidly expanding cotton industry of the Manchester district.

Politics interrupted the career of two Catholic cotton manufacturers, Peter Mosse and John Holker, who were partners. In 1745 they left their business to join the Manchester regiment raised for Prince Charles; after the defeat at Carlisle they were taken prisoner and sent to London, but managed to escape from Newgate on the day before they were to be tried. Mosse fled to Spain, Holker to Flanders, where he served as a soldier for some years. In 1753 he was invited by the French government to start a cotton factory in Rouen. The idea of encouraging a rival industry abroad did not appeal to him, so he wrote to the English government informing them of the plan and offering to refuse to co-operate if he were given a pardon and allowed to return home. His letter was ignored, so the next year he came secretly to Manchester and smuggled 25 first-class cotton operatives over to Rouen. The venture was so successful that in 1755 he was given a government post as inspector-general to all such factories in France. His son founded a chemical factory in Rouen, so the enforced emigration was fruitful both for the Holkers and for the French.[4]

It was during the troubles of 1745–46 that the strength of the Catholics in Liverpool was revealed. Early in the eighteenth century they had built a chapel of their own; before that, they had

[1] C.R.S., VI, 118, 205.   [2] C.R.S., XX, 95, 139.
[3] C.R.S., VI, 155.   [4] Ibid., 225.

been served by priests who lived with the Catholic squires round about the town. By 1727 the Liverpool congregation was a large one; at the service on Palm Sunday 256 palms were distributed. A 'No Popery' mob invaded the chapel in 1746; they allowed the priest to remove the sacrament and take it to the house of a Presbyterian friend, and then burned the chapel and four houses adjoining it. A new centre was promptly opened, in a house adjoined on either side by the home of a Presbyterian. For some time great precautions were taken; the congregation slipped in singly to hear Mass. Soon they grew bolder, and asked the mayor and corporation to build them a new chapel: this was refused, as was to be expected, but that such a request should have been made at all shows how much the Papists were respected in Liverpool.

Their leader, Henry Pippard, or Peppard, who had married a daughter of Nicholas Blundell of Crosby Hall,[1] then announced that he would build a warehouse. The true purpose of this enterprise was no secret to the town authorities; subscriptions were collected, but it was felt prudent that the new chapel, St. Mary's, should not be too obvious to passers-by. It was on the upper floor of a large two-storey building, in a yard closed by doors, and was surrounded by small houses, one occupied by the priests and others let to Catholic tenants. The property was owned by well-known laymen, acting as trustees, and until 1778 worship went on there peacefully.

A Spanish Jesuit had come to Liverpool in 1773, after the suppression of the Society in Spain; he changed his name of Hormasa to Harris. He joined the senior priest at St. Mary's, Father Gittins, also a Jesuit. Father Harris made friends with some of the wealthy slave-traders of Liverpool, and did excellent work among the foreign prisoners who were brought in from ships captured in the wars. Unfortunately he and Father Gittins fell out over some business connected with the management of the chapel, and in 1778 their quarrel became public; the congregation joined in, some supporting one priest and some the other. Letters appeared in the local press, and Catholics all round the district joined in the argument. Legal proceedings were threatened, and in 1783 both priests were suspended by the vicar apostolic. Father Harris printed an 'Appeal to the Public'; his opponents threw brickbats into the windows of his lodging, and the magistrates offered a reward for their arrest. The bishop then proposed that Harris should go to Ugthorpe;[2] he refused, and was therefore deprived of his faculties for administering the sacraments. He

[1] See infra, p. 188.   [2] See supra, p. 161.

stayed on in Liverpool as a private person, producing in 1788 a book, *Scriptural Researches on the Licitness of the Slave Trade,* which doubtless pleased his friends among the merchants, although it provoked many replies. Next year he died. He seems to have been a vigorous and able man, though singularly lacking in the virtue of obedience usually thought to be a hall-mark of the Jesuits. His opponent, Father Gittins, was sent to Worcester, and the charge of St. Mary's given to the Benedictines.[1]

The story is a melancholy one, but it shows clearly how far removed were the Papists of Liverpool from the timid people, seeking obscurity, that later observers believed them to have been. In contrast, about 1760 there was a plan to open 'a public Mass-house' at Bristol, under the protection of the Duke of Norfolk.[2] Fierce opposition was roused, and the plan was dropped; from 1724 there had been priests active in or near the city,[3] and from 1743 the Jesuits had a chapel in a back street. As long as there was no publicity, there was no interference.

Not only in the north were wealthy Catholics to be found acting as merchants or heads of flourishing businesses. Many names could be given; there was, for example, John Sone,[4] a miller of Bed-hampton, who was a great benefactor to the Catholics of Hamp-shire. He made himself responsible for sending promising boys to school in England or abroad; he constantly acted as godfather for babies; he settled an annual income on the chapel at Brockhamp-ton, and gave £2,000 to his bishop, promising a further similar sum. When he died in 1795 he left £10,000 towards the building of St. Edmund's College at Ware, £1,000 to his parish priest to cover the expenses of the boys for whose education he was responsible, and annuities to many of the people who had worked for him.

The Whebles, who bought Woodley Lodge near Reading, were very wealthy merchants. Throughout the centuries such men had bought land and had married daughters of the aristocracy; the Whebles seem to have done the same. Lady Jerningham reported in 1802 that Maria Talbot was to marry 'Mr Wheble, son to the Catholick merchant who died last year worth upwards of £100,000.' It may have been of men like him that Bishop Challoner was thinking when, speaking of the discourtesy shown to the bishops by some of the Catholic aristocracy, he said to Bishop Hay, 'There

---

[1] C.R.S., IX, 188 ff.

[2] Carpenter, S. C., *Eighteenth Century Church and People* (1959), 5, footnote.

[3] C.R.S., III, 181.

[4] C.R.S., XLIV, several references, see Index of this volume.

[5] *Jerningham Letters,* Vol. I, p. 218,

will be a new people'.[1] He himself was on intimate terms with a
London woollen draper, William Mawhood.[2] This man was a
wholesaler, dealing in cloth on a large scale; he had been educated
at the Jesuit school at St. Omer. During the Gordon Riots, Bishop
Challoner took refuge with the Mawhoods at their house at
Finchley.

There were many Catholics working in and around London;
great fortunes might be made in the expanding areas of the north,
but London was the centre for finance and fashion, as all through
the penal times it had been the chief centre of Catholicism. It was
there that the ambassadors of the Catholic powers gave political
and spiritual aid to their co-religionists. The penal system tended
to collect both priests and laymen in the London prisons, and, in
spite of all the laws, their friends lived round about them, so that
it was usual for priests coming from overseas to go first to London
for help and direction. As well as in the Inns of Court and the town
houses of great families, refuge might be found with the many
craftsmen, traders and innkeepers, though it seems that there
were proportionately fewer Catholics in this last trade in London
than in country towns.

In 1706 the Bishop of London asked detailed questions of his
clergy, and from their replies a very interesting picture of the
Catholics of London appears.[3] There was a concentration of them
in two parishes, St. Clement Danes and St. Giles in the Fields;
about 150 names are listed in each, and as only householders were
included, the total number of Papists would have been higher.
St. Paul's, Covent Garden, reported over 40, and most of the
central London parishes had a few. In the suburbs, Hammersmith
and Chelsea contained a good many, but the majority of the out-
lying parishes sent in 'nil' returns.

In nearly all lists, the occupations of those named were given.
Several of them were men of substance; there were seven goldsmiths. Not included in the returns is Gilbert Whitehall, an exceptionally wealthy man; he had suffered severely, like other London
bankers and dealers in gold, when in 1672 Charles II suddenly
stopped paying interest on the money he owed—the so-called
Stop of the Exchequer.[4] Instead of receiving the huge sum of
£248,866 3s. 4d. due to him, Whitehall, like the other creditors, was
promised annual interest on it at 6 per cent, which amounted to
nearly £15,000 a year; but after a few years not even this was

[1] Burton, *Challoner*, Vol. II, p. 214.
[2] C.R.S., L, *The Mawhood Diary*.
[3] They are now in the Guildhall Library, MS. Box 9800, 1 CSR 63.
[4] See supra, p. 97.

paid.[1] The money thus forcibly 'borrowed', but in fact confiscated, was not all the personal property of the unlucky goldsmiths; much of it had been deposited with them on trust, and interest had naturally to be paid on it or the funds returned. The whole London money market was badly shaken by Charles's action, and it was not until after the founding of the Bank of England in 1693 that borrowing and lending on reasonable terms became possible. The seven goldsmiths mentioned in the 1706 returns may not have been, as Whitehall was, really bankers, though Wright of Covent Garden certainly was; but they were substantial capitalists. So, too, were the many jewellers and watchmakers included in the lists.

In the parish of St. Ann, Blackfriars, lived a group of workers in the luxury trades. Some had French names, often oddly spelt— Dupile, Boutander, Remier; others were English—Wood, Simons, Bryan. These men were engaged in the making of fans; it was a highly specialized trade, including fan-stickmaking and painting. Twenty-two of the 27 recusants listed in the parish were in the fan business; the others were two button makers, one silversmith, one shoemaker and one 'Glass Scolloper'. In other parishes there resided tailors, hatters and milliners, and a very considerable number of makers of periwigs. There were dancing masters, an embroiderer, a pencil maker, many victuallers and keepers of coffee-houses, vintners, a 'brandy-man' and a 'strong water man' —in fact, Catholics are represented in most trades.

These people were all known to the parsons and churchwardens as recusants, but there is no evidence that any action followed on the reports. Nor, probably, were the lists complete. Not many comments were made; R. Ashley, a tailor in Wapping, was described as 'a poor and very harmless man', and R. Morphey was 'master of a merchant ship.' This last occupation might have seemed potentially dangerous to the government, as it gave opportunities for communication with Catholic centres abroad. A stage coach driver might also have been useful to priests; but now the authorities were not worrying overmuch, it seems, or they might have prevented the Edgerleys of Romayne's Court in Oxfordshire from acting as carriers between Oxford and London.[2]

The most dangerous of all trades for Catholics was, from the point of view of the English government and from that of their own security, the printing, publishing and distribution of books. There can have been little monetary gain for the men who produced and imported Catholic works of devotion and controversy

---

[1] Payne, J. O., *Records of English Catholics 1715* (1889), p. 10.
[2] Stapleton, B., *Post-Reformation Catholic Missions* (1906), p. 267.

during the years of active persecution, yet they were to be found in many parts of the country, and Papist literary output was considerable.[1] Although many suffered imprisonment, the pillory, even a traitor's death—as did William Carter in 1584[2]—a Yorkshireman in 1581 was able to buy a Catholic Catechism from a barrow at a fair in Beverley.[3] The Countess of Arundel acted as agent for the priests she assisted; she employed a printer called Charlewood. He was in sufficiently good repute to be granted the valuable monopoly of printing play bills, and probably assisted in erecting the press on which Southwell's works were produced.[4]

William Wrench had part of his press destroyed in Whitefriars in 1597, as the Stationers' Company discovered that he had been 'printinge papisticall bookes'. He moved to Staffordshire where he set up a press, but went back to London where he was frequently indicted for recusancy between 1605 and 1611. It was only natural that some of these printers and publishers should emigrate to France or the Netherlands, where they could be of more permanent use. There were plenty of available presses, but a good deal of technical help was needed in seeing English works through the hands of foreign printers. In 1603 John Heigham went over to Douay, whence he smuggled Catholic books into England—a letter to him from an English Jesuit complaining that part of an order had not been fulfilled was intercepted by Cecil's agents in 1604. He was quite well known to the government; in 1609 he sent his wife over with 'seditious' books written by Jesuits. She was captured, but as she was a Frenchwoman from Arras she only 'remayned XV days in the pursuivants keeping' and was then released. During the years when King James's negotiations with Spain and France led to a slackening in the persecution of Catholics in England, Heigham published and exported a considerable number of works.[5]

Outstanding among the English publishers was Richard Verstegen. He came from a Dutch family which had settled in London; for four years he was a sizar at Christ Church, Oxford, but as a Catholic he could not take his degree. When he came back to London he worked for a time with a goldsmith, and learned the

[1] See Allison and Rogers, *A Catalogue of Catholic Books printed . . . 1558–1640* (1956). Specimens of these publications will be found in Southerne, A. C., *Elizabethan Recusant Prose*, and Guiney, L. I., *Recusant Poets*.

[2] C.R.S., V, pp. 8, 30, 39.

[3] Aveling, H., *Post Reformation Catholicism in E. Yorkshire*, E. Y. Local History Series, No. 11 (1960), p. 31.

[4] Devlin, C., *Robert Southwell*, p. 141.

[5] *Recusant History*, Vol. 4, No. 6 (1958). Article on Heigham by A. F. Allison.

art of engraving. Then he set up as a publisher in association with a printer, Thomas East, another Papist. In 1582 he was responsible for the production of the account of Campion's martyrdom; when this was discovered, he escaped to France. In Paris in 1583 he published an account in French of the persecution of Catholics in England; the English ambassador got him arrested, but William Allen secured his release. After visiting Rome and again Paris, he settled down in 1587 in Antwerp.

He worked for very many years as a publisher, seeing books through the press, often illustrating them with engravings, translating and himself writing several works. Like other Catholic exiles, he was granted a pension by the King of Spain; like them, he suffered from the irregularity or non-payment of the income he had been promised. His most successful effort was the production of a *Primer or Office of the Blessed Virgin*; this continued to be sold, in various editions, all through the penal times. In 1612 he secured a licence to import English cloth; this not only gave him a steady profit but also a regular means of communication with England. Verstegen was constantly corresponding with Catholics in England and in various European towns. He kept Father Persons and others informed of events in London; he was even able to secure the texts of acts of parliament and of proclamations. In fact, in all sorts of ways he may be counted as a major figure in the Catholic resistance movement. He lived to see many changes in England and on the continent, for he was 90 years old when he died in 1640.[1]

By the end of the seventeenth century there were numerous Papist printers and booksellers in London and in the provinces. When Nathaniel Thompson purchased his entry into the Stationers' Company in 1669, he had already openly acknowledged that he was a Catholic 'and thanks to God for it'. At first he had a partner, but from 1678 to 1687 he worked independently, and about a quarter of his whole output was definitely Papist. In 1678 he published 30,000 copies of a Catechism; this led to his arrest, but he was released on bail. When he was in trouble again in 1680 he was sufficiently prosperous to be able to offer bail in £1,000. Even when he dared to print attacks on Oates and his Popish Plot, he escaped with a fine of £100 and an appearance in the pillory. When he died in 1687 his wife carried on his business for a time. He ignored 'the wrath of the State and the scorn of his Guild. With resolution and courage Nathaniel Thompson pursued his trade, his faith and his conviction.'[2]

[1] C.R.S., LII, Verstegen Papers.
[2] *The Library*, September 1955. Article on Thompson by L. Rostenberg.

James II was a great buyer of books; large sums appear in his secret service accounts[1] as paid to booksellers. Catholic books were naturally bought, for distribution to the bishops, sometimes from men who were not themselves Papists, like Robert Scott, whose bills came to £76 14s. in 1688 and £199 1s. next year. James ordered a special work, an *Assurance of Abbey and other Church lands to the Possessors*, from Henry Hills, who sometimes made a show of Catholicism; he was paid £50 13s. for the publication, but as a result his shop was wrecked in the riots that followed James's flight. Catholic books and pamphlets ordered from Robert Brant cost over £1,000. That the last Stewart king was not a narrow bigot, and that he felt he had a duty to the national church, was shown by his arranging for a supply of Bibles and books of Common Prayer to be sent to the 'Plantations of Virginia and New England' at a cost of £139 15s. 11d. Almost as much was spent on Bibles for Jamaica.

Though Thomas Meighan of Drury Lane was not included in the 1706 returns of Papists in London, as were James Gardener in Cary Street and Thomas Metcalf in Drury Lane, he was by 1717 well established as a publisher of Catholic literature. In that year he produced an edition of Verstegen's *Primer of the Blessed Virgin* with additional matter so voluminous that the book contained no fewer than 560 pages; there were litanies, summaries of doctrine, prayers for various occasions, hymns, 'the Manner how to Serve at Mass', and a calendar with a table of feast-days for the years 1714–40.[2]

A remarkable feature of this volume is the inclusion of a catalogue of other publications, a substantial list of books of devotion, instruction and controversy, varying in price from 8s. 6d. to 2d. A surprising feature for a publication of 1717 is the inclusion of a Life of James II (at 2s.) and an Oration on him (price 8d.). Meighan's activity was known to the government; in 1745 Thomas Wells, writing to the Duke of Newcastle, referred to 'treasonable libels' printed by Iles, a Papist in Wild Street: 'he is constantly employ'd by one Mayam, a Papist and noted Bookseller in Drury Lane, whose shop (its said) is daily frequented by the most wealthy Papists, Priests in particular'.[3]

Meighan dealt in all sorts of books. There is a bill of his among the archives of the Constables of Burton Constable, now in the record office at Beverley; the total of £3 6s. 6d. included the

---

[1] Camden Society, 1851.

[2] The copy I have seen belongs to Mr. F. B. Smith, 166 Victoria Road, Swindon.

[3] P.R.O., George II S.P.D., MS. Calendar, SP/37/77, No. 22.

supplement to Dugdale's *Monasticon* and the continuation of
the *Philosophical Transactions* as well as a controversial book at 2s.
In 1773 he wrote to Cuthbert Constable, who liked his books to
be nicely bound, but wanted to have the latest publications:
'There is no more than 2 voll of Foggs Letters published so as to
be bound and there is non of the Grubstreet Papers printed in
any other size or form but as they first came out in Broad Sheets.'

Several of the books of Bishop Challoner were published by
Meighan; it is not known whether it was he or one of the many
other printers of Catholic devotional books who first produced
his famous prayer book, *The Garden of the Soul*. This work was
constantly reprinted, in the provinces as well as in London; the
modern versions have been very much added to and altered.
The vicar apostolic's translation of the Bible, and his many other
histories, books of devotion and of controversy, were printed by
various firms. After Meighan's death another Catholic publisher,
Coghlan, bought his stock and continued his business. One
remarkable publication was the *Laity's Catholic Directory*, which
from the 1760s gave the sort of information which had brought
rewards for priest-catchers in earlier times. Needham, of Holborn,
was producing controversial works in 1755; in fact, the demand
for books by English Catholics was so great that Bishop Challoner
worked day and night to supply them, and their sale was a steady
and profitable undertaking. Gone for ever were the days of secret
presses and smuggled Testaments and prayer books. Many of the
gentry were stocking their libraries, as their neighbours did, with
expensively bound books; Richard Arundell of Lanherne bought
in 1717 an abridgement of the Statutes of the Realm and also,
very wisely, a dictionary of legal terms; perhaps his bookseller,
R. Lewis, was a Catholic, as W. Lewis certainly was; but gentlemen by no means confined their dealings to their co-religionists.

Ephemeral pamphlets and broadsheets were issued by all these
printers, both in London and elsewhere. Newspapers were by the
eighteenth century common in the provinces as well as the capital,
and there is an unusual case of a local paper being published by
a Catholic woman. When Christopher Smart, the poet, died in
1771, he left his Papist wife and two daughters without any means
of support; indeed before his death Mrs. Smart had in 1762 been
helped by her stepfather, who owned a newspaper, the *Reading
Mercury*. On his death in 1767 she took control, altering the
name to the *Reading Mercury and Oxford Gazette*. It appeared as
being owned by Anna Maria Smart and Co., and publication continued successfully for in 1923 it celebrated its bicentenary.[1]

[1] C.R.S., XXXII, 120 ff.

On the borderline between tradesmen and 'gentry' came the doctors. There were numbers of Papist apothecaries who sold drugs and often prescribed for their customers, and men who would now hold the rank of physician were frequently called apothecaries. The professional status of doctors had been recognized in 1518 when the College of Physicians was founded; the surgeons had to wait until 1540 before their charter was granted. Both colleges gave licences after examination. But there was no necessity for a man to hold a licence to practise medicine, and training might be had in various ways. Many doctors—after 1559 mainly Catholics—attended the famous medical schools on the continent, especially Padua. Others learned their trade (for as such it was generally regarded) by the usual method of apprenticeship, being taught empirical methods by established practitioners.

Under Elizabeth there were complaints about the College of Physicians, which in 1571 elected as its President John Caius of Cambridge.[1] Five years later it was stated that 'the papistes have constantly occupied the *Cheefe roomes*',[2] which suggests that their influence was considerable. Among the Elizabethan recusants were many doctors, several of whom were imprisoned; in 1582 J. Halsey, a physician of Tewkesbury, was moved from the Fleet prison to the Clink 'bycause the said halsey was a man thought to doe muche harme at the ffleet emongst the Papists there'.[3] Such men, moving as they did among the sick, could do much to assist priests in 'reconciling' those of their patients who had given up the practice of their religion; John Southcote in his *Note Book* (1623–37) included nine physicians in his list of useful English Catholics.[4]

Several younger sons of the landed families became doctors, like Lewis Chichester, of the Chichesters of Arlington; he lived at Cruwys Morchard in Devon and held land, possibly in trust for other members of the family, for he joined with other men in arranging a mortgage in 1649.[5] John Troutbeck, a physician of York, was a friend of the Fairfax family,[6] and another York doctor, P. Vavasour, was rich enough to give a donation of £50 to the Yorkshire clergy fund when it was established in 1660.[7]

[1] See supra. p. 7.

[2] Lansdowne MS., XXI, 123. Quoted by Swan, C., in his unpublished thesis cited supra., p. 18 ff.

[3] C.R.S., II, 223.

[4] C.R.S., I, 116.

[5] Chichester MSS., Exeter City Library, 50/11/17/9.

[6] *Recusant History*, Vol. 4, No. 2, p. 80.

[7] Rev. Vincent Smith, unpublished History of Yorkshire Clergy Fund.

Richard Lathom, of Aintree near Liverpool, was entered in the 1672 list of recusants convict as a husbandman; he was in fact a surgeon and of good standing in local society. He had a chapel in his house, and in 1686 his wife got a licence to keep the school she had already started, which had led to her prosecution.[1] Among his friends were the Blundells of Crosby Hall; on 2 July 1703, when Nicholas Blundell was on his way home with his bride, he arranged to meet Lathom and was 'treated by him in ye Rode'.[2] In 1713 he sent his coach to carry the doctor's body to the grave, and acted as one of the executors of his will. One of Blundell's sisters married another physician, one of the Gerards of Garswood.

The professional status of Catholic doctors was possibly affected when in 1679 Parliament ordered the College of Physicians to eject all Papists. It was not until after the Revolution of 1689 that the college sent to the House of Lords a list of its members who were 'Papists, reputed Papists, or Criminals'. Five well-known men were deprived of their privileges as members; one had been physician to James II's Queen; another, Charles Conquest, was ranked among the leaders of his profession.

The expulsion did not prevent their continuing in practice, and all through the eighteenth century there were numbers of Papist doctors. In 1707 there were in Liverpool three brothers from Lancaster of an old Catholic family; one was a grocer who gave a home to a priest, one was captain of a merchant ship, and the third a doctor.[3] Edward Charleton, who had taken a degree in medicine, was the son of a landowner in Northumberland; he was among the prisoners taken at Preston in 1715.[4] A relative of the Welds of Lulworth was reported in 1760 to be aiming at a medical career; Clementina Jones wrote to Edward Weld, who was at school in Rheims, 'our cousin Berkley is gone to Edinburgh to finish his studies & will make such a Physician as you or I shall, but such is ye scheme'.[5] Walter Blount studied 'with a view to the practice of Medicine, but his brother dying in 1765 he succeeded to his estates' and the baronetcy.[6]

This 'practice of medicine' seems to have served as a social bridge in the eighteenth century between the middle classes and the landed aristocracy. Professional men were still regarded as

[1] C.R.S., VI, 129.

[2] Blundell, M., *Blundell's Diary* (Liverpool, 1952), p. 15.

[3] C.R.S., IX, 181.

[4] Kirk, J., *Biographies of English Catholics 1700–1800* (London, 1909), p. 43.

[5] Weld MSS. at Dorset County Record Office.   [6] Kirk, op cit., p. 29.

inferior members of a society which in England maintained fairly
rigid class distinctions. So few, however, were the employments
open to the younger sons of Catholic families that many of them
were forced into an occupation which the advance of science was only
gradually making 'respectable'.

13

MARRIAGE, PROPERTY AND THE LAW

The marriages of the sons and daughters of English Catholic landowners normally followed the pattern of the society in which they lived; they were carefully planned by parents and relations; romance played no part in them. Exceptions were to be found, for example among the members of the Vaux family, who were strong individualists. When William, Lord Vaux, was released from prison[1] in 1583 he tried to 'advance my house by some good marriage' and was 'offered a very worshipful match and no small portion of money for my son'. George Vaux refused the match, and insisted on marrying Elizabeth Roper, the granddaughter of St. Thomas More. His father disinherited him. Merill Vaux was as disobedient as her brother; in 1597 she was living with the Treshams, who were arranging a match for her; she was 27 years old and wanted her own way, so she secretly married the man of her choice, a member of the Tresham household.[2]

The normal procedure was that, after a bargain had been struck between two families, the prospective bridegroom was sent to woo his lady. Sometimes he was still very young, as was the William Blundell of Crosby when in 1635 at the age of 15 he went to Haggerston in Northumberland, 'a pretty straight young thing, all dashing in scarlet'.[3] Anne Haggerston and he went over the border into Scotland for their wedding, for greater security, and their union proved very happy.

Later Blundells paid more heed to their children's wishes, not always with the best results. William's daughter, Emilia, fell in love with a young Irishman, Richard Butler, the son of Lord Mountgarret. He had come to Crosby with her father when they had been released from prison in Liverpool. The parents on both sides were anxious for their children to marry 'well'; Richard

---

[1] See supra, p. 36.
[2] Anstruther, *Vaux of Harrowden*, pp. 205, 233.
[3] Blundell, M., *Cavalier*, p. 4.

Butler was penniless and in debt, and the Blundells had had to pay heavy fines to the Commonwealth. So Emilia was sent away to stay with relations, and William Blundell got her suitor's debts paid so that he could leave Crosby, though 'on foot and with twenty shillings in his purse'. But three years later, in 1661, he reappeared 'in a most distressed and indigent state'. The lovers got their way and married, but Lord Mountgarret ignored his son's existence for five years. Emilia's father, who had had to spend about £22 on the bridegroom's clothes, now had to support her and her husband and children. When they did return to Ireland, they constantly wrote for help, and sent two of their children to Crosby to be brought up and educated. Even after Richard Butler succeeded to the title in 1679 they were extremely poor. Emilia died, worn out, in 1682.[1]

William Blundell's grandson, Nicholas, succeeded to the Crosby estates in 1702.[2] He was then 33, and so far all attempts to secure a wealthy wife for him had failed. Now he determined to do well for himself and the family property. 'Many Ladyes,' he wrote, a week after his father's funeral, 'have been proposed with fifteen Hundred Pounds', but he hoped for more. It was probably a Jesuit priest who conducted the negotiations that led to his receiving the news in April 1703 that 'I might wate on Mrs Frances Langdale as soon as I pleased'. So the wooer set off, with his chaplain and servants, for Oxfordshire.

On 19 April Nicholas first met his intended wife; two days later he 'discoursed Mrs Frances Langdale in the Kitchen Garden', and on the 28th he gave her a diamond ring. When the engaged couple went for walks, the chaplain accompanied them. It was a good match for Nicholas Blundell, who was to get £2,000 in instalments, and his wife was assured of an income of £100 should she be left a widow. An aunt also gave her £100 a year, so she went to her husband well provided. The marriage took place on 17 June; the ceremony was performed by a secular priest, but the parish church bells were rung and the parson got 10s. 9d. for his dues.

Nicholas brought his wife to Crosby, and then they went on pilgrimage to Holywell. Frances did not prove a perfect wife; she quarrelled with her husband's female relatives, was usually on bad terms with her servants, and finally got the chaplain turned out of the house, so that a new dwelling had to be built for him. Nor did she provide a male heir; only daughters were born at Crosby. Of these, the eldest, Mary, usually called Mally, gave

[1] Blundell, M., *Cavalier*, pp. 84 ff, 120 ff.
[2] Blundell, M., *Blundell's Diary* (Liverpool, 1952), passim.

trouble over her matrimonial affairs. She seems to have been a wilful lass; after being at school abroad till she was 18 she said that she would be a nun. Her father suggested that she should see something of society before making up her mind, and pledged himself not to force her into marriage against her will. Suitors appeared, some most eligible, but Mally hesitated and refused one after the other. Her father apologized, but said, "Tis but reason Mally should be left entirely to her own Choyce'. At last she decided upon an Irishman, John Coppinger, whose father had sent him to England to secure an heiress. Her sister Fanny married Henry Peppard (or Pippard) of a Liverpool family of merchants;[1] her wedding, in 1733, seems to have been a simple one compared with Mally's, and her father's wedding present to her was a dictionary costing 17s. 6d.

Another marriage of which details survive was that of Sir Francis Throckmorton.[2] The negotiations were carried on by his steward. He first met his bride-to-be in London, when he was 18; her mother brought her up from Surrey, and he came down from Warwickshire. She was Anne Monson, the sole heiress of her father Sir William, and an excellent match. Though the month was November and Cromwell had just died, the engaged couple and their relatives were able to enjoy a gay time in London, including a visit to the Opera. Six months later the marriage was celebrated in London. Sir Francis wanted to take his wife home in style, and ordered a new coach; but the vehicle was not ready in time, so the return to Coughton Court was neither as comfortable nor as splendid as he had hoped. However, the villagers turned out to greet the bride, and the bells of the parish church rang peals of welcome. That the lord of the manor was a Papist did not matter at all.

Sir Francis's good fortune in securing a fine estate as his wife's dowry was not exceptional. In many of the Catholic families the direct line in 'tail male' failed in the eighteenth century, and women inherited the property. Occasionally, to preserve the family name, the husband took that of his wife, or a daughter's son might change his name when he inherited. It was the duty of every eldest son to marry and ensure the succession, unless he chose to become a priest, when his next brother took over the estate and the obligation. When Sir Carnaby Haggerston succeeded his grandfather, his kinsmen busied themselves to find him a suitable bride. Edward Haggerston wrote to his uncle Sir Marmaduke Constable in June 1720 on the subject: 'I would

---

[1] Supra, p. 175.

[2] Barnard, E., *A Seventeenth Century Country Gentleman*, Chap. IV.

willingly persuade Sir Carnaby . . . to go to York races, if Mrs. Fairfax or any other person were there, that might be thought a proper lady for him & might be seen thereby, it might not be impossible to prevail with him to go to them, thinking the sooner he is settled the better.'[1] He chose Elizabeth Middleton, and his son Tommy was born in 1722.[2] When in his turn Thomas went courting, in 1745, the first attempt was a failure; he took with him not only his Jesuit chaplain but a number of other helpers, with the result that, as Sir Marmaduke Constable wrote, 'so many, and almost all strangers, was enough to discompose a young lady.'

It was not until 1754 that Tommy married Mary Silvertop of Minsteracres, whose kinsman had done well in the coal trade.[3] Widowers too were urged to remarry; when Cuthbert Constable, of Tunstall and Burton Constable, lost his wife, a friend wrote to him that, as he had only one son, he was 'not suprised at yr Friends Sollicitations to re-enter ye holy state; you owe ye world a young Tunstall or two, and at least 3 sons to Burton'. For the sake of the family and 'some zeal for ye Catholick cause', he ought not to remain long 'without a good lady'.[4]

Sometimes duty pointed in one direction and inclination in another. Thomas Weld wrote in 1771 to his brother Edward:

> You will be glad perhaps to know what I think of Miss Massey; I think she is a very sensible, lively, good natured, vertuous young lady. She is just turned 19 her face is plain & marked with the small pox, she looks very healthy and strong she has a number of very pretty accomplishments. . . . If you wish me happily settled. . . . I dare say it is a thing that may be brought about very agreeably.[5]

But the wedding did not take place.

Probable marriages between members of leading Catholic families were a happy source of speculation to gossiping ladies. Mrs. Winifred Stonor wrote a letter to Richard Arundell in August 1719 telling him of the latest news and giving a vivid description of a wooing:

> Mr Fuller of Sussex makes up to Lady Falconbridge, he is come down to Richmond and has brought a preist with him to make him more acceptable, he is resolved to get ye widdow and follows her everywhere, if he be denyed going up Staires he setts at ye dore till Twelve at night but he will stay till ye Lady comes out, she visits no

[1] Transcript of MSS., Ampleforth Abbey.
[2] See supra, p. 158.   [3] See supra, p. 173.
[4] East Riding Record Office, Beverly. MSS. 146, Box 310.
[5] Weld MSS., Dorset Record Office.

body but has all ye Court Ladyes at Hazard two or three times a week.

If, as seems likely, the lady was the widow of Lord Fauconberg, who died in 1718, she was a matrimonial prize, for he owned land in many counties. The Arundell family were themselves very successful matchmakers; the fifth Lord Arundell's wife brought him valuable property in London. Wardour Street and Arundel Street bear witness to the connection, though the land was sold long ago. His son secured a bride with an income of £1,000 as well as a capital of £8,000.[1]

Until the Act of 1753[2] these marriages were generally recognized as valid in law. The Archbishop of Canterbury even issued a licence for the wedding of Lord Petre to Anna Maria Radcliffe in 1732 'by reason of their both being under age';[3] yet both were known to be Catholics—indeed, she was the daughter of the Earl of Derwentwater who had been executed for his share in the 1715 rebellion. 'Mixed' marriages, between a Catholic and a Protestant, were disliked by the clergy of both churches; on both sides it was feared that a member might be lost to the other flock. Rome had always discouraged such unions, and still does; if both husband and wife take their faith seriously, there can be no spiritual harmony to support them in their life together. Bishop Leyburn, who became vicar apostolic in 1685, always refused to conduct a 'mixed marriage' ceremony; he said that it was 'consenting to profane a sacrament'.[4] The condition was always made that the Protestant partner should promise that all children of the union should be brought up as Catholics; but as long as Catholics were under so many disabilities, the danger that such a vow would be broken was obvious. Sometimes the sons followed their father's religion, while the mother reared her daughters in her own faith. Even a parson, when his Catholic wife died, sent his daughter to her mother's parents to be brought up as a Catholic.[5] Often one of the spouses joined the church of the other; among people of property, it was more likely to be the Catholic who surrendered. A good deal, however, depended on circumstances as well as on the strength of character and conviction of the Papist partner. In places where Catholicism was strong, as at Egton, pressure was considerable. There Parson

---

[1] Arundell MSS. at Wardour Castle.   [2] See supra, p. 126.
[3] Petre MSS., Colchester Record Office, F/1/83.
[4] Hemphill, B., *Early Vicars Apostolic*, p. 15, footnote.
[5] Teversham, T. F., *History of Sawston*, Pt. II. Privately published 1947, p. 124.

Robinson reported to the Archbishop of York, in 1765, that a Protestant wife 'tels me she could not live a quiet life till she consented to become a Papist.'[1] Many examples can be found in which the husband was received into the Catholic church some time after the wedding.

Most Catholic priests felt it their duty to perform the maimed rites of matrimony between a Protestant and a Papist; almost every surviving Catholic register includes records of some such weddings. In that of St. Peter's, Lancaster, there is one rather touching entry for the year 1805:

> Nov. 22nd. Confirmed this day the natural contract which for many years had existed between John Winder and Anne Byron, both being in extreme old age & infirm & utterly incapable of facing the expence of a marriage at church, & in order to prevent scandal and put some sort of plaster on an old sore, married them according to the rite of our Church though against my principles relative to the marriage of Protestants & Catholics, sacrificing in this single instance to the opinion of those who think differently. by me. J. Rigby.

A marginal note was added: 'N.B. Anne Winder afterwards became a Catholic.'[2]

One such marriage, at the end of the eighteenth century, could not have been a very happy one for the Catholic wife. Captain Farquharson, a wealthy seaman engaged in trade with China, fell in love with Mary Vinn, who was employed as a servant in a bank. They were married at the Catholic chapel in Winchester, but did not go through the additional ceremony in the parish church. After a while, the Captain began to think that he might have made a better match. The story is recorded among the archives of what is now the Diocese of Portsmouth.[3]

'He arranged to marry the daughter of another Captain, and had to pay many thousands to appease the father's disappointment. While from home he always left spies to watch her but could not find anything against her. Although of a most violent temper he was very fond of her but when trying to get rid of her would call her Miss Polly.' . . . 'Mrs. Farquharson was always in terror until dinner was over, at times he would kick the butler downstairs and stuff a ten pound note in his mouth. He woud rise at three or four in the morning and throw handfuls of silver to the scavengers in the street.' The captain does not seem to have kept his wife short of money, for she contributed £2 2s. a year to the Catholic church in Winchester for her seat rent. She fell ill with cancer,

[1] Bishopthorpe MSS., York, Bundle 5.
[2] C.R.S., XX, 135.　　[3] C.R.S., XLII, 150, 175.

and died in London in 1829. Her husband had her buried in the Catholic cemetery at Winchester; he paid for a wall to be built round it, and put up a lodge which he endowed. 'He was very anxious to be buried with her and tried all the catholic bishops in England but without success. . . . From his bedroom he could see her tomb and used to say My Angel can see what I am doing this would be while he was doing so much for her family.' On her tombstone he inscribed the following lines:

> A friend yea more than a friend a wife rests here
> And sad remembrance claims the tribute tear
> By nature kind with every gift endued
> That tends to form the just the wise the good
> True to her word in every thought sincere
> Who knew no wish but that the world might hear
> To name her virtues ill befitts my grief
> What was my bliss can NOW give no relief
> A husband mourns the rest let friendship tell
> All owned her worth her HUSBAND knew it well
> Peace to her gentle soul and endless rest
> Blest in her genius in her faith too blest.

It seems that in the end this highly temperamental sea captain fully appreciated his wife. It would, however, have been possible for him to repudiate her had he not written a letter in which he acknowledged the marriage; perhaps even this would not have been good at law.

Many Catholic marriages were technically invalid, but great care was taken to ensure that the weddings of the wealthy were properly registered. Often they were entered in the parish register; when the incumbent got his dues he was generally willing to make the official entry, and after 1753 two ceremonies were arranged. In 1799 one of these double weddings took place in the Jerning-hams' London house; the Bishop of Exeter 'married them in the Dining Room', and an hour later 'arrived the Archbishop of Narbonne and he performed with great dignity below in the Parlour'.[1]

Almost invariably settlements involving the transfer of land or payments of income accompanied such weddings; the wife was secured, should she become a widow, and when children were born it was not unusual to provide for them by a settlement of land. To have legal obligations attached to property was definitely advantageous for a Catholic landowner; even if all those interested were Papists the authorities would be involved in several separate actions if they wished to levy fines or sequester land, so the

[1] *Jerningham Letters*, Vol. I, p. 151.

chances of escape were increased. Protestant friends often acted as trustees in marriage settlements, sometimes even being nominal owners. A document among the Petre archives[1] shows the plan at work. The date is 1713, and the parties concerned are referred to by initials only; this safeguard is not unusual. J.N., the husband, died two years after his wedding; his widow, K., was still legally an 'infant' under 21, but was named sole executrix in her husband's will. His estate had been 'placed out at Interest upon Bonds and Mortgages . . . in the hands of some friends.' £10,000 had been paid in ready money as security for the wife's marriage portion 'to which the Protestant ffriends before mencioned were prive and consenting'. The question was asked of counsel, Did this dowry form part of the estate? The opinion given was that it did not, for as the widow was not yet of age she could not legally acquire her jointure.

On such points the services of sympathetic lawyers were most valuable. Until the Disabling Act of 1696, which prevented Catholics from being called to the bar, many barristers were Papists: the Inns of Court had several Catholic members throughout the penal times. Not only in London were there qualified men ready to help their co-religionists; for example, a succession of lawyers in the Needham family was active in drawing up deeds and conveyances in the border country beween Wales and England.[2] Important transfers and serious problems were, however, usually submitted to men who were constantly occupied in the central courts, and the services of skilful lawyers, trained in the tradition of More and Plowden, were in demand not only by Catholics. Langhorne, who, like many other innocent men, was executed during the fever of the Popish Plot,[3] did business all over the country. When the act of 1696 was passed, a group of Protestant clients presented a petition that John Wolfe should be exempted and allowed to continue his practice at the bar; he was a man of standing, from an Oxfordshire family, and was brother-in-law to Lord Petre.[4]

Another famous lawyer was the Irishman Denis Molony.[5] He was already 38 years old when he joined Gray's Inn in 1687 and was the 'only person of his country and principle' to remain studying law in England after the Revolution. He was about to be called

---

[1] D/DP F. 102, Essex Record Office.

[2] C.R.S., IX, 163.   [3] See supra, p. 101.

[4] Stapleton, *Post-Reformation Catholic Missions*, p. 259.

[5] C.R.S., II, 312. Molony's name was spelt in many ways by his clients and by officials; in the 1706 returns he appears as Belone.

OCE

to the bar when the 1696 act was passed; he petitioned Parliament to exempt him, but in vain. He stayed on in practice 'under the bar'. Men like him had chambers in one of the Inns of Court, where they could be consulted and could draw up deeds and conveyances, though they could not plead. In 1710 he gave wise advice to Richard Arundell of Lanherne, whose cousin was thinking of presenting a petition to Parliament:

> Little do these people that talk so foolishly know how cautious a Roman Catholicke must be att this time of day who complains in print of ye proceedings of one Parliamt to another Parliamt & expects to be relieved, if he does not take care he may meet with punishment instead of Redress, it is no subject for Romancing or flourishing.[1]

There were a number of men like Molony whose ability and learning were recognized. Had they been willing to conform, they might have attained high rank in their profession, but loyalty to their faith prevented them from reaping the full harvest of their reputation. Nathaniel Pigott[2] had been called to the bar before 1696; his knowledge of law led many Protestant young men to come to him as pupils. Another conveyancer, Mannock Strickland, who was employed by many prominent families, including the Petres, Constables and Jerninghams, bore witness to Pigott's eminence when he wrote in 1723 that Lord Petre had told him at the Duke of Norfolk's that he

> spoke to his Grace about employing me for his Counsel. His Grace said that he had just agreed with Mr Pigott upon the same terms as the last Duke had. His Lordship said he did not recommend me with a view to displacing Mr Pigott but that if Mr Pigott should fail his Grace would then employ me. To which his Grace answered, he would, as thinking me an honest man and a good Lawyer.

In another memorandum, Strickland again referred to Pigott. His cousin George's sister was getting married to Mr. Constable, and he hoped to draw up the marriage settlement. He found that it had been arranged for Pigott to do the work. If he were not able to undertake it, then 'he would take effectual care that I should be re-employed in all the Affairs of the family.'[3]

James Booth was another recusant famous among lawyers; he has been called 'the patriarch of the modern school of conveyancers.'[4] William Murray, afterwards Lord Mansfield, who became Lord Chief Justice in 1765, learned his law from Booth;

---

[1] Arundell MSS., Wardour Castle.   [2] Or Pigot, or even Picket.
[3] Bodleian MS., D. D. Blount e 52.
[4] O'Sullivan, R., article in *The Catholic Lawyer*, New York, January 1957.

it was natural therefore that he should show in court sympathy for Catholics. One brilliant Catholic conveyancer followed another. Duane had Lord Eldon as his pupil; Charles Butler's edition of the great textbook 'Coke upon Littleton' was in constant use. He was the first Catholic to be called to the bar when the act of 1791 removed the obnoxious oath.

A principal duty of all these learned men was to find ways of evading the consequences of Catholicism. Assistance for those charged before the courts was, by the seventeenth century, possible as it had not been in the sixteenth. In 1641 Dame Joan Vaughan, widow, of Kinnersley in Herefordshire, was indicted for harbouring a priest, John Broughton, who was nominally her steward. Her son John was in London; he had himself been listed as a recusant and threatened with prosecution. He wrote to the judge who was conducting the assizes at which his mother would be charged, saying, 'there is not any prooffe more than the prosecutors owne that the said Broughton is a priest'. In fact Broughton had already been charged and sentenced to outlawry, though he had not actually been tried, as he had escaped capture. Moreover, wrote John Vaughan, his mother, 'whoe is a very weake and sickley gentlewoman', ought to be allowed time to prepare her defence. Counsel's opinion was obtained from Henry Rolle, who gave full instructions for the defence. The main points were: 'They must Prove Broughton to be a Priest'. That he had been outlawed, in his absence, was no proof that he was; unless the prosecution could show documents—and, if they did, they must be asked if they could read Latin—or produce a witness who had actually been present when Broughton said Mass, there was no valid evidence. Second, they must prove that he was English, not born in Scotland or overseas; everyone knew that he was a Shropshire man, but in those days firm evidence was not easy to obtain. Third, how did they know that Dame Joan was aware that he was a priest and had been outlawed? 'These or anie one of these Lefte out are suffitiente to quash the Indictmente'. As a result of her son's activity, the Lord Chief Justice withdrew the warrant for the lady's arrest, and Charles I issued a mandate to prevent the execution of any penalty were she in fact tried and found guilty. The case is of interest, for many points raised by counsel were used successfully in later trials, when it was no longer easy to get direct intervention from the king.[1]

Another ingenious device was to challenge the accuracy of the indictment if the name of the accused were misspelt. That this was often effective is shown by an entry in the register of the

[1] C.R.S., XIII, 150 ff.

Privy Council on 21 December 1679. The Attorney-General was ordered to examine the lists of Popish recusants 'that there may be no false Spelling, or misnomer, or any other Errour that may impede or delay the prosecution of the sayd persons therein mentioned unto Conviction.'[1] The old complaint was repeated a month later, that 'by the favour & conivance of their Neighbours, or by ye abuse of officers' many Papists 'have escaped unpunished & very few of them are returned convicted'; those who are 'have found means by secret Conveyances of their Estates to protect themselves from any considerable forfeitures.'[2]

To escape formal conviction as a recusant was very important for a man of property who might be involved in a civil law case. Richard Arundell of Lanherne was appointed by Mrs. Creagh, a well-to-do widow, as her sole executor and residuary legatee, and on her death had to prove her will. On 10 February 1718 the lawyer Edward Webb wrote to him, 'from ye Person I have Imployed in Doctrs Commons to procure you the Probat, I find Mr. Stephen Creagh the Mercht has entered a Caveat, pretending himself to be next of kin to ye deceased, and designs I presume to give you all ye trouble Imaginable & perhaps may pretend to get you Convictd of Recusancy, in order to render you incapable to take upon you ye Executorship'. He thought it a pity that Mrs. Creagh had not appointed a Protestant friend as co-executor.

Fortunately Creagh did not accuse Arundell of being a recusant, but he did claim that some of the legacies in the will were for 'superstitious uses'. It is by no means unlikely that Mrs. Creagh intended Richard Arundell to use some of her money to help priests; one priest did write to him saying that she had given him money for a vestment, and asked that from her estate help should be given to his own 'Dr Mother' and other poor widows. The lawyer advised that Creagh should be bought off; it seems likely that this was done, for Arundell got his commission to administer the estate.[3] Such difficulties were likely to occur over wills; frequently testators left secret codicils or private letters to their nominal heirs stating the 'superstitious uses' on which their money should be spent; occasionally such instructions were inserted in the will.

Protestant executors and trustees were very useful, and often employed. The case of Mrs. Fenwick, however, made public the weakness of the legal position of Catholics. She was an heiress who had married for love a Protestant, who was burdened with

[1] Public Record Office. Privy Council Register 68, p. 335.
[2] Ibid, pp. 367–8.   [3] Arundell MSS., Wardour Castle.

debt. On their marriage in 1752 she made over her property to him to help him out of his troubles; he tried to have it re-conveyed to her, but there was difficulty in finding a legal way of transferring land to a Catholic. In 1757, before he succeeded in doing it, he was killed out hunting, and his brother, Thomas Fenwick, a lawyer, laid claim to the estate. An arbitration gave her some relief; she was awarded the use of her house and £250 a year. Her brother-in-law did not pay her the income, so she brought an action against him and was awarded £18,000. Still Thomas Fenwick refused to pay, and her religion made it difficult for her to enforce her rights. She made a personal appeal to the Lord Chancellor, Lord Camden, and in 1772 he obtained a private act of parliament to legalize her claim. This was an effective but costly procedure, and it is quite likely that Mrs. Fenwick's case, and the sympathy it aroused among leading lawyers, was one of the factors which led to the Catholic Relief Act of 1778.[1]

Such victories were rare, and the chief aim of the Catholic lawyers was to keep their clients out of the courts, and by skilful use of their knowledge of the laws of real property to save them from claims, fines and confiscations. In the later seventeenth century Thomas Jackson of Knayton wrote to his wife 'My Dear Hart . . . As for Mr Anthony Meynell . . . I have Rubbed upp my ould experyence and have found out a way and an Invencion how to clear his Land from Sequestration. . . . This is more than I can doe for my self but it is gods goodness to that house for the great good they have done. Wee are now goeing to Councell about it.'[2]

These evasions were made very much more difficult when the act of 1717 ordered all Catholics to register their estates and to report all further acquisitions. Bryan Salvin, when in 1723 he succeeded his father, tried to escape the obligation, but failed. He wrote to Sir Marmaduke Constable: 'I have consulted Rudd and Pigott about Registering, and both say nothing to be done, but to register the real Rent, they are, or shall be let at this next Mayday, tho' advanced since my Father did Register.'[3]

The registers of Papists' estates give valuable information of the extent and distribution of property owned by Catholics; one interesting point is the number of small properties held in various counties by great landowners like the Arundells, the Cliffords and the Webbs. Most of their land lay near their chief seats, even if in another county; in Somerset, for instance,[4] the

---

[1] C.R.S., IV, 322.   [2] Meynell MSS., transcript at Ampleforth Abbey.
[3] Constable MSS., Ampleforth Abbey.
[4] Register Rolls in Somerset Record Office, Taunton.

list of Arundell properties covers three long rolls and parts of others; the Cliffords' land, mostly held on lease, occupies a roll and a half. Lord Waldegrave's Somerset estates fill 19 rolls, and he also registered land in Essex and in Kent; in 1741 Lord Waldegrave conformed, and was thus freed from the onus of recusancy. Charles Fairfax of York had rents worth £60 a year from his wife's Somerset estates.

Many estates are stated to be mortgaged, or burdened with payments due to some person other than the owner. This was one of the ingenious devices employed to escape double taxation. Sir Marmaduke Constable found it to his advantage to borrow money on the security of his land and keep large sums available to lend out to others, or on short term loans 'at call'—that is, on deposit with a merchant or banker who had to repay cash on demand. In 1740 he told Sir Carnaby Haggerston that he had at call '3000 and perhaps 4000', as well as 'a 1000 that I thinke is in my servants hands.' These were enormous sums for a private person to hold as liquid capital in the eighteenth century.[1]

When Catholics succeeded to property under a will, it often brought plenty of work for the lawyers 'under the bar'. In 1728 Bryan Salvin wrote to Sir Marmaduke, 'One Dorrell's business makes a good deal of Noise at least among the Pap. lawyers.' Dorrell, a boy of seven, had inherited an estate from a kinsman, who also bequeathed £1,000 each to three female relatives. 'The Ladys demand their Fortunes, the Trustees make difficulty to pay them, one of the Ladys is a Nun.' The indignant ladies brought an action against the boy 'Posessor', 'upon which they pay the Ladys their £1,000 but refuse paying the Nun' . . . 'saying according to such a statute of superstitious uses, they could not answer the paying of it.' The claimants quoted a recent case in which a special verdict had been given in favour of a Catholic, but this 'the Judge was very tender of, and even the Ladys Counsell say we must be very carefull how it is worded, because it will be trying the case of all the Catholicks of England . . . the Grand question whether a Papist can inherit.'[2]

Several such cases came before the courts in the eighteenth century;[3] but the judges were now wholly independent of the government, since they were appointed for life, and their respect for the faith held by the Catholic lawyers with whom, or even under

[1] Constable MSS., Ampleforth Abbey.
[2] Ibid.
[3] For instance, Mary Evans held land in Wells. She and her heir were both Papist. On her death, Brailsford Hughes claimed the property. See Goddard, W., *An Extract of the Sessions Rolls of Somerset* (1765), pp. 63, 65.

whom, they had learned their law made them sympathetic to the claims of Papist heirs. Tolerance and natural justice often weighed more heavily than the law as set out in the penal statutes, and the way was prepared for their repeal, although political considerations brought this about in a slow and fragmentary fashion. As the friendship of Church Papists had saved the Catholics in the seventeenth century, so did the skill of their lawyers conserve their wealth in the Age of Reason.

14

THE NOBILITY AND GENTRY

The Rev. William Deane of Woolhampton, Berkshire, wrote in 1767 to the Bishop of Salisbury:

As the Papists are, by our Laws, wisely excluded from all lucrative Offices in ye State, & from all high Posts in the Civil, Military or Ecclesiastical Establishments in ye Kingdom (whereby good Estates are often raised) & are exposed to all ye usual ways of Dissipation, arising from Pride & Pomp, indulging expensive Pleasures, Gaming &c as much, if not more than other People; & are also exhausted by secret invisible Drains, They are generally Poor, and their Estates are daily wasting, & consequently their Power decreasing. Sometimes they spend and run out of their Estates; & sometimes Families being extinct, their Estates devolve to Protestants. And when that happens to be ye case, we see all ye Popish dependants soon fall off and disappear. Many such instances, within memory, may be produc'd in this county.[1]

Bishop Challoner would have agreed with the parson's views. Several of the old families had given up the struggle; the Gages of Firle, where he himself had been brought up, had conformed and Thomas Gage had been rewarded with an Irish peerage.[2] Lord Waldegrave and many others did the same. Even in Lancashire 16 Catholic chapels were closed during the late seventeenth and early eighteenth centuries; some of the landowners who had supported them conformed, though often younger branches of the family remained constant to their faith; or the direct line failed and the property passed to Protestants.[3]

In 1737 Bishop Petre prepared a report for Rome on the situation in England. The number of Catholics was diminishing, he said; he ascribed this to the 'apostacy of many nobles', to the ruin of some families after the rising of 1715 and the subsequent prosecutions, and to the extravagant living of others. He blamed his clergy for lack of enthusiasm, and thought that more care

[1] Salisbury Diocesan Archives, Return of Papists, Box 1.
[2] Burton, *Challoner*, Vol. I, p. 68.
[3] C.R.S., VI, 112–243.

should be taken over the selection and training of candidates for
the priesthood.[1]

The 1715 rebellion had certainly made things difficult for many
people. Bishop Giffard was always in sore straits for money;
his imprisonments had been costly and his priests in London were
poor. In 1722 he wrote that he had had to borrow £50, which he
would have to repay as soon as possible, to meet the debts a good
priest had incurred for bare necessities. Lay people also needed
charity; in another letter he said, 'Just as I was writing this, came
to me a Gentlewoman of a very ancient and honble Catholick
family, who, with her sisters, are in a most miserable condition;
so far, that with extraordinary acknowledgements, and tears of
joy, she accepted of half a crown for their relief.'[2]

Robert Carnaby of Durham wrote on 3 September 1720 to
Cuthbert Constable, of Burton Constable, asking his help for
John Collingwood of Eslington, whose land had been confiscated
because his nephew had been convicted for sharing in the rising
of 1715. Collingwood had managed to save £100 and wanted to
lend it to someone for seven years in return for £20 a year. This,
Carnaby knew, was far too high a rate of interest, but he asked
Constable to accept the offer as an act of charity.[3] Many small
landowners were very hard hit when they or members of their
families had paid the penalty for their loyalty to the Stewarts;
the greater proprietors escaped more often than the lesser, for
they had influential friends.

The 'secret invisible drains' mentioned by Parson Deane were
a serious charge on even the largest incomes. The upkeep of
chapels, the support of chaplains and the poor Catholics of the
neighbourhood (a charity often mentioned with disapproval by
the local parsons), the expense of sending children abroad for
education—each of these involved a large annual expenditure.
Sons and daughters who entered religion did to a certain extent
relieve the family budget. A lump sum was usually paid to a nun
for her 'dowry', in return for which her order supported her for
the rest of her life, but this was generally less than a suitor would
have expected as a marriage portion. Sons who became priests
usually surrendered all claim to the family estates except a small
annuity secured on a piece of land. It was the sons who stayed at
home who were a burden.

Henry, sixth Lord Arundell, had large estates but heavy
expenses. He cut down his household to 10 servants; he sold

[1] Burton, *Challoner*, Vol. I, p. 80.
[2] Westminster Cathedral Archives. Series B., File 13, Nos. 130, 134.
[3] Constable MSS., E. Riding Record Office, Beverley. Box 310, MS. 146.

timber, horses and hounds. He allowed his three sons who lived at home £100 a year each, and wrote from Paris in 1740 directing that a doctor in Salisbury who was good at drawing horses should make pictures of the handsomest of the Wardour colts to decorate their chimney-pieces. Yet, as he wrote to his steward, the young men were asking for increased allowances, and were drinking too much strong beer; if this went on, they would have to pay for their beer themselves.[1] Normally, in such families, younger sons were provided for by the transference of some portion of the estates, often those at some distance from the family seat. One therefore finds collateral branches quite widely scattered. Where this was not possible, and no good marriage was available, there was no career open to them save medicine or the law.

Some Catholic landowners had rights and duties connected with the parish churches on their estates: they enforced their claim to burial within the church; they had proprietary rights over an aisle or a chapel; they were responsible for payments to vicars or curates; they received income from alienated tithes. Frances Kennet, widow, of the city of York, registered her property in 1724.[2] For £100 a year she leased from the dean and chapter of Carlisle the rectories and churchyards of Wetherall and Warwick in Cumberland; she got £15 a year rent from the rectories, 10s. for one churchyard, and 6d. for the other. She had to repair the chancel of the 'said church of Wetherall and Warwick', and pay the curate £52 a year. Her profit came from three large barns and tithes amounting to about £300 annually. Such pecuniary rights and responsibilities in connection with parish churches can only have emphasized to their possessors the disadvantages of their own religion; their friends' sons could take orders and enjoy good livings, theirs, if they became priests, were bound to celibacy and comparative poverty. Other careers were open to men whose fathers had political influence; the desire to be on equal terms with their neighbours, to be members of parliament or even justices of the peace, was a strong reason for that abandonment of the faith deplored by Bishop Petre.

Emigration to the new world was considered by Catholics even in the reign of Elizabeth. A plan for a Catholic colony was stopped by the strong opposition, not of the English government which would have been glad to be rid of Papists, but of Spain.[3] Every school child knows that in 1620 the *Mayflower* took a group of

[1] Wardour Archives, box labelled 'Correspondence 1740–1742'.
[2] Huddleston, C. R., article in *Transactions* of Cumberland and Westmorland Antiquarian Society, Vol. LIX, p. 121.
[3] Tenison, E. M., *Elizabethan England*, Vol. IV, p. 252.

Puritans to the inhospitable shores across the Atlantic; few people are aware that in that same year Edmund Plowden, grandson of the great lawyer, settled on Long Island. For years this was known as 'Isle Plowden', but in 1640 family problems forced him to return to England and he was unable to come back to his American home.[1]

In 1621 an enterprising man, George Calvert, tried to found a colony called Avalon in Newfoundland; though in 1625 he became a Catholic, he was nevertheless created Lord Baltimore for his past services. He revisited Avalon between 1629 and 1631, and attempted to start a new plantation further south as a refuge for Catholics. The Virginia company had by then succeeded in establishing about 4,000 settlers, who included several Papists, on and near the coast, and they objected to Calvert's scheme. King Charles gave him a charter to settle lands north of the Potomac River; here in 1633 his son established the colony of Maryland. An English Jesuit went with the first settlers, and another went to Virginia. Besides these main centres, there were English Catholics in other places on the mainland, and in the West Indian islands; in 1684 the chapter of the English clergy noted that 'Care was taken to provide the Catholicks in Jamaica with spiritual help by sending a Pastor thither.'[2]

Richard Langhorne and William Blundell, when in 1666 they were very depressed, both thought of going to Maryland.[3] A grandson of William Blundell did in fact go to Virginia as agent for a merchant, but fell ill and, instead of looking after his business, married a rich widow and went to live in Maryland.[4] The colony developed steadily; no religious tests were imposed, and Puritans from Virginia and Episcopalians from New England found refuge there from their mutual persecutions. Gradually they outnumbered the Catholics; Lord Baltimore's heir conformed in order to regain the estates which had been confiscated, and Anglicanism became the official religion of the colony. Protestant dissenters were tolerated, but not Catholics; they were prohibited from hearing Mass except in private houses, and forbidden to teach. There were, it was calculated, about 16,000 of them, but under these conditions Maryland did not offer a hopeful prospect to the younger sons of Catholic landowners. There was no bishop resident in the Americas: in 1757 Bishop Petre was made responsible for the 'colonies and islands subject

[1] Stapleton, *Post-Reformation Catholic Missions*, p. 310.
[2] Old Brotherhood Papers, Ward's MS.
[3] Blundell, M., *Cavalier*, p. 117.
[4] Blundell, M., *Blundell's Diary*, pp. 39, 46.

to the English crown in America', and this duty fell on his successor, Bishop Challoner.[1] But it was not until the colonies became independent that freedom was secured by Catholics, and, oddly enough, the only Englishman who had any authority in the new Republic of the United States of America was the vicar apostolic for the London district.

The English Army and Navy contained many Catholics as private soldiers and ordinary seamen; priests near the barracks and the naval dockyards were kept busy looking after them. In theory, no Catholic could hold a commission unless he took an oath against his conscience; not until 1793 were Irish officers exempt. The oath was by no means always proffered, even to Protestant officers, and several Catholics evaded it. They were still, however, liable to prosecution and severe penalties; the general oath of loyalty taken by Catholics after 1778 was not sufficient. The situation was generally recognized as preposterous, but the obstinacy of George III prevented a reform.

When invasion by the French was threatened in 1794 prominent Catholics joined their neighbours in offering to raise forces for local defence. Mr. Thomas Corby had striven in vain to get into the British army; he had been trained in a military school in Vienna, but was refused leave even to serve as a volunteer when troops were sent to America. His reputation in Cumberland was high; he wrote that 'a seat in Parliament . . . was offered to me in a very flattering manner, with other advantages, which the law forced me reluctantly to decline.' Mr. Corby formed a volunteer force, the Cumberland Rangers, but could not obtain his heart's desire; he said sadly that his had been an 'inefficient life'.[2] At the other end of the country, a meeting of Devonshire gentry in Exeter decided to raise a troop of horse, and Lord Clifford of Chudleigh was elected its chairman. Two troops were raised of 'gentlemen, yeomen, and other respectable persons'; they had no pay and provided their own horses and uniforms, with the help of £10,000 raised by voluntary subscription. All that the government supplied was arms and ammunition. But Lord Clifford could not hold a commission. In 1798 he therefore formed a purely private force, at his own expense, of men from Chudleigh; he was captain, and appointed his own lieutenant and a cornet. This little group joined in the field days and exercises of the Devonshire Yeomanry; it was believed locally that the French were afraid of these active men and that therefore no invasion was attempted. On the Peace of Amiens in 1802 Lord Clifford was presented with a silver tray

---

[1] Burton, *Challoner*, Vol. II, p. 128.

[2] Quoted by Gwynn, D., *The Second Spring* (1944), p. 11.

by the subscribers to the defence fund, and the officers of the
yeomanry gave him a silver urn in recognition of his valuable
services. A portrait exists in which he appears with these testi-
monials to his popularity; he is wearing the uniform of his own
force which he had designed himself—a long blue coat with buff
collar and cuffs and silver buttons and braid, white knee breeches
and white court shoes. When war was renewed, the yeomanry was
reconstituted, including Lord Clifford's 'private army'; he now
called himself major, and had seven officers under him—but only
94 men. This force was not disbanded until 1827, when the smart
uniforms were given to the Christmas waits.[1]

Lord Petre, in Essex, also planned to raise a troop in 1798. He
was on the friendliest terms with the king, but George refused
to sign the commission for his son to command the force. In vain
it was pointed out that the king had signed commissions held by
other Catholics; the stubborn old man said that he had not been
personally aware of the religion of the gentlemen concerned.[2] In
1807 his refusal to sanction a bill allowing Catholics to be officers
led to the fall of the ministry.

In fact, as many people knew, through the connivance of their
commanding officers there were several Catholics serving in the
armed forces, both local and national. Mr. Weld in Dorset, and
two of the Huddlestons in Cambridgeshire, held commissions in
the local yeomanry. In 1800 Lady Jerningham's son was gazetted
as an ensign; 'a little favour may then get him Leave to purchase
a Company'. In 1802 the young man told his mother that 'most of
his Regmt are Catholicks and that on St Patrick's Day Mass was
positively said in the Barracks.'[3]

William Mawhood was a substantial London merchant; his
father had become a Catholic, but most of his relatives were
Protestant. He had a cousin in command of a regiment, and
supplied clothing for it to the value of £4,000—not a very good
piece of business, for he had to wait four years before he was fully
paid. His son, also a William, did not want to enter the family
business, and in May 1777 the merchant wrote in his diary, 'Son
Wm and Self had much talk about his choice he is most desirous
for the Army.' Inquiries were made; there were rumours that
regiments of Catholics were to be raised. A military friend advised
William to join the Austrian army; service in the forces of another
country was still quite usual. He told William that in the English

[1] Freeman, B., *The Yeomanry of Devon*. Privately printed, 1927.

[2] Western, J. P., article in the *English Historical Review*, July 1955, pp.
428 ff.

[3] *Jerningham Letters*, Vol. I, pp. 179, 211.

army 'the officers must go to Church'; but another friend said that
'a young man may Enter the Army without taking the Oths.'

William did manage to evade the difficulties, and got his commission as a lieutenant in 1778. His regiment went to America,
and he was taken prisoner; when he returned in 1782 he soon went
back across the Atlantic to marry a lady whom he had met there,
so the war office placed him on half pay. This was only £42 per
annum—but he drew it for 60 years. It was suggested that he
should find some work to do, but he said that he was a gentleman;
he preferred to live—generally out of England, to escape his
creditors—on what his family could allow him. From 1796 to 1801
he came home and served in the militia; probably with little
success, for on the renewal of war he was not re-commissioned.
He died in France in 1845.[1]

Many young men of this type, too proud to work in a business
and lacking in energy and ability, were to be found in the army,
for it was possible to buy a commission, and promotion was
largely by patronage. The low standards of the ordinary young
officers probably influenced the attitude of Catholic clergy like
Bishop Walmesley, who in 1788 strongly deprecated the wish of
the Catholic gentry that their sons should be free to enter the
forces; he thought that they would probably abandon their
religion, for they would be subject to great social pressure to
conform.[2] There were very many privates who were openly Papist,
and the Duke of Wellington held a high opinion of them; a few
Catholics did succeed as officers, but as a career His Majesty's
Commission offered but the slightest of prospects to younger sons
until in 1817 the religious tests were abolished.

Even then, offices under the state were closed to Catholics; Sir
Henry Jerningham spoke in 1821 of the 'Hardship of a Parent who
seeing a Son with every intelligence to make a figure in Life, is
obliged to say to Him; You must be satisfied with your own
Correctness . . . as drawing Breath in your own Country is all that
is allowed of.' For men like him, the impossibility of pursuing
a political career was a humiliation.

Although it was difficult for Catholics to add to their incomes,
several of them had estates which brought in handsome returns.
Of the great Papist houses that remain, some, like Sawston Hall
near Cambridge, have kept their original sixteenth-century form
with little alteration; others, for example Hazlewood Castle near
York, were largely rebuilt. Wealthy Catholics, like their Protestant
friends, wanted mansions in the new style, with great rooms, fine

[1] C.R.S., L, 113, 118, 119.
[2] Archives of the Bishop of Clifton, Vol. II, p. 101.

gardens, and spacious parks. Lord Petre, though Ingatestone Hall was, and still is, most beautiful, built at Thorndon a practically new residence in 1770; it was burnt down about 100 years later. Lord Arundell's castle at Wardour had been greatly damaged, so he had more reason for the erection of a new castle. He employed the leading architects of the day; James Paine began it in 1771 and Sir John Soane was consulted. The original scheme was so grandiose that it was never fully carried out, but a fine mansion was ready for occupation in 1776. These palaces were costly to maintain; large numbers of servants were required to keep them cleaned and warmed. Many an eighteenth-century family was ruined by such capital expenditure and such an addition to the costs of living, and their parks and the preserving of game for sport reduced the amount of their profitable land.

A Catholic gentleman had an extra charge to meet, for his house always contained a chapel. Even when, as at Hazlewood Castle, the original chapel which had been built in 1286 was still in use, it was redecorated and embellished in keeping with the additions to the castle itself.[1] When the new chapel was built at Wardour Castle, an Italian architect designed it, and a Jesuit in Rome was employed to buy a magnificent altar, rich marbles, and all sorts of adornments. When these things were despatched from Italy, pieces of ancient Roman sculpture were placed at the top of the crates, lest the customs officers at the ports should seize the objects designed for 'superstitious uses'. The expense was enormous.

Even smaller chapels, especially after the act of 1791 permitted Mass to be said publicly, were enlarged and embellished with imitations of classical pillars and mural paintings. Pictures of religious subjects were bought abroad or commissioned from local artists; many remain in private collections. In one interesting picture at Wardour holy and secular subjects are ingeniously combined. One of the daughters of the third Baron Arundell was a Poor Clare in a convent overseas; she longed to have portraits of her father and mother, but such enjoyments were prohibited by the strict rule of her order. Her father therefore employed an artist to paint a large picture of the crucified Christ. The Cross was depicted as seen from the rear, and kneeling in front of it, facing the viewer, were Lord and Lady Arundell in their very best clothes.

The provision of altar plate was an anxiety for owners of chapels all through penal times. When the communion cup replaced the pre-Reformation chalice after 1562,[2] second-hand chalices could

[1] *Country Life*, December 1957, illustrated article on Hazlewood by A. Oswald.
[2] Oman, C., *English Church Plate* (London, 1957), pp. 133 ff.

be bought fairly cheaply, though most of them were melted down and converted to the new style. Occasionally a recusant secured the chalice of the parish church. It was dangerous to possess such things, but essential if Mass were to be celebrated. Many new chalices, patens, pyxes and so forth were made by the goldsmiths for Catholics, and when persecution slackened in the eighteenth century, well-known designers were employed and the vessels sometimes hall-marked.

Priests moving from place to place carried with them the necessary outfit for saying Mass—an altar stone, a tiny chalice and paten, and a supply of Hosts. In the seventeenth century chalices were often made in two or three pieces, which could be screwed together, so that their purpose was less evident. Several of these still exist, including one at Ugthorpe. In the same way, altar cruets were made with separate tops, so that they looked like ordinary little jugs when the lids with their sacred emblems had been removed. Some superb altar plate from recusant houses survives; most of it was made in England, for it was not safe to bring it in from the continent until near the time of emancipation. There were Catholic goldsmiths, but much was made by non-Papist designers who did not, as they should have done, report their clients to the authorities.

The plate and vestments in a private chapel were usually the property of the householder. When he died, if he had no Catholic heir they could be sold. In 1782 on the death of Sir H. Hunloke a box of vestments and other articles became the property of the secular priests of Derbyshire: it included 'a silver chalice with paten said to have been bought by subscription of the congregation'.[1] Frequently such collections were left to individual priests: the bequest was generally in a secret codicil along with other gifts to seminaries or to clergy funds.

A list was drawn up, probably about 1701, of 'Persons of Quality and their Chaplains'. It included 22 priests supported by peers or peeresses, 24 by baronets and knights, 34 by 'Gentlemen of considerable estates', and 63 by gentlemen and ladies whose incomes ranged from £400 to £600. It was noted that in Lancashire between 30 and 40 secular priests were maintained by the gentry. In all, 154 secular priests, 44 Jesuits, 12 monks and 6 friars were known by the person who made the list, and he was aware that his information was imperfect; it is probable that at that date there were about 250 priests active in England.[2]

[1] Midland Archives.
[2] Westminster Cathedral Archives. Series A, Vol. XXXVIII, No. 2. Transcript by J. A. Williams.

Father Sympson, a Benedictine who was priest to Mrs. Throckmorton of Weston Underwood, was on friendly terms with local society; he went to dinner with the Rector of Bletchley, and showed him his chapel at Weston.[1] Indeed, that chaplains should forget their main purpose, concentrate overmuch on the service of their patrons and so play too large a part in secular life, was a constant anxiety to their bishops. For their right to administer the sacraments, all priests depended on the vicars apostolic, but a withdrawal of such faculties, once granted, was made as a rule only for some very grave cause. When a patron chose as chaplain a 'secular' priest, the bishop had to be consulted; but often a member of one of the orders was selected, and over him the bishop had less immediate control. Indeed, a long struggle had gone on before the vicars apostolic won the right to grant or withhold faculties from the 'regular' clergy, and such men could be dismissed by their patrons or recalled by their superiors without the bishop's consent or even knowledge.

While some heads of Catholic families paid due reverence to their spiritual fathers, others were apt to treat the chaplain as a servant —of higher standing than the steward, perhaps, but in the same category. In one house there was a long dispute—whether the chaplain could have a silver candlestick for his bedroom, or whether that would not place him on an equality with members of the family.[2] In a book of household hints written by Lady Petre,[3] the list of necessary servants begins 'Two chaplains'; no wage is stated for them, as it is for the lay staff, and one footman is deputed for duty in the sacristy. Everyone was supposed to attend Mass daily in this household, but not all patrons set a good example. Bishop Hornyold wrote to his clergy that every priest 'who lives in a family' ought to read evening prayers at a fixed time and see that all the servants attend. 'A great omission which I observe in some Families' is 'yt we very seldom find ye Master there present; this has a very ill aspect.'[4]

Perhaps it was to check the temptation, which beset domestic chaplains, to fall in with the extravagant easy-going ways of the period that the bishops settled their stipend at £20 a year. This was below the wage of a head cook, fixed at £30 by Lady Petre, and did not permit unnecessary expenditure. The chaplain's duties, if carried out conscientiously, went far beyond the estate

[1] Cole, W., *Blecheley Diary*. Vol. I, p. 144.

[2] Burton, *Challoner*, Vol. I, p. 144.

[3] Printed in *Notes and Queries*. Introduction by Dom John Stéphan, August 1958, text March and April 1959.

[4] Midland Archives.

PCE

on which he lived. He cared for the Catholics all round the district, riding or walking long distances to visit the sick. Sometimes these priests were well known and even loved outside their own flock. Father Wheble, S.J., was noted as a preacher; when he died, as chaplain at Wardour, in 1788, the *Salisbury Journal* referred to him as 'a Gentleman universally loved & respected by all that knew him; endued with Christian virtues, he was the true friend to the friendless, whatever their persuasion, & in charity with all mankind'.[1]

One useful function that a chaplain could fulfil was that of correspondent when his patron was away from home. The Jesuit Father Thornton at Everingham wrote to Sir Marmaduke Constable a number of jolly letters with news about the estate, and about local races and fox hunts. Both these sports were in high favour with the Catholic gentry; the pack of hounds at Wardour was famous, and Lord Arundell's puppies were in great demand. Games, as they developed, were taken up by the Papists as by the rest of the country; the Nyren family of cricketers at Hambledon appears in the Catholic registers of Gosport.

The theatre, too, had its devotees, and many actors were Catholics. In the early seventeenth century a travelling company from Egton near Whitby toured the Yorkshire countryside; their repertoire included *King Lear* and *Pericles* as well as lighter productions. They seem to have escaped arrest as recusants, and as vagabond players; probably they were well protected by the local gentry. In 1609 at Christmas they performed a morality play at the house of Sir John Yorke in Nidderdale in the West Riding; it was a popular piece, and several Protestants, including the local parson, were in the audience. An Interlude was added, in which a priest worsted a Protestant clergyman in argument, and then 'he that plaid the Divell did carry the English minister away. Whereat all the people laughed and rejoiced a long time together.'[2] An enemy of Sir John reported this to the Star Chamber; many other charges were added, and a fine, paid off by instalments, was eventually imposed.

An Interlude such as this must have formed part of the ordinary repertory of the company; it could scarcely have been improvised for one performance, for the Devil's appearance was accompanied by flashes of fire, and the theological arguments must have been well studied by the actors. Doubtless it aroused applause in many other places besides Nidderdale. A 'strolling gang of players' is mentioned in the Catholic register of Holme-on-Spalding-Moor in

[1] C.R.S., XLII, 137.
[2] Howard, C., *Sir John Yorke of Nidderdale* (1939), p. 25.

1755,[1] so the Egton company had a successor. This form of amusement was not approved by Catholic moralists; Alban Butler in
the eighteenth century, like the Archpriest Harrison in the
seventeenth,[2] did not wish priests to go to the theatre. He wrote
in 1752, 'I am much surprised that a Jesuit in Oxford carried a
young Gentleman to a comedy.'[3]

Music had its recusant votaries; numbers of fiddlers and other
musicians appear in the lists and registers of Papists. The great
organ builder, Renatus Harris, who between 1686 and 1710
built 39 organs for cathedrals and other churches, appears as a
known recusant in the London returns of 1706. Masses and other
music for use in church were composed; in 1784 Mawhood, the
merchant, himself a keen musician, noted that the organist of
St. Paul's had given the music of a new Mass, lately brought
from Rome, to the choir master of the cathedral to 'reharse over
with his boys.'[4]

By this date the position of Catholics in society was fully
established. King George III himself gave them his sanction in
the social sphere, though he was adamant in refusing to remove
their political disabilities. His visit to Lord Petre's new mansion
at Thorndon was a tremendous occasion. On 22 September 1778
Lord Petre heard that the king had consented to stay with him
when he came to Essex to hold a review on 2 October. That very
evening he 'sent for Mr Bracken my upholsterer': this competent
man was asked to 'new furnish the Great Drawing Room' and a
bedroom and two dressing-rooms for the king and queen, all in
English damask, by 2 October; 'his answer was that it should be
done'. It turned out to be impossible to get enough English
damask, so Indian was used. Painters were brought in to 'Repair
and Beautify the staircase', and gold plate for the king's use and
new candlesticks and tableware were ordered. On 30 September
two coaches arrived from London with nine French cooks 'with
their moulds their Troufles &c.'

That very day Lord Petre was told that the review had been
postponed to 19 October. The 'great Hurry' was at an end; the
cooks were sent back to London; but 'those dishes that would not
keep, very good things' had to be consumed by officers of the
troops at a dinner party at Thorndon. When at last the royal
party arrived, all the tenants of the estate '& every Body Els'
that the steward could muster were drawn up before the house;
the soldiers were on parade in the park, the guns firing salutes.
The 'Rapidity with which the King's Chaise run the lawn . . .

[1] C.R.S., IV, 272.   [2] Supra, p. 70.   [3] Midland Archives.
[4] C.R.S., L, 213.

the Horses panting made the whole resemble an inchantment.'
Everything went off well; after a grand dinner cards were played
till almost midnight, when supper was served and their majesties
retired. Next day the troops were reviewed; the queen was on a
stand specially built by Lord Petre. Dinner that night included
130 dishes, and next morning the royal visitors departed, thanking
their hosts 'in the most obliging manner' and leaving 100 guineas
for the servants and 'some money for the poor'. The affair cost
the Petres over £1,000; of this more than £100 was for the French
cooks and their dishes. The £279 18s. for the silversmith did at
any rate produce something of permanent value.[1]

When in 1789 George III visited the Welds at Lulworth Castle
there was much less ostentation and expense. Weld's suggestion
of a visit while the king was at Weymouth had been accepted,
but only on a Sunday afternoon did he hear that the royal visitor
would arrive in a frigate on Monday morning. Carpets were laid
on the steps of the castle and 'two Great Statues' held a 'Vestoon'
of Garter blue with 'Long Live the King' inscribed on it. As the
king came up the children sang 'God save great George', the
organ played and cannon were fired. A 'collation' was served to
the royal party, who were then shown over the castle with its
little old chapel. Walking in the garden, the king saw the large
new chapel in the grounds and went to inspect it; the children
gathered inside and sang 'God save the King'. The altar, and
church plate, displayed in the sacristry, were admired. Weld
sent an account of the visit to his friend Lord Arundell. 'I am
very glad this business is over,' he wrote. 'I hope it will answer
the purpose I had solely in view I think the King's seeing the
Chapel in that publick manner must be a kind of sanction to it.'[2]

Lady Jerningham's gossipy letters show how considerable a
part Catholics were playing in London society at the end of the
century; in 1786 she wrote, 'I think the Catholick Ladies seem to
be in fashion!' and by 1819 she could say, 'It is really fashionable
to be a Catholic. *Tempora mutantur.*'[3]

The change could not have come about had there not been a
solid basis of friendship between Catholics and their neighbours
all through the years since Elizabeth I ascended the throne. In
spite of the severity of the laws, of many executions, deaths,
tortures and imprisonments, Catholics remained an integral part
of English society in all classes, though not, perhaps, in all districts.
There was no period when the ordinary people turned against

[1] Petre Archives, D/DP F 322/22, Essex Record Office.
[2] MS. at Wardour Castle.
[3] *Jerningham Letters*, Vol. I, p. 43, Vol. II, p. 130.

those who held to the old ways; persecution was due to government policy or to personal spite, not to any antipathy felt by fellow craftsmen or traders or landowners. On the other hand, their sense of belonging to their own country led many to conform to the English way of worship, particularly when no priests or instruction were available. The remarkable thing is that so many people did hold on to their faith when every human influence would have led them to conform. Undoubtedly, the nobility and gentry were the main supporters of Catholicism; had all of them fallen away, Papistry would have ceased to be 'respectable'. Their heirs have every right to cherish their memory; their influence, their generosity, ensured that Catholics continued, in spite of every handicap, familiar figures in the society of their native land. They might resent the restrictions imposed by the law or by their own bishops, but in spite of everything they succeeded in keeping their faith while remaining 'pure English'.

INDEX OF
SUBJECTS, SOVEREIGNS, STATES

SELECTIVE INDEX OF
FAMILIES, PERSONS, PLACES